KINGS
of the
JEWS

KINGS
of the
JEWS

The Origins of the Jewish Nation

NORMAN GELB

2010 • 5770
The Jewish Publication Society
Philadelphia

The Jewish Publication Society
2100 Arch Street, 2ⁿᵈ floor
Philadelphia, PA 19103
www.jewishpub.org

Cover design by Claudia Cappelli

Manufactured in the United States of America

10 11 12   10 9 8 7 6 5 4 3 2 1

ISBN: 978-0-8276-0913-6
eISBN: 978 0-8276-0953-2

Library of Congress Cataloging-in-Publication Data

Gelb, Norman.
  Kings of the Jews : exploring the origins of the Jewish nation / Norman Gelb.
    p. cm.
  Includes bibliographical references and index.
  ISBN 978-0-8276-0913-6 (alk. paper)
  1. Jews—History—To 70 A.D. 2. Bible. O.T.—History of Biblical events. 3. Jews—Kings and rulers—Biography. I. Title.
  DS121.G42 2009
  933.009'9—dc22
                         2009025800

In memory of my father,
Samuel Gelb,
a good and gentle man

**King David Leading the Procession
Bringing the Ark of the Covenant to Jerusalem**

If, after you have entered the land that the Lord your God has assigned to you, and taken possession of it and settled in it, you decide, "I will set a king over me, as do all the nations about me," you shall be free to set a king over yourself, one chosen by the Lord your God.

Deuteronomy 17:14–15

Contents

INTRODUCTION

Kings feature prominently in the annals of most countries. Major historical events are commonly portrayed as having been achieved or perpetrated by kings or in their names: the wars they fought, the projects they undertook, the riches they accumulated, the reverses they sustained, how their people fared under them. That was as true for the Jews as for, say, the English or the Chinese.

Before the emergence of their monarchy, Jews were a divided, fragmented people despite being linked by their shared worship of their one God Yahweh, by a shared heritage dating back to the Patriarchs who founded their faith, and by geographic proximity. Those who led them then, called Judges, were regional notables, tribal rather than national figures. In time, pressures exerted by hostile neighbors made them succumb to a craving for a king who would promote their common security and interests. That craving set the stage for the creation of the Jewish nation.

Of the more than fifty monarchs who sat on the throne of the Jews, over a period spanning more than a thousand years, the memory of only a few has passed into the popular imagination. Among those few are King David, the harp-strumming warrior who first molded the Jewish tribes into a nation, and King Solomon, who was said to have conjured up marvels of wisdom and dispensed wonders of justice while administering an empire. In the thirty centuries that have passed since their time, tales of their accomplishments have been richly embroidered by legend and embellishment.

> *King David and King Solomon led merry, merry lives,*
> *With many many lady friends, and many many wives.*
> *But when old age crept over them, with many many qualms,*
> *King Solomon wrote the proverbs and King David wrote the psalms.*[1]

Despite the puffed-up yarns, David and Solomon were men of historic achievement. Though some of their royal successors were figures of little sub-stance who would have been forgotten if they had not been mentioned in passing in the Bible, others who wore the crown of the Jews in ancient times were, like David and Solomon, figures of considerable significance in the evolution of the

Jewish nation. The rival monarchs Rehoboam and Jeroboam were the first to preside over the twin kingdoms of Israel[1] and Judah into which the Jewish nation split after Solomon's death. King Omri's impact on the region was great enough for the kingdom of Israel he ruled to become commonly known to its neighbors as the House of Omri. King Ahab's own considerable achievements were overshadowed by his wife Jezebel's abortive campaign to eradicate Jewish worship. A man of the soil as well as a military engineer, King Uzziah revolutionized the agrarian economy of his often drought-stricken people. Reversing the spiritual decline of his kingdom, King Josiah renewed the faith of the Jews in their seemingly lapsed, defining covenant with God.

A gap of four hundred years divided the two periods when the Jews were ruled by their own kings. That interval began with their expulsion from the land of Israel by the Babylonians, one of the devouring regional superpowers that succeeded each other in dominance in ancient times—Egypt, Assyria, Babylonia, Persia, Greek-Syria, Parthia, Rome. That forced exile proved a crucial test in which the Jewish nation could have been blotted out forever, the fate of other small lands in the region.

But that nation was reborn after the Jews returned to their ancestral homeland, and their monarchy was subsequently revived by the Hasmonean descendants of the guerrilla fighters who had rebelled against a foreign attempt to snuff out Jewish worship. The Hasmoneans, in turn, gave way to the highly accomplished, infamous King Herod the Great, an Arab Jew who rebuilt the diminished international standing of the Jewish nation. But by then, a two thousand-year period had begun in which the survival of the Jews as a people would depend, not on geographic boundaries, but on the tenacious identity they had forged under their kings and through a sequence of galvanizing developmental experiences.

*   *   *

The history of the Jewish people is said to have begun at a place called Haran in the southeast of what is now Turkey. It was there that a herdsman named

---

1.   As a place name in ancient times, *Israel* had two very different meanings. It was the generic name of the homeland of the Jews in what would later be called Palestine. But when Solomon's kingdom divided in two after his death, the southern kingdom of the Jews, with Jerusalem at its heart, was called *Judah* while the separate northern kingdom, in the region later to be called Samaria, took the name *Israel*.

Abram (later to be commonly known as Abraham), formerly from Ur, in what is now Iraq, was chosen by God to go to a different place where, God told him, "I will make of you a great nation."[2]That place was a narrow crescent of land called Canaan on the eastern shore of the Mediterranean. Abraham's son Isaac and grandson Jacob (later called Israel) subsequently also received divine assurances that the land would belong to their descendants for all time. Jacob's sons were the founders of the twelve tribes from which the Jewish nation later emerged.

The story of those three Patriarchs is the earliest chapter in the history of the Jewish people. The word *Jew* (or its equivalent in various languages) is derived from the name of the tribe and tribal territory of Judah, though not till much later did it come to signify someone of Jewish faith and culture.[2] Jews were earlier called Israelites, Children of Israel, and Hebrews. Abraham is identified as a Hebrew in the Bible, a designation that may have been derived from the name Eber, an ancestor of his.

Few large cities existed in those days, and the distances between them were great. A small number of them were sophisticated urban centers like Babylon and Thebes, with intricate class structures and magnificent edifices. But, like Abraham, most people lived off the land. Many moved from place to place wherever crop cultivation, grazing, and hunting provided sustenance. Those migrations—whether massive or very gradual—were a major feature of ancient times. When, in Jacob's old age, famine descended on the land of Canaan, he and his family migrated to Egypt.

Joseph, Jacob's favored second-youngest son, who had previously been sold into slavery by his resentful brothers, had achieved a position of authority and influence in the court of the pharaoh. With Joseph's patronage, Jacob's family and household, numbering seventy in all, settled on land in the fertile Nile delta. They stayed in Egypt the rest of their days and their descendants stayed on also, generation after generation, for some four hundred years, according to the Bible.

Multiplying over time, they inevitably lost cohesion as a single family. Each came to identify with his or her clan or tribe. They knew themselves as descendants of one of Jacob's sons: Reuben, Simeon, Levi, Judah, Dan, Naphtali, Gad, Asher, Issachar, Zebulun, and Benjamin, and of Joseph's two sons, Manasseh and Ephraim.

In time, the sanctuary they had found in Egypt turned onerous and oppressive. In search of freedom, they fled, led by Moses, the charismatic lawgiver who

---

2. For clarity, in these pages devotees of Yahweh are called Jews and Jewish when referred to even in times before those names were in usage.

gave order and method to Judaism as a living faith. They departed, not yet as a nation, but as linked tribes, and made their way across the Sinai desert to Canaan, the land promised by God to their patriarchal forebears.

There was no immediate triumphant homecoming for the migrating descendants of Abraham, Isaac, and Jacob, as Joshua, who had succeeded Moses as their leader, led them into the promised land. It is likely the tribes—those repelled by the Canaanites at first, and those who settled in without strife—entered the land in waves rather than *en masse*. Some settled peacefully on unclaimed territory in Canaan, notably in the thinly settled highlands north and east of the Jordan River. For others, it was an absorption process in which the resilient Children of Israel gradually adapted to the more advanced Canaanite culture while the Canaanites, under pressure as well from Philistine[3] settlers, went into decline.

Jewish settlement in Canaan was a protracted process. The tribe of Judah gradually settled on territory west and northwest of the Dead Sea. The tribe of Simeon retained a semi-nomadic existence in the Negev Desert to the south and was later largely absorbed into Judah. The tribe of Naphtali settled in the central Galilee, that of Asher in the western Galilee, Issachar in the southeastern Galilee, Zebulun in the southwestern Galilee, Manasseh across a wide region in the center of the land on both sides of the River Jordan, Ephraim in hill country south of Manasseh, Benjamin on the plain of Jericho, and Reuben and Gad on the east bank of the Jordan. Members of the tribe of Levi had no fixed territory but served as priests and guardians of religious artifacts throughout the land.

While some tribes expanded the territory in which they sank roots, others, failing to claim land on which they had tried to settle, had to migrate elsewhere, or were reduced to enclaves existing under the shadow of Philistine or Canaanite dominance. The tribe of Dan first settled on the Mediterranean coast in the south but finally established itself in the sparsely settled north of the land, beyond the Sea of Galilee.

While the settling process took place, the Jews remained a fragmented people. In those days, says the Bible, "there was no king in Israel; every man did as he pleased."[3] They still identified with their tribes rather than with a Jewish national entity, and with the smaller extended family groups that composed their clans. Rivalries, especially between the northern tribes (which formed a some-

---

3.   The Philistines, from whom the name *Palestine* was much later derived, were originally from Asia Minor and the Greek Islands. They had begun migrating to the region around the twelfth century BCE. Their efforts to establish settlements in Egypt having been repelled, they had moved on to colonize Canaan's southern coastal region.

times close-knit alliance) and Judah in the south would later be of great consequence for the Jewish nation.

The "Judges," the charismatic figures who led the Jews during those turbulent
times, were regional chieftains, local dignitaries or tribal elders rather than
national figures. Their emergence was a response to the need for an instrument
for maintaining order and administering justice, as permanent communities
evolved. Agrarian life predominated, but towns sprang up as commerce and its
interactions increased. This was a transitional period of adjustment and accom-
modation between the arrival of the Jews in Canaan and the emergence of the
Jewish monarchy.

It was also a period when the tribes were exposed to severe external pressures.
They were under threat of subjugation and dispersal. That is why the warriors
among the Judges are the best known. Ehud of the tribe of Benjamin fought off
the neighboring Moabites. Othniel of the tribe of Judah led the defense against
an attack from Mesopotamia. Shamgar repelled a formidable Philistine assault.

Most famous was Samson, of the tribe of Dan, the brawny nemesis of the Philistines who, though captured and blinded through the wiles of Delilah, brought
down the roof of the building in which his enemies were celebrating his capture,
killing them as well as himself. The Judge Deborah, believed to have been of the
tribe of Ephraim, was a poet and prophet as well. Like others, she performed both
a judicial and a military function.

Gideon, of the tribe of Manasseh, became so popular as a unifying military
leader that some proposed he be the first to sit on the throne of the Jews. He
declined, saying that only God could be their king, perhaps suspecting that the
unity he inspired among the tribes might be of only brief duration.

If that was his belief, it was borne out by the experience of his son Abimelech,
who attempted to rule as king, crowned as such by the elders of the city of
Shechem. After he had slaughtered many of his subjects, including all but one of
his many brothers, the people of Shechem and nearby villages rebelled. He was
killed trying to suppress their uprising, his kingship never having taken hold.

However, facing the persisting threat posed by the Philistines and other neighboring peoples, the tribes finally succumbed to a craving for a king to promote
their security. He was also to provide the glamorous, prestigious trappings of
royal leadership prevalent among other peoples of the region. The moment had
come for the establishment of a Jewish monarchy.

ISRAEL IN CANAAN
Joshua to Samuel and Saul

▲ Cities of Refuge
■ Philistine Cities

SCALE OF MILES

0   5   10 15 20 25 30

The Great Sea

Sidon

MT. HERMON
●Damascus

Tyre●

Dan
(Laish)

DAN

ASHER

▲Kadesh

Hazor●

BASHAN

ZEBULUN

NAPHTALI

Sea of
Chinnereth

Golan●

MT. TABOR

ISSACHAR

MANASSEH

▲Ramoth-gilead

Megiddo●

MANASSEH

HILL
COUNTRY
OF ISRAEL   ▲Shechem

River Jordan

THE ARABAH

GILEAD

MT. GERIZIM

EPHRAIM

GAD

AMMON

Shiloh●

DAN

Bethel●
●Ai

Jericho●

Shittim

Gibeon●

BENJAMIN

MT. PISGAH

▲Bezer

Jerusalem●

Ashdod■

Ashkelon■

PHILISTINES

HILL
COUNTRY
OF JUDAH

Sea of the Arabah
(Salt Sea)

REUBEN

Gaza■

Lachish●

Hebron
▲

●Aroer

River Arnon

J
U
D
A
H

●Debir

●Beer-sheba

MOAB

SIMEON

The Negeb

EDOM

BEGINNINGS

We must have a king over us that we may be like all other nations

1 Samuel 8:19

Samuel Blessing Saul

SAUL

1020–1000 BCE[4]

The story of Saul is a tragedy of Shakespearean proportions. It is a tale of glory and fame turning to despair, madness, and ultimate doom.

Saul was chosen the first king of the Jews at a time when they were fully recognizing the emasculating consequences of their tribal divisions and rivalries. Some of their land was under Philistine subjugation and the rest was threatened with the same.

Despite the growth of their towns, the Jews, almost all farmers and herdsmen, were still a Bronze Age people who could arm themselves only with Bronze Age weapons. The weaponry of the Philistines was far more advanced than anything they could field in combat. The military superiority of their adversaries had been demonstrated when they were routed in battle at Aphek, not far from present-day Tel Aviv, and their sacred Ark of the Covenant was captured. Built to house the tablets of the law handed down by God to Moses in the Sinai Desert, the Ark had been in the care of priests at sacred shrines but was brought onto the battlefield in times of war to help protect His chosen people from the power of their enemies.

But it failed to avert defeat at Aphek. The Philistines also destroyed the sanctuary at Shiloh where the Ark had last been housed. It seemed a fitting punishment for a people who had been straying from their faith and therefore no longer worthy of either the Ark or the sanctuary. Even the sons of the prophet Eli, who were guardians of the Ark and who were killed in the clash with the Philistines, had begun flirting with the worship of other deities.

However the Ark was soon returned by the Philistines, who blamed a series of subsequent misfortunes that befell them on their theft of this sacred booty from its rightful owners. But its initial loss and the destruction of Shiloh had important ramifications. It generated a unifying backlash among the Jews, of a kind that was to recur repeatedly at times of tragedy.

*   *   *

Despite tribal disunity, despite flirtation with the pagan observances of the Canaanites, and despite occasional fratricidal territorial clashes between tribes

---

4.   The dates of the earliest kings are approximate.

and clans, recognition of a common Jewish heritage had endured. People from all over the land had periodically gathered to worship at the shrine at Shechem which the Patriarch Abraham had sanctified and where Joshua had renewed the covenant with God. Those gatherings helped sustain the residual sense of common identity. They also nourished shared despair at the impotence of the tribes in the face of territorial pressure from the Philistines and others, and they contributed to the emergence of trans-tribal sentiments with nationalist overtones.

Crossing tribal boundaries, itinerant preachers, priests, and prophets wandered among the Jews, as they would in later times of anguish, admonishing people to shun foreign ways and sinfulness. Among those who foretold disaster unless the people followed the path of piety was the revered sage and prophet Samuel, formerly a priest at the shrine at Shiloh. His warnings, and those of others, also promoted a sense of shared uniqueness and fate.

By Samuel's time, the Philistines had extended their domain up along the coast from Gaza as far as Sidon in Lebanon and were extracting tribute from the militarily outmatched Jews inland. To the east, the Ammonites, in what is now Jordan, having recovered from earlier setbacks, were encroaching on nearby Jewish areas. Problems with desert tribes had developed in the south of the land as well.

Subjected to marauders, territorial loss, and extortion, and influenced by growing national feelings, the Jews succumbed to the craving for a king, a monarch like other nations boasted, a leader who would unite the tribes and organize armed resistance to their enemies.

Samuel objected. The prophet maintained God was the only king the Jews required. He may also have feared the emergence of a figure who would challenge his authority as spiritual leader.

He warned that under a king Jews would no longer live as equals. A king would be an oppressive tyrant who would take away their sons to be soldiers and their daughters to be servants. He would take their best cornfields, vineyards, and olive groves. He would demand a one-tenth part of their livestock and would stand between them and the Lord.

But popular demand for a king was overwhelming, and Samuel conceded that such widespread feeling had to be a reflection of God's will. He thereupon went in search of an individual capable and worthy of wearing the crown of the Jews.

His choice fell upon Saul, a farmer and shepherd of forceful personality and commanding appearance, tall, and powerfully built. Saul also had the political advantage of being of the small tribe of Benjamin. The larger tribes were less likely to feel shamed by such a choice of a king from outside their own ranks.

Nevertheless, the decision was not completely welcomed throughout the land. Accustomed to independence, some of the tribes—particularly those in remote northern regions of the land less threatened by outsiders—bridled at the suggestion that they now owed allegiance to a monarch. Saul was required to prove himself worthy of leadership.

The opportunity for him to do so was provided by the Ammonites when they laid siege to the Jewish city of Jabesh, east of the Jordan River. The Ammonite king threatened to conquer Jabesh and inflict harsh punishment on its inhabitants. The terms of surrender would include the loss of an eye for each of the men of the city.

The elders of Jabesh were able to negotiate a temporary ceasefire. They would be permitted to dispatch messengers to appeal for help from other Jews. If such help was not forthcoming within a fixed period of time—and the Ammonites were certain it would not be—the city would surrender without a struggle and its inhabitants would put themselves at the mercy of their conquerors.

Little help was, in fact, forthcoming, until word of the plight of the Jabeshites reached Saul. In assuming authority over the Jews he had also accepted responsibility for protecting them. He hastily went about recruiting a militia to rush to the aid of the people of Jabesh.

It proved no simple task. Despite their common heritage, mutual assistance had never been a matter of course among the tribes. They had usually been caught up only in their own pursuits and generally had coped alone with their problems.

There was no standing Jewish military force, not even within any of the separate tribes. The call to arms had always been answered by men putting aside their normal activities and picking up their weapons, mostly farm tools. The summons from their new king to rally to the aid of the beleaguered Jabeshites for reasons of common heritage drew little response.

But Saul was not easily denied. What would not be given freely would be extorted. When he threatened to destroy the livestock of Jews who declined to join his rescue army, recruits came soon enough. Saul then led his reluctant conscripts on a forced march to Jabesh. There they threw themselves into battle against the Ammonites who had bivouacked around the city walls. They killed many and dispersed the rest.

Word of the victory swept through the land, stirring a wave of gratification and pride. The Jews reveled in their trans-tribal hero. Demands were made that those who had opposed Saul's coronation should be punished, even put to death. But recognizing the occasion as an opportunity for unity, he regally proclaimed forgiveness for all who had challenged or doubted him. For the first time, the Jewish people had begun to assume a national as well as religious identity.

The prophet Samuel recognized the significance of the moment. Though he had already anointed Saul king, he had not yet ceremonially proclaimed him monarch. Now he made good that omission at the altar at Gilgal, near Jericho, sparking popular rejoicing.

Officiating at this coronation was not a task Samuel enjoyed. He now publicly and with little grace relinquished his position of highest eminence in the land, accepting that he had been superseded in authority. He conceded that the Jews had affirmed their allegiance to their king and that God had agreed to the choice. But he forecast that when difficulties arose in the future, they would realize they had sinned in demanding a mortal ruler.

Riding a crest of popularity, Saul paid little attention to that grim prophecy. Nor was he initially bothered by the withdrawal of Samuel's spiritual guidance. He considered himself the representative of Yahweh, though his primary task was secular. It was to lead the military resistance against the enemies of his people, especially the Philistines who were still either dominant or threatening across large parts of the land. He prepared to take the fight to the enemy in a surprise raid against Philistine positions near Michmash, north of Jerusalem, still a Canaanite city at the time.

He recruited a corps of warriors, providing the Jews with their first standing corps of fighting men. It was led by his cousin Abner and included his own son Jonathan, a man of considerable strength and shrewdness. This elite band was drawn mostly from Saul's own tribe of Benjamin, a potentially divisive matter. The Benjaminites would be held responsible if the campaign against the Philistines failed, which was more than possible. The enemy was equipped with swords, spears, and shields while the Jewish fighters had few of those.

The enemy also had chariots which initially permitted them to take command of the battlefield. But a cunning move by Prince Jonathan, a skilled archer, transformed the battle. Positioning himself above a rocky defile as a troop of the enemy passed through, he killed several, driving the others into panic flight. Accounts of the incident were exaggerated in Philistine ranks, spreading confusion that permitted the main body of the scattered Jewish fighters to regroup.

As the dust of battle settled and the extent of Saul's victory became clear, the king almost condemned himself to a grotesque personal tragedy. He had earlier commanded that none of his men touch so much as a morsel of food until victory. Not having heard the order, Jonathan had disobeyed. Only a chorus of pleadings from his victorious warriors dissuaded Saul, a stern disciplinarian, from having his son put to death for insubordination. The incident foreshadowed the torment that lay ahead for the king. But for the moment all was hope and glory.

The triumph permitted Saul to turn his exertions to clearing the land of other enemies: the Aramaeans in Syria, the Ammonites and Moabites in Transjordan, and the Edomites in the southern desert territory. He also embarked on raids against the nomadic Amalekite marauders who had harassed the Jews when the tribes were migrating from bondage in Egypt. But throughout his reign, it was the Philistines, with their seasoned professional warriors and superior weaponry, who remained Saul's primary adversaries.

For the security of his kingdom as well as its unity, he began recruiting men from each of the tribes to be officers in his army. He took several wives and concubines during his reign but shunned luxury and ostentation. He continued to live at Gibeah, where Samuel had found him, established his court there, and invited his officers to a banquet at his house on each new moon. He also summoned them to councils of war there when circumstances warranted.

However, his efforts to promote unity did nothing to calm the disquiet that troubled the ageing Samuel. To the prophet's dismay, Saul's military successes, the emergence of a new class of privileged military officers and royal advisers, and the king's concentration on secular rather than religious matters undermined the special role of priests.

Samuel sought to retrieve the situation by publicly questioning Saul's spiritual qualifications and, by implication, his right to rule over God's people. He grew increasingly critical of the king, his disapproval turning to outrage when, not having arrived in time prior to a crucial battle, he saw that the impatient Saul had taken it upon himself to offer the animal sacrifice to God that was to precede the commencement of combat.

Samuel's rebuke over this transgression, and his prediction that Saul's reign would be brief, deeply troubled the temperamental king. Coming from someone with great spiritual authority, and echoed by other malcontents, it turned the king morbid. Saul's mood was also clouded by his continuing failure to gain the wholehearted support of the northern tribes whose enthusiasm for a united Jewish nation had never been great.

Saul had not sought the crown, but now he began to fear that he was being spurned, not only by the revered Samuel, but also by God. He grew distrustful, even of those he had chosen for his entourage. A notable exception was David, a young man from the tribe of Judah who not only had fought heroically and victoriously against the Philistines but who played the harp pleasingly. In addition to being a favorite of the king, David had become a close friend of both Prince

Jonathan and of Saul's daughters, one of whom, Michal, he was permitted to marry.

How, as a youth, he had slain the Philistine giant Goliath with his slingshot was already a legend throughout the land. His other talents and his piety were also widely known. But as David's fame and popularity spread, Saul grew jealous and suspicious. He was furious when David was welcomed with greater acclaim than he was upon returning from battle. People cried out, "Saul has slain his thousands; David his tens of thousands!"[4] The young man's ability to charm all with whom he came into contact angered the king, plunging him to the depths of gloom and despair and driving him into tantrums of rage. At a royal banquet, in a sudden spasm of jealousy, he hurled a spear at David, meaning to kill him.

The spear went wide of the mark, but Saul was now determined to rid himself of the popular young warrior. He dispatched David into what he thought would be hopeless combat against strong Philistine positions. But David triumphed against extreme odds, deepening the king's fury and consternation. He grew ever more anxious to destroy this threat to his peace of mind and eliminate this challenge to his throne, as David had become to his increasingly fevered imagination.

When informed by Jonathan that Saul planned to have him murdered, David fled first to Samuel to seek the prophet's guidance and protection and then to the priestly sanctuary at Nob. There he pretended to be on a mission for the king and was well received. But when word of it reached Saul, he ordered the execution of those at the sanctuary who had welcomed David. Aside from their not having known that the king considered their guest an enemy, it was a grave violation of established standards of refuge. It was a sign of Saul's increasing desperation and an act that appalled already alienated priests whose support he needed more than ever.

David had meanwhile fled to hills to the south, where he gathered a band of rebels, malcontents, and adventurers. Living off the land, they were continually in motion, eluding the efforts of Saul's troops to track them down. Those hunting him were sometimes joined in their efforts by the king himself.

One night, David infiltrated the royal bivouac while Saul was asleep and could have killed him, as one of his men advised. But David held back, saying it was not for him to decide the fate of the man chosen to unite the tribes.

For an ambitious man such restraint probably had a political dimension as well. Despite his difficulties, Saul retained considerable popular support. He had, after all, been ritually anointed king of the Jews on behalf of God and had fought heroically against their enemies.

In continuing to evade the king's efforts to destroy him, David was assisted by country folk increasingly disenchanted with Saul's reign and charmed by the image of this dashing rebel. When Nabal, a local dignitary in territory south of Hebron, who had refused to supply David's men with food, died of a stroke, David courted local popularity by marrying Abigail, the dead man's widow.

She had gone to him to apologize for her husband's disagreeable behavior, though Abigail's beauty may have been an even greater attraction than her graciousness. She was said to have been so beautiful that the mere thought of her aroused the lust of men. David would later take many more wives, who, with their offspring, would prove a source of intrigue and conspiracy much later in his life.

Charming and shrewd, David methodically cultivated friendship and support wherever he went, compounding Saul's rage. At a time when his forces were still locked in sporadic combat with the Philistines, it was a dangerously distracting obsession for the king and for the fledgling nation he had been chosen to rule.

So intent was Saul on tracking down his former protégé that David found it advisable to seek sanctuary among the enemy Philistines who held a string of confederated city-states on the coastal plain. He offered his services and those of his band of Jewish outlaws to the king of Gath who hoped to employ this resourceful leader of men as an ally against Saul. However, according to the Bible, David confined himself to predatory raids against Bedouin marauders and other enemies of the Jews while pretending to serve the Philistines against his own people.

Meantime Saul found it increasingly difficult to deal with the Philistine military threat. After a series of particularly damaging setbacks, he decided in desperation that he required greater assistance than had been provided by his fighters on the field of battle and by his priests.

Early in his reign, Saul had issued a decree banishing wizards and magicians from the land because, he said, they desecrated the spirit of God with their pretensions. But now, as his army advanced on the Plain of Jezreel to meet a powerful Philistine force, he went in disguise to the town of Endor to call on a local sorcerer. He asked her to summon the spirit of Samuel, who had died and whose counsel he now sorely missed. She was to extract from him a forecast on how the battle would go. She was unable to invoke an image of the prophet but conjured up his voice from beyond the grave. It told Saul, "Tomorrow you and your sons will be with me."[5]

Though reduced to despair, Saul went with his troops into battle on the Plain of Jezreel the next day. As he expected, his forces, more suited to fighting in the hills where the enemy's superiority in numbers and weaponry could be neutralized, were badly battered by the Philistines with their chariots. Though withdrawing up into neighboring Mount Gilboa, they continued to be mauled by Philistine archers. Jonathan and two of Saul's other sons were among those cut down. Distraught and grieving, and his army routed, Saul ordered his armor bearer to kill him before the Philistines could capture him. The armor bearer refused and Saul took his own life, throwing himself on his sword. When the Philistines found his body, they cut off his head as a trophy and hung the dead king's body on the walls of a nearby town.

David had never underestimated Saul's contribution to the Jewish people, both in uniting the tribes and as a royal symbol. Nor, ambitious himself, did he discount the high regard with which the king had been held at the height of his popularity. Upon hearing of Saul's death, he publicly grieved:

> *Your glory, O Israel, lies slain on your heights. How have the mighty fallen! Tell it not in Gath. Do not proclaim it in the streets of Ashkelon lest the daughters of the Philistine rejoice.... Daughters of Israel, weep over Saul who clothed you in crimson and finery, who decked your robes with jewels of gold.*[6]

Saul had been a tragic figure. But despite the continuing Philistine military preponderance, during the two decades of his reign he initiated the process of welding the Jewish people into a nation. For historical purposes and for purposes of legend, that accomplishment outweighed his personal torment and bizarre behavior. David would build upon his achievement.

ISHBOSHETH

1000–998 BCE

Saul's life had ended in the war with the Philistines, as had the lives of three of his sons. But he had been ritually ordained ruler of the Jews and his last surviving son Ishbosheth claimed to be his successor as king by right of inheritance. Abner, who had been Saul's military commander, arranged the coronation. Abner was a forceful figure, in contrast to the weak-willed Ishbosheth (also called Ishbaal). He intended to be the actual ruler of the Jews, monarch in all but name.

Despite Saul's efforts, Ishbosheth's legacy did not include a united kingdom. Military defeat and the suicide of his father had divisive consequences for the people. David, once Saul's favorite and then his adversary, had emerged as a popular rival to Ishbosheth. Through force and diplomacy, he had done much to shield the southern Jewish tribes from Philistine subjugation and nomadic marauders. In the process, he had become a popular, respected figure among them.

David also received strong backing from the priests. He had long sought their advice and counsel, in contrast to Saul, whose neglect and disregard had alienated the influential priesthood. When word of Saul's death spread, the people of Judah, the largest of the southern tribes, scorned Ishbosheth's claim to the throne and instead chose David, one of their own, to be their king.

Declaring Hebron, Judah's main city, his capital, David sent emissaries to other tribes to solicit their loyalty and submission. He met with a measure of success, but some of the northern tribes, largely remote from the struggles for security in the south, rejected appeals for backing from both David and Ishbosheth. They chose instead to assert their separateness, demonstrating that whatever unity Saul had achieved during his reign had been fragile. It was an inauspicious beginning for Ishbosheth's reign. With so little popular support for him, Abner, the power behind the throne, was careful to establish the new monarch's capital at Mahanaim, east of the Jordan River, away from the regions loyal to David, the areas dominated by the Philistines, and the territories of the dissenting northern tribes.

At this secure outpost, Ishbosheth, angered by David's refusal to acknowledge him as ruler, charged him with criminal mutiny. As his army commander, Abner was supposed to do something about that.

He had long considered David an enemy for having been a challenger to Saul's authority and to his own. But his position at Ishbosheth's court was undermined by his grasping quest for a higher station than he had already achieved.

He presumed to take a woman, the beautiful Rizpah, who had been Saul's mistress, as a concubine. It was an act of impudence, seen as revealing Abner's own monarchical aspirations. Had Ishbosheth truly been in command, such impertinence would have cost Abner his life. But all he could do was admonish him for the insult to his father's memory and for this blatant challenge to his own position.

Though the rebuke was comparatively mild, it infuriated Abner. Disgruntled, and realizing after an inconclusive clash that David's army was superior to his own, he considered transferring his allegiance from Ishbosheth. He met secretly with David in Hebron, and with the elders of several of the other tribes, hoping to end the divisions in the Jewish nation and make David its ruler. It was understood his reward would be command of the army of this once-more-united kingdom.

David agreed with the proposed arrangement but demanded proof of Abner's good faith. He insisted that he bring him Saul's daughter, Michal, Ishbosheth's sister. She was the wife from whom he had been separated years before when Saul began thinking of young David as his nemesis. Though Michal had helped David flee her father's wrath, he was motivated now by ambition rather than love. Being reunited with her would strengthen his claim to be Saul's legitimate successor as king.

Abner agreed to assist David in pursuing this plan. He prevailed upon Ishbosheth to command that his sister be taken from the man to whom she had been given in marriage by her father years before (despite still being married to the then-renegade David). He then delivered her back to her first husband in Hebron. Michal's feelings about this change in her fate are not known though her resumed relationship with David was not to be a happy one.

Abner lived up to his part of the deal with David but all did not go as intended. Joab, David's military commander, had not been apprised of the secret diplomacy in progress. He would not have been pleased by the plan for Abner to replace him as commander of David's army. Besides, Joab was known to hate Abner, who had killed his brother in internecine combat some time before. Spotting him on a secret visit to David's court, Joab overtook him when he left and cut him down.

David was furious. He feared the killing might jeopardize the plans for his becoming king of a united Jewish nation. Seeking to retain the following that

Abner would have brought with him when he changed sides, he had him buried with full honors and wrote a stirring elegy to his memory.

He need not have worried about complications. With Abner gone, Ishbosheth was seen by all to be weak and ineffectual. Soon after Abner's death, he was murdered by two of his own officers. They brought his head to David in Hebron as proof and as a token of submission.

Claiming to have acted in accordance with the will of God, the assassins expected to be rewarded. But David had them executed. He did not want to share responsibility for killing the son of Saul, a man who had been anointed king in God's name. It might have been considered sacrilege and provoked popular resentment.

With Ishbosheth gone, the only surviving male among Saul's descendants was Ishbosheth's young nephew Meribaal. The boy had been crippled by disease and was considered no threat to David or to his claim to be king of all the Jews.

The elders of all the tribes, who had already been consulted by David or his emissaries and were much impressed by David's achievements and bearing, conferred among themselves. They then went to Hebron to offer David the crown and to have him anointed their king.

In name at least, Ishbosheth had been monarch for two years. Sandwiched between such significant figures as Saul and David, he is obscured in history by their deeds and achievements.

King David

DAVID

1000–961 BCE

King Saul had been a tragic figure and Ishbosheth a feeble one. But David, who came to the throne of the Jews around the year 1000 BCE, was a figure of heroic proportions—warrior, musician and dynamic ruler. He vanquished the enemies of his people and did much to weld the Jewish tribes into a nation, with Jerusalem at its heart and center. Through force of arms, he turned that nation into a power to be reckoned with in the region. He established a royal dynasty which lasted more than four centuries, and despite character flaws that tested Yahweh's wrath and threatened the unity of his people, he generated such intense mystical spirit that he is still seen by religious Jews as the forerunner of the Messiah still to come. The New Testament suggests Jesus Christ was descended from him.

The youngest son of Jesse, a farmer in fields near Bethlehem, David had been a youthful shepherd when first sought out and secretly anointed by the prophet Samuel at God's behest after the prophet had turned against Saul, the first king of the Jews. But Saul was still king at the time, and David was summoned to his rustic court at Gibeah because of his reputation as a talented harpist. It was thought that, through music, this young warrior might revive the king's spirits during the fits of gloom to which he was increasingly subjected, as the promise of glory he brought to the fledgling Jewish kingdom remained frustratingly unfulfilled. Saul grew fond of David and made him his armor bearer.

But Saul was a man of violent moods and David's popularity at the royal court, and among the people generally, provoked his intense resentment. When the king attempted to kill him in a jealous fit, he fled into the Judaean wilderness. There he formed a band of outcasts, men who were "in distress ... in debt, and ... desperate."[7] Pursued and almost caught by Saul and his army, David offered his services to and was befriended by Achish, king of the Philistine city-state of Gath. In return for Achish's patronage, he and his band were to raid Jewish settlements. David pretended to do so but confined himself to raiding nomadic tribes of the southern desert which had been harassing his people.

When Saul took his own life after failing to crush the Philistines in battle, the brittle ties that had linked the Jewish tribes under him shattered. The situation reverted to being much the same as it had been before his attempt to unite the

Jews and free much of their land from Philistine dominance. David turned that moment of adversity to his own advantage.

Escorted by his small army of irregular desert fighters, he made for Hebron, the main city of Judah, his own tribe. Under threat of Philistine subjugation, the Judaeans welcomed him as a defending champion. The Philistines he had previously served, and whom he was careful not to offend at this stage, raised no objections when he was proclaimed king of Judah.

The Jews now had two kings. Saul's son Ishbosheth had been proclaimed his father's successor as monarch and had established his capital at Mahanaim, east of the Jordan River, beyond the reach of the Philistines. But Ishbosheth was a weak ruler and uninspiring leader. Though hoping to command the support of all the Jewish tribes, he could count only on the loyalty of his own small tribe of Benjamin, those in Transjordan and, less reliably, some in the north (which, through much of the history of ancient Israel, would prove constitutionally resistant to submission to anyone).

However, by the time Ishbosheth was removed from the scene by assassins, David had gained admirers and adherents among all the tribes through careful cultivation of their leaders. Their religious dedication also worked in his favor; priests throughout the land held David in high regard because of his piety and his respect for their status and prerogatives. In contrast to Saul, who had antagonized and alienated them, David included some in his entourage as trusted advisers.

The alternative to David as king would not have seemed overly attractive. The tribes would have had to abandon the quest for national unity while large parts of the land were still dominated by the Philistines and threatened by other neighboring peoples. Even tribal leaders who pointedly recalled that David had seditiously served under the Philistines when he was fleeing from Saul's wrath grudgingly accepted that he displayed the personal qualities essential for someone leading the nation in that stage of its development. Accordingly, at the age of thirty, with the agreement of all the tribes, David was anointed king of all the Jews.

He had already been king of Judah for seven years. But just as ruling that smaller kingdom had been too limiting for a man of his energy and drive, neither was the crown he now donned enough to satisfy his aspirations and objectives. To formalize the emergence finally of a truly indivisible kingdom under his rule, he wanted to establish a religious and national nerve center for the Jewish people.

Hebron, from which he had governed only Judah, was too far to the south. To remain there would have exposed him to accusations that he favored his own tribe over the others. To choose a different location in another tribal area might also have been interpreted as a form of favoritism by tribes not honored that way. The only solution was to pick a location where none of the tribes could claim dominion and where such charges could therefore not be leveled[5].

Jerusalem was not well situated to serve as political hub of the kingdom. It was not on the main trade arteries that ran along the coast and along the fringe of the eastern desert. However, it was more centrally located than Hebron, and it towered imposingly over the countryside.

An ancient sanctuary in existence for at least one thousand years, it was a place of wonder and regard. As capital of the Jewish nation, it would lend David's reign added majesty. In its elevated position—its high point was a fortified citadel called Zion—it was likely to be able withstand even the fiercest of enemy assaults.

The Jebusites, the Canaanite inhabitants of Jerusalem (which was also called Jebus), had previously fought off attacks by Philistines and Jews. So impregnable did their city appear that when apprised of David's intentions to capture it, they boasted that it would withstand any assault even if its walls were manned only by the blind and crippled. That was never put to the test. After seizing control of surrounding lower ground, David's commanding general, Joab, discovered a conduit leading up under the city's walls. Clamoring through it, his soldiers took the defenders by surprise and captured the citadel with neither slaughter nor great exertion.

Established in his new capital and confident of his powers and authority, David became even more of a hero to his people. By beginning to construct a professional army drawn from across the land, and with trans-tribal priestly support, he did much to subdue the separatist inclinations of the northern tribes.

The Philistines were alarmed by what was happening. They had faced little effective resistance from the Jews when the tribes had been divided and often distrustful of each other. Nor had Saul proved a great challenge to them when he was king. But the unification and strengthening of the Jewish nation under David, their former vassal and ally, was a threat they could not countenance.

Not long after David's conquest of Jerusalem, they launched a campaign to destroy him, dispatching a strike force to storm his new royal city. Unprepared as yet for battle and unwilling to expose Jerusalem to the potential ravages of a powerful enemy, David withdrew from the city and led his army southward into Judah, territory he knew well from his marauding days.

---

5.   The Founding Fathers of the United States employed similar reasoning when they chose Washington rather than a city in any of the states to be capital of the new American nation.

When the two armies finally met in a series of engagements, the Philistines were badly trounced. However, the reverses they suffered were not enough to end the menace they posed. So, rather than remaining permanently on the defensive, David took the battle to them. Pursuing the Philistines well into their own territory, he took control of a large area of the coastal strip they had long dominated.

His campaign was so thorough and successful that, though they would at times again be troublesome for the Jewish nation, it largely spelled the end of the Philistines as an expansionist power. Their decline was symbolized by the humbling of Achish, the Philistine king whom David had served as a mercenary when he had been a fugitive from Saul's wrath.

The Philistines now were required to pay tribute to David and, reversing the previous order, Philistine mercenaries began to serve in his army. Indeed, David chose among them for his elite bodyguard.

His military achievements were greatly acclaimed by his people. But he recognized that more was required to overcome the persistent, divisive appeal of their separate tribal identities. Unifying charismatic spiritual leadership was essential and he redesigned the priesthood so that it would serve his goals and purposes. The high priests Abiathar, who had rallied to David when he was an outlaw, and Zadok, the first high priest of the Jewish monarchy under Saul, were to be part of David's entourage, as was the prophet Nathan. Levites throughout the land, members of the priestly non-territorial tribe, were to act for the king as well as perform the work of the Lord so that the two functions were intertwined.

Though he had secured the allegiance of the priests, the tangible core of Jewish spirituality lay elsewhere. The Ark of the Covenant containing the tablets of the law handed down by God to Moses had long been kept under the care of priests at the shrine of Kiriath-Jearim, west of Jerusalem. Especially sacred to the Jews, the shrine was a place of pilgrimage and worship, as were other revered holy places. But David recognized that any alternative focus of religious interest in the land might challenge Jerusalem's supreme status. Having established it as his political capital, he wanted it to be the religious capital of his people as well.

He therefore arranged for the Ark to be brought to Jerusalem and vowed it would find a proper abode there. In accordance with his instructions, it was transferred in a richly ceremonial procession of a kind his people had never before witnessed. Transported on a cart drawn by oxen, it was flanked by priests, accompanied by pilgrims, and escorted by thousands of troops. Trumpets, cymbals, and drums announced their passage. Choirs sang hymns to praise and sanctify the event. Dancers danced along the route, including David himself who, having shed his royal robes to don a simple linen cloth around his waist for the occasion, leapt and danced in frenzied joy and worship.

Those lining the route were awed by their king's display of religious intensity and devotion. His only rebuke came from his wife, Michal, daughter of the deceased King Saul. She scolded him for exhibiting himself in such an unseemly fashion before even slaves and servant girls, debasing his royal dignity. Outraged by her haughtiness, David told her he would never be ashamed to behave in a way that was acceptable to God who, he reminded her, had preferred him to her own father.

She had not grasped the political dimensions of David's extraordinary public religious display. It left no doubt among the populace that the Ark of the Covenant, which belonged to God's people, had come under David's personal protection in a way that it had never been under Saul's. What was more, he intended to build a temple in Jerusalem to house the Ark. It would further glorify his capital and weld the seams that joined the tribes into a single nation.

But his hopes to build such a temple were to be frustrated. The prophet Nathan told him that God had forbidden it because he was a man of war and had shed blood. It was a severe disappointment. But Nathan conveyed to him assurances from God that he would be blessed with even greater glory.

> *I will give you renown like that of the greatest men on earth.... I will subdue all your enemies.... When your days are done and you lie with your fathers, I will raise up your offspring after you, one of your own sons ... and I will establish his throne forever.*[8]

With his capital founded in Jerusalem and popularly called the City of David, the Ark under his personal protection in a specially erected shrine tent, his dynasty established forever by word of the Lord, and his newly built royal palace arousing wide acclaim, David was able to turn his attention to other concerns of the nation.

His priority was to strengthen the bonds with which the loose confederation of tribes had been transformed into a unified state. Borrowing from Egyptian procedures, he appointed administrators with specific duties. Many were based in Jerusalem rather than in tribal centers. They were made responsible and loyal to the king rather than to the elders of the individual tribes.

As David went about consolidating the unity of his people and his own position, he did not confine himself to picking Jews for administrative assignments or to serve as senior military officers. Though careful not to neglect regional political considerations, he considered the skill, experience, and likely reliability of candidates rather than religion or patronage to be the key criteria when making appointments. Non-Jewish officials and mercenaries, proved to be among his most valued appointees.

David became judge as well as king to his people. Disputes between tribes and individuals that could not be settled by his officials were put to him to resolve personally. Petitioners journeyed to the capital to ask him to right wrongs and to beg regal favor. Thus, in addition to being the political, religious, and military nerve center of the land, Jerusalem became the center for the administration of justice.

A census was taken for the first time among the Jews to assess taxes and for conscripting young men from all the tribes into David's standing army (which also had a continuous intake of non-Jewish mercenaries). Unlike the pharaohs of Egypt, David was not deemed divine by his subjects, and he made no claim to divinity. But serving him was made to seem the same as serving God. When his army went into battle at his command, it was confident it enjoyed divine sanction.

Under David, the Jewish nation began assuming ever-greater ascendancy in the region, and he dealt firmly with neighboring peoples who might challenge it. In a series of campaigns, he overwhelmed Edom to the south and Moab and Ammon to the east. Alarmed at his victories, the Aramaeans of Syria went to the aid of their neighboring Ammonites, but they too were subdued. Remaining Canaanite enclaves in the land also came under David's rule.

The Jewish nation grew so formidable that Egypt and Assyria were the only regional powers that might have seriously challenged it. But both were in decline at the time, their capabilities hobbled by domestic problems and their other difficulties in the area. The power vacuum thus created contributed to the emergence of the Jewish state itself as a regional power during David's reign. He built an empire extending from the Mediterranean to the Euphrates in Mesopotamia and from the mountains of Lebanon to the borders of Egypt.

Though he established military garrisons in conquered territory, his treatment of the lands he conquered varied according to the degree of threat they might pose, the resistance they had mounted to him, and the personal relations he had established with their rulers. He deposed some of the kings he vanquished; others he permitted to remain on their thrones as vassals pledging their allegiance and paying tribute. Neighboring rulers found it advisable to avoid offending him. Toi, king of Hamath in northern Syria, was among those who are known to have sent David gifts by way of congratulations for his military successes.

Hiram, king of Tyre on the Phoenician coast—pleased that he no longer had to fear the expansionist aspirations of the Philistines and seeking to live in peace and harmony with David—dispatched emissaries to Jerusalem to offer him an alliance and seal his friendship with the Jewish state.

An alliance with David was also sought by Talmai, ruler of Geshur in the Golan Heights, whose daughter Maacah he married. She bore him his beloved son Absalom, who would almost bring about David's ruin.

God had told Abraham He would make of him a great nation. On God's behalf, David fulfilled that promise, making the nation united, strong, and prosperous. Wealth poured in from tribute and from profits accruing from the busy trade routes through the land of Israel that linked Egypt and southwest Asia commercially.

*   *   *

Throughout his reign, David sought to observe the religious laws regarding ethical conduct and, though king, he felt bound by the standards of justice he had established for his people. Nevertheless, at the high point of his reign he exploited the privileges of his exalted position to transgress against those standards.

While on an upper balcony of his palace one evening, looking out at the panorama beneath him, the king spied the beautiful and shapely Bathsheba on a nearby roof. She was naked, being bathed by a maidservant. Bathsheba was the wife of Uriah, a Hittite officer in the Jewish army stationed with troops fighting the Ammonites. Unable to restrain his lust for her, David exercised his royal prerogative. He sent for her, lay with her, and made her pregnant.

Fearing she would be stoned to death for adultery, Bathsheba pleaded with him to save her. Deeply in love with her, David had Uriah summoned back from the front. As a pretext, he questioned him about the campaign against the Ammonites before suggesting that he go home, take his rest, and sleep with his wife so that it would appear that her husband had impregnated Bathsheba. But Uriah, a soldier of great integrity and dedication, slept instead on the floor of the palace alongside David's bodyguards. He explained that he could not indulge in domestic comforts while his fellow soldiers were making camp on hard ground in enemy territory.

David next invited Uriah to his table and tried to get him drunk so that he might be less resistant to Bathsheba's sensual attractions. But Uriah still would not succumb. Enraged at having his scheme foiled, David sent him back to the front carrying a sealed message for his commanding officer. It contained an order that Uriah be placed in a sector of the attack line where the enemy's resistance was likely to be fiercest. The soldiers who were to fight alongside him were to be ordered to withdraw when the enemy appeared. This they did, but Uriah, true to his warrior creed, stood his ground alone, fought hard, and killed many of the Ammonites before he was himself cut down.

Bathsheba made an ostentatious display of grief over the death of her husband. But when the required period of mourning was over, David and she were married. Their son was born soon afterward. However, the prophet Nathan learned—presumably through palace servants—of the premarital liaison between the king and his new bride and of how Uriah's fate had been sealed. But for all his sense of justice, David was not a man to be confronted with accusations about his own sinful behavior. Fearing his wrath, Nathan resorted to a stratagem.

He asked the king's advice in a case involving a rich man who had mistreated a poor man. The rich man had vast flocks of cattle and sheep but had taken the poor man's only possession—a single lamb of which he was very fond—and had it slaughtered for food, though he already had more than enough to eat. As Nathan had expected, the rich man's arrogance and greed appalled David. He called his behavior wicked and said the culprit deserved to be put to death.

Emboldened by this judgment from the king, Nathan revealed his tale had been a parable, that the rich man was in fact David himself, and that he had committed a grievous crime in taking a man's beloved only wife and calculatingly sending the husband to his death in battle. Nathan said God was angry with David and would exact vengeance. He said he had been instructed to pass on to David a divine judgment against him.

> The sword shall never depart from your house because you spurned Me by taking the wife of Uriah the Hittite and making her your wife.... I will make a calamity rise against you from within your own house. I will take your wives and give them to another man before your very eyes and he shall sleep with your wives. You acted in secret but I will make this happen in the sight of all Israel and in broad daylight.[9]

There was also to be more immediate retribution for David's transgressions. Nathan told him that God would take from him the son Bathsheba had borne him. Anguished by that prospect, the king begged God's forgiveness through prayer and fasting and showed deep remorse. But the baby fell ill and died.

Bathsheba soon conceived by him again and gave birth to another son, who was given the name Solomon. But well before Solomon came of age, Nathan's prophecy that David would have to pay for his misdeeds through violence and humiliation became a reality.

In keeping with prevailing conventions governing inheritance, it was expected that Amnon, the oldest of the king's seventeen sons, would inherit his father's throne in due course. Amnon had been borne to a woman David had married when he was a young man fleeing from King Saul's jealousy and vindictiveness. This crown prince of the Jews was neither a warrior nor a man of rectitude. Accustomed as eldest son of the king to having his every wish and whim satisfied, he lived a dissolute life, the low point of which was forcing himself on David's daughter Tamar, his own half sister.

He had fallen in love with her, but that love evaporated after he had violated her innocence. In its place, he felt deep contempt for his victim and drove her from his home. Disgraced, Tamar tore her clothing in mourning, sprinkled ashes over her head, and displayed her shame in the streets of Jerusalem for all to see.

Though displeased by Amnon's sin and offense, David loved his eldest son, obviously much more than he did Tamar. He was also preoccupied with affairs of state at the time, and Amnon escaped having to answer to him for what he had done. No one else in Jerusalem dared to fall foul of the heir to throne, though his crime and Tamar's shame were public knowledge.

It aroused the fury of her brother Absalom, another of David's sons. He was Tamar's full brother and obliged by custom to exact vengeance. Absalom was second in line to the throne after Amnon, and, in the atmosphere of intrigue that had developed at David's court, he was already bitter about the crown prince's privileged rank. It fed his resolve to avenge his sister's disgrace.

To mark the occasion of a sheep-shearing festival, Absalom organized a lavish feast. As his guests, entertained by musicians and dancers, ate and drank, Absalom's servants, acting on his instructions, crept up on the lecherous Amnon and stabbed him to death.

David was aggrieved and infuriated by the murder of his oldest son. To escape his father's wrath, Absalom fled to the court of his grandfather, King Talmai, in the Golan Heights. Palace intriguers urged David to send an army to bring him back for punishment and to punish Talmai for providing the fugitive with sanctuary. They were alarmed by Absalom's new status as heir to the throne and hoped to have him replaced by someone less headstrong and more pliable.

But losing this son as well as Amnon was more than David would countenance. Nevertheless, Absalom felt it prudent to remain away for three years. Even when it seemed safe for him to return to Jerusalem, David banished him from his court for a further two years, after which, penitent and vowing obedience and love, he was reconciled with his father.

However, Absalom believed his banishment had been unjust and that David should have recognized he had acted properly in avenging his sister's dishonor. It also seemed to him that David was taking far too long to vacate the throne in his favor. He may have feared his father might decide to name a different heir, most likely Solomon. Though younger, Solomon was the offspring of Bathsheba, the king's favorite wife, and was favored by some senior members of David's entourage who believed he would be easier to manipulate after the king died than the strong-willed Absalom.

To press his threatened right to succeed his father, Absalom sought to involve himself increasingly in matters of popular interest. He stood at the city gate each morning to meet people who had come to present David with petitions or grievances but had been unable to see the king. After hearing their requests and complaints, Absalom would assure them that right was on their side and that if he were empowered with the necessary authority, they would receive the justice being denied them. Of agreeable appearance and ingratiating personality, he surrounded himself with advisers, bodyguards, and other trappings of a royal presence and grew enormously popular. In the words of the Bible, Absalom "won away the hearts of the men of Israel."[10]

It was not surprising. David had by then been on the throne a long time. Though he had united the nation, antagonism between the tribes in the north and those in south had continued to smolder not far below the surface. The census he had ordered, to fix taxes and determine how many young men would be available for army conscription, was hugely unpopular. It was considered tyrannical and provoked concern that the king was planning new military campaigns, which indeed he was. When an epidemic of disease broke out and caused many deaths, it was widely believed to be God's retribution for the wickedness of holding the census, and David was held responsible.

Even before Prince Absalom's self-seeking interest in affairs of state had manifested itself, David's image as benevolent despot had begun to tarnish. His imperiousness and growing neglect of political realities blunted his popularity. Grievances and indignation simmered among those who objected to how the authority and role of tribal elders had been undermined. Impatient to rule the land, Absalom seized upon those resentments to depose his father.

With the permission of the unsuspecting David, he left Jerusalem for Hebron, David's old stronghold. Gathering an army of dissidents, malcontents, debtors, and adventurers—much like the men of the marauding force young David had gathered when he was fleeing King Saul—he raised the flag of rebellion.

Many who were loyal to Saul's memory rallied to his cause. Other rebels had been among David's followers but had become disenchanted with the king. Many felt they had been slighted by him or resented his assumption of dictatorial powers or believed he had sinned in calling the census. Absalom drew support even in Judah, David's original power base. Many there had been embittered by David's refusal to favor his own tribesmen and his reliance on trusted foreign mercenaries.

Absalom prepared his rebellion with thoroughness. Through secret emissaries, he had acquired supporters in many parts of the kingdom and received pledges of allegiance from envoys from all the major towns. As the movement toward insurrection gathered momentum, "King" Absalom was openly and widely acclaimed.

David did not at first realize that a coup was in the making. But once apprised of the situation, he acted quickly. Informed that Absalom had gathered forces strong enough to storm Jerusalem, where his renegade son also had many adherents, he fled the capital accompanied by his family and escorted by his troop of bodyguards. Hushai, one of his most valued and loyal advisers, was instructed to stay behind in Jerusalem and pretend he had been recruited to Absalom's cause. He was to keep David alerted to developments after Absalom marched into the capital to establish himself there.

As a secret agent in Absalom's court, Hushai performed a crucial service for the king. Gaining the confidence of the would-be usurper, he urged him to disregard advice to pursue David before he could rally support. He advised Absalom that his father, who was on the run and vulnerable, still commanded an army that was capable of defeating his enemies on the field of battle. He urged Absalom to gather stronger forces of his own, drawn from the entire nation, "as numerous as the sands of the sea,"[11] before going in pursuit of the king.

Absalom agreed to hold back as he reveled in the regal pleasures of Jerusalem. To demonstrate that he had now replaced his absconding father as king, he disgraced him by taking possession of his concubines, left behind in the royal party's hasty departure from the capital. Long before, when David had maliciously sent Bathsheba's husband Uriah to his death in combat, the prophet Nathan had said that as punishment another man would lie with his wives. Now that was happening.

Though Absalom did not hurry in pursuit of his father, David's flight was not without its dangers. Though ritually ordained king of the Jews, he was received with scorn and neglect on his flight through the territory of the tribe of Benjamin—kinsmen of Saul and Ishbosheth, the first two kings whose royal dynasty he had defied and then extinguished. But he fled safely into Transjordan, where he examined the situation in comparative safety, tallied up his resources, and judged his prospects.

David was not without adherents. His military commander, Joab, remained loyal, as did the forces under Joab's direct command. So did the mercenaries who had sworn personal allegiance to the king and had fought battles for him. He was again offered welcome in Transjordan where he had been given shelter while fleeing from Saul much earlier. Based there, he rallied the Transjordanian Jews to his side, so that when Absalom finally pieced together an army which he believed strong enough to deal with his father, he was able to meet his son's challenge on the field of battle.

Absalom's army was larger, but David had the advantage. His rebellious son's army commanders were inexperienced, while David's officers, led by Joab, were seasoned warriors. Absalom's soldiers, mostly new conscripts, were deployed without coherent strategic order and had no plan of battle. David's army, which included many combat-hardened fighters, was well deployed in flanking and frontal assault contingents. Holding to prearranged offensive tactics, they savaged their foes.

Absalom was not spared. Fleeing from defeat, he was wrenched from his mount when his long, thick hair became tangled in overhanging branches. David had given instructions that his son was not to be harmed. But, enraged by the rebellion and the lives it had cost, Joab, who had gone in pursuit, found Absalom still trapped in the tree, his body twitching helplessly off the ground as he struggled desperately to free himself. Joab ran the would-be king through with his sword and his soldiers finished the task of ending his life.

Word of Absalom's death left David in agony. He cried out in anguish, "My son Absalom! O my son, my son Absalom! If only I had died instead of you. O Absalom, my son, my son!"[12] His mourning was so unrelenting that Joab dared to rebuke him. He told the king that he was humiliating his own loyal warriors who had saved his life and the lives of other members of his family. Joab told David that he showed his "love for those who hate you and hate for those who love you. You have made it clear today that the officers and men mean nothing to you. I am sure that if Absalom were alive today and the rest of us dead, you would have preferred it."[13]

Joab warned David that unless he joined his soldiers in celebrating their triumph in battle, they would depart, leaving him to find his way back to Jerusalem without an army. Recognizing that his position was still uncertain, David masked his grief and went to sit with his soldiers.

He was dismayed that though his reign had begun in glory, he now ruled a kingdom in which discord had resurfaced and which had been subjected to civil war. The immediate challenge to his crown had been crushed, but recrossing the River Jordan to return to Jerusalem, he fumblingly sowed new seeds of discontent.

He had received pledges of renewed allegiance from all the tribal elders but made a special effort to regain the affection of the people of Judah, his own tribe. Many of them had long felt neglected by him and had rallied to Absalom's rebellion. To regain their affection and allegiance, he arranged for Judaeans to provide the vanguard escorting him back to his throne in triumph.

That act of favoritism had damaging consequences, stirring resentment among tribes that had remained loyal to him. He also fueled bitterness by forgiving his nephew Amasa, the warrior who had led Absalom's mutinous army. He appointed him commander of his own army in place of the faithful Joab, who was never to be forgiven for Absalom's death.

The rebellion had been crushed, but the unity of the nation which David had done so much to forge as a younger man had become tenuous. Unable to heal the reappearing rifts, the king became old in spirit as well as age. His body grew creaky, and he shivered with cold, even in the summer heat of Jerusalem. His servants chose Abishag, a comely young girl, to lie close to the king in bed to comfort him and keep him warm.

His oldest surviving son, Adonijah, now took on the attitudes and many of the duties of crown prince, confidently expecting to succeed his father on the throne before much longer. Like Absalom before him, he gathered counselors, advocates, and hangers-on at David's court. He presumed to dress in regal fashion and acquired chariots, mounted courtiers, and heralds who ran before him to announce his coming wherever he went.

A change in leadership of the kingdom seeming imminent; several of the other princes, Joab, and some senior priests supported Adonijah's claim. Just as the rise of Absalom had been preceded by public declarations of acclaim for him, so cries in praise of "King Adonijah"[14] could be heard in the streets of Jerusalem and in other parts of the land.

David mourning the Death of His Son Absalom

However, the revered prophet Nathan was not among Adonijah's advocates. Doubting that he would make a suitable ruler for the Jews and having conspiratorial loyalties elsewhere, Nathan urged Queen Bathsheba to go to David and convince him that he had promised her that their son Solomon would be his royal heir.

Bathsheba was also to tell him his marriage to her would retrospectively be deemed an abomination if Adonijah inherited the crown and that both Solomon and she would be put to death. Nathan then followed her into the presence of the elderly, forgetful David to confirm Bathsheba's story about his promise that Solomon would inherit the kingdom and to advise him to keep that promise.

Nathan and Bathsheba also persuaded him that Adonijah, impatient to mount the throne, was about to attempt to seize it by force. David had already heard rumors to that effect and ordered his mercenary bodyguards, who had remained immune to the pressures of palace politics, to guard Solomon from assassination. The favored young prince was then dispatched in procession to the consecrated spring of Gihon in the Kidron Valley, where, at David's instructions, Nathan and the high priest Zadok anointed him king to the sound of the ram's horn. According to legend, God's approval was signified by Solomon riding to his coronation mounted on a she-mule, a creature which, unlike others of that species, was not a product of crossbreeding between a horse and a donkey, but was deemed a special act of creation.

After Solomon had been anointed, David summoned all senior officials of the land, including leaders of the clans and senior military officers, to Jerusalem and instructed them to honor and obey their new king. He told them God had chosen Solomon to build a temple in Jerusalem to be a shelter for the Ark of the Covenant, an edifice he himself had been forbidden to construct because he had been a man of war. He said that God had told him that Solomon's kingdom would last forever if he continued to be true to His sacred laws and commands.

By acting so resolutely, David averted a new civil war. Faced with his father's decisiveness, Adonijah realized he would have been unable to gather sufficient forces to vanquish those which had already vowed allegiance to David's chosen successor, and he abandoned his hopes of replacing the newly anointed Solomon.

Solomon sent word to his frustrated older half brother that as long as he was loyal to him he would not have to fear for his safety. Fearing for his life nevertheless, Adonijah sought sanctuary near the Ark of the Covenant in its temporary tent abode in Jerusalem.

From the time of Solomon's coronation, David played little role in affairs of state or palace intrigue though ostensibly ruling the nation together with

Solomon. Having reigned for forty years, he was now seventy years old and exhausted from the triumphs and grief he had experienced and endured. He grew increasingly reflective and philosophical, seeing life as something humans pass through as exiles and strangers.

When he died, he was buried in a mausoleum he had built in Jerusalem. His achievements had been monumental. He had turned a loose federation of tribes into a thriving kingdom. He had destroyed the previously dominant power of the Philistines, subdued Israel's other adversaries, and built a formidable standing army. Despite his shortcomings, transgressions, and the persisting grumblings of discord in the land (some of it still deeply implanted), he had led his people to greater unity and a greater sense of security than they had ever known. He had imbued them with a vibrant sense of common identity that has persisted to this day.

According to the Bible, the Lord bestowed on David a special divine covenant, distinct from the one established earlier with the Children of Israel, making them the chosen people. David and his direct descendants were picked by Yahweh to reign over them for all time: "I will establish his line forever, his throne, as long as the heavens last."[15] No figure in the history of the Jews—not Abraham the founding father, not Moses the lawgiver, none of the great prophets—has left as profound an impression on the Jewish people as David. Without David, there might not have been an enduring Jewish nation.

King Solomon

SOLOMON

961–931 BC

When Solomon became king of the Jews, the situation was hugely different than it had been when his father, David, had donned the crown. Within a relatively short period of time—roughly forty years—David had created a unified nation of the land in which tribes had jealously guarded their separate identities. What was more, that nation had humbled its adversaries, expanded territorially, and become confident and secure.

The emergence of the land of Israel as a regional power had been assisted by the decline of neighboring superpowers Egypt and Assyria which previously would not have tolerated such impudence. But whatever the reasons, as successor to his illustrious father, King Solomon was to become the first Jewish leader of international distinction.

Building on David's accomplishments, Solomon transformed Israel into a highly centralized, bureaucratized state, administered by civil servants of various ranks and guarded by a beefed-up army with up-to-date weaponry and facilities. He hugely increased the nation's wealth through commerce and the exploitation of natural resources and turned Jerusalem, so recently only a hilltop town, into a major city. Within it, he built the temple that was to become the central focus of Jewish worship. His royal court was a place of legendary luxury and indulgence, and he himself was said to leave visitors breathless with admiration of his wizard-like wisdom.

Solomon—also called Jedidiah (beloved of God)—was twenty years old when he was anointed king by the prophet Nathan and the High Priest Zadok. For the first two years of his reign, he shared the throne with his increasingly feeble father. During that time, he discreetly refrained from major exercise of his royal prerogatives. But he was alert to the implications of the strained circumstances of his succession.

Palace intrigue had played a central role in his elevation. Influential court and army figures had opposed it. Therefore, when David died, Solomon acted quickly to consolidate his position and stamp his personal mark on the throne, the way David had advised him: "Be strong and show yourself a man."[16]

Among his first acts after David's death was eliminating the two figures who might have posed a threat to him. At his command, both his half brother Adonijah and David's army commander, Joab, who had supported Adonijah's claim to the throne, were executed.

High Priest Abiathar, who had also preferred Solomon as king, was removed from the scene as well. Solomon banished him from Jerusalem, sending him to live out his life in the country town where he had been born and where palace conspiracies were unlikely to develop. Zadok, on whose allegiance Solomon could rely and who had shared the high priestly role with Abiathar, would occupy that position alone. Blood descent from Zadok would confer legitimacy on the high priests of the Jews for centuries to come.

Another loose end that Solomon tied up at the beginning of his reign concerned Shimei, an elder of the tribe of Benjamin who had assailed David with insults and scorn when he was in flight during his son Absalom's thwarted coup. David had subsequently forgiven him, but in the atmosphere of suspicion that now prevailed, Solomon acted to minimize the possibility of renewed tribal rivalries. He confined Shimei to Jerusalem, where his movements and actions could be monitored, and soon contrived a convenient reason to have him executed as well.

"Thus," says the Bible, "the kingdom was secured in Solomon's hands."[17] Solomon had demonstrated his determination to crush divisive tendencies that could tear the Jewish kingdom apart and had acted ruthlessly to establish the invulnerability of his position. But sustaining the fragile national solidarity required more than that.

Unlike his father, Solomon was neither an acclaimed warrior nor yet a charismatic figure. David had overwhelmed or cowed potential enemies among neighboring peoples, so a call by his son now for unity among the Jews to ward off external threats would have had little credibility. He had to find other means to cultivate the allegiance of his subjects and sustain their commitment to an undivided kingdom with its center in Jerusalem. To that end, he set to work constructing the Holy Temple in the city. It was to be a monumental tribute and place of homage to the God of the Jews as well as their awe-inspiring center of worship, and it would steeply downgrade the role and attractions of local shrines.

To others as well as to the Jews themselves, their religion and heritage identified them as essentially one people. The Temple would be the symbol of both the living faith that bound them together and the nation David had shaped and made mighty. It would also symbolize the historic link between that nation and the wandering tribes with whom God had made a covenant as they had made their way through the desert wilderness to the land He had promised them.

This grandiose structure was to be built on a rising above the city at a place which is still called the Temple Mount. It was to be worthy of God, of the people chosen by God and of the proud potentate who had inherited David's kingdom.

For this, Solomon needed appropriate materials and skilled artisans, both of which were in short supply within the borders of Israel. However, Hiram—king of Tyre on the coast to the north, the son of a Jewish mother and a Syrian father, and an ally of the deceased David—provided both timber from the cedars of Lebanon and craftsmen to help design and construct the Temple.

The cedars for the Temple were cut down in the hills above Tyre, carted down to the sea, tied onto rafts, and floated down the Mediterranean coast to the port at Jaffa forty miles west of Jerusalem. All preliminary stonework for the Temple was done where the stone was quarried, so the Temple compound would not be contaminated by the use of metal tools, and the finished stone was hauled overland to the construction site. For this, and other tasks related to the project, Solomon conscripted an army of forced labor, including one hundred and fifty thousand able-bodied Ammonites, Hittites, and other non-Jews.

Thirty thousand Jews were also conscripted for forced labor related to the building of the Temple. They were divided into three divisions of ten thousand men each. Each division spent one month felling trees and shifting timber, followed by two months at home.

It was four years into Solomon's reign before actual construction commenced and it took seven years for it to be fully realized. The finished edifice was richly decorated with precious wood and metals. Its high ceiling was of cedar, and its walls were finished with cedar panels. The stone superstructure was totally concealed.

The temple's furnishings, candleholders, basins, dishes, censers for incense, various ornaments, and furniture were of gold, silver, brass, or cedar. Gold chains were stretched across the entrances of the central passageways linking the inner halls. Harps and other instruments used in religious ceremonies both within and outside the Temple were made of precious wood and a gold and silver alloy. Temple priests wore garments of fine linen belted with rich purple girdles. Senior priests were attired in long robes studded with precious stones.

For the Temple's dedication ceremony, Solomon called together the elders of all the tribes and the entire priestly tribe of Levi. When they had gathered in the Temple's monumental courtyard, priests carried the Ark of the Covenant to its new resting place in the Temple's Holy of Holies, the chamber to which only the high priest was permitted access and only on the holiest day of the year, the Day of Atonement (*Yom Kippur*). Presiding over the ceremony with great flair and pomp, Solomon told the assembled dignitaries that God had chosen Jerusalem to be at the heart of the nation. He reminded them that God had also chosen his father, David, to be king over Israel, and that he himself had been chosen to build the Temple to house the sacred Ark. For those in attendance, this was living history, tribal memory, divine identity, national pride, and personal glorification all in one. It linked the covenant between God and the Children of Israel to the covenant between God and the House of David and, by logical progression, to a special relationship between God and Solomon.

Solomon's royal palace close to the Temple, flanked by exquisite gardens, was a magnificent structure as well, consisting of several linked buildings, including the royal residence and the House of the Forest of Lebanon, an armory whose roof was supported by a "forest" of cedar pillars. Elsewhere in the palace was the throne room and judgment hall which housed Solomon's throne of ivory overlaid with fine gold, perched on a raised platform six steps up, each step flanked by statues of lions. It was there that Solomon received distinguished visitors and petitioners.

By building his palace near the Temple, Solomon further followed David's example of identifying himself and his reign with the spiritual life of the nation. Acting as a priest himself, he performed sacred sacrifices and conveyed the blessings of God to his people. With High Priest Abiathar dismissed and exiled to the countryside and High Priest Zadok retaining his position only through royal favor, no religious figure could undermine the king's position as the prophet Samuel had undermined King Saul's.

Solomon maintained a large royal bodyguard consisting of more than one thousand picked men armed, at least for ceremonial purposes, with spears and shields of gold. Among their duties was to attend the king when he made his way the short distance between his palace and the Temple.

Under Solomon, the face and character of Jerusalem was transformed. David had made it the capital of the people. Under Solomon, it was turned into a much-expanded, stately royal city. Following his example and the requirements of fashion, his courtiers, senior officials, and wealthy merchants in Jerusalem built majestic homes for themselves. Solomon had the walls of the city repaired and strengthened and surmounted by lookout towers.

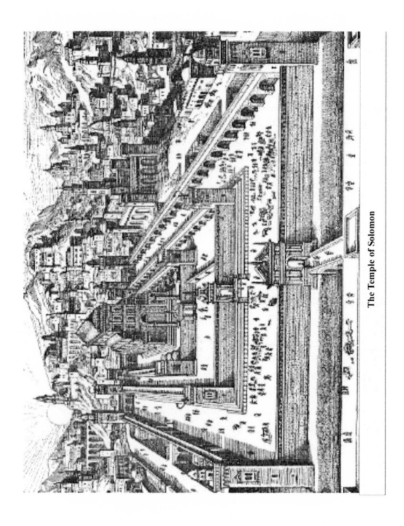

The Temple of Solomon

Jerusalem became a flourishing metropolis. Great numbers of people abandoned the surrounding countryside and nearby towns to take up residence there and partake of its thriving economic and cultural life. Religious pilgrims converged on it from all parts of the land. Visitors from foreign lands were drawn to Jerusalem by word of its wonders and Solomon's growing reputation.

Unlike David, Solomon fought no wars of great territorial or political significance and never personally engaged in combat. Unlike David's rise to power, which had been studded with conspiracy, wars, and adventure, most of Solomon's time on the throne (after he had eliminated possible challengers at the start) was tranquil. Nevertheless, he built a formidable fighting force to guard the empire he had inherited from David, far more powerful than the one David had fashioned for the security of the fledgling Jewish nation.

This army was equipped for the first time with chariots and boasted an elite corps of charioteers. They were deployed in fortified garrison towns which Solomon erected throughout his realm. These strongholds were meant to provide both a perimeter defense for his kingdom as well as an internal security network. The town of Tamar, near the Dead Sea, guarded the southern approaches of the land. Hazor, south of the Sea of Galilee, was transformed into a fortress town on the approaches from Syria. Megiddo (the fabled Armageddon) secured the main pass of the Carmel Mountains.

The design of these outposts displayed an imaginative flair for military architecture. In addition to being strategically positioned, they were built in such a way as to be easily defended, while at the same time it was possible for the chariots garrisoned within their walls to be quickly dispatched on offensive operations.

Solomon had warehouses positioned in different parts of the land to store grain against recurring scarcity, an overdue precaution in a region chronically afflicted by drought and famine. He had new roads built and punctuated them with guardhouses to guarantee the safety of the trade routes crossing his domain and the caravans that traversed them.

Mindful of the experiences of his predecessors, Solomon sternly stifled disaffection and discontent wherever they surfaced as he went about his massive modernization programs. But for those accepting the king as rightful ruler, the administration of justice appeared to be impartial and evenhanded. Ordinary people came before the monarch with their problems and petitions, and dignitaries from far-off places were said to have converged on Jerusalem to consult him. Included among them was the Queen of Sheba (in what is now probably Yemen), who came, bearing sumptuous gifts, "to test him with hard questions,"[18] the answers to which dazzled her.

It was said he needed no witnesses to make a judgment in a dispute, that he could tell right from wrong merely by looking at the faces of the parties involved, could cure disease by uttering incantations which only he knew, could grow all types of plants which the soil of the region had never before been able to sustain, and was capable of conversing with animals, settling disputes between them.

It was said that beasts and fowl trooped and flew happily to the palace kitchens for the honor of being prepared for the king's dinner. It was said he had power over spirits and demons which served him as personal attendants and brought him precious gems from remote corners of the world.

The Bible credits Solomon with having composed three thousand proverbs. Because of his reputation for wisdom and perception, composition of both the philosophical Ecclesiastes and the haunting love poetry of the Song of Songs were subsequently attributed to him, though scholars examining their linguistic qualities and derivations have cast doubt on his authorship. Nevertheless, rich cultural activity was a feature of Solomon's reign.

The Bible's accounts of the period are likely to have been based on extensive records compiled by the king's scribes. They testify to the likely flowering of literary activity at the time, the product of which was subsequently mainly lost. It is also likely that the wealth and grandeur of Solomon's court attracted musicians and savants of all sorts from across the land and from further afield.

In addition to acting assertively to protect his kingdom and his reign, Solomon cultivated extensive trading arrangements with other nations of the region and elsewhere. Like David, he controlled what the Romans would later call the Via Maris—the heavily trafficked overland route running along the Mediterranean shore linking southwestern Asia with Egypt and North Africa—as well as the equally busy so-called King's Highway which traversed Transjordan. Caravan routes to and from the eastern deserts also came under his royal sway. Along those routes, patrolled and controlled by Solomon's officials and soldiers, the treasures of the region were transported: gold, silver, and other precious and non-precious metals, grain and spices, timber and fabrics, livestock and such exotic animals as monkeys and peacocks. His subjects became deeply engaged in commerce. They bought horses from Cilicia and chariots from Egypt and sold them to the Aramaeans of Syria and other neighboring peoples.

Solomon built a merchant fleet and, with the assistance of Hiram of Tyre, who contracted shipwrights and sailors out to him, he dispatched his traders along the eastern Mediterranean shore and as far as Spain in search of goods and markets. He had the harbor of Ezion-geber (Eilat) constructed on the Gulf of

Aqaba to send his ships through the Red Sea to ports of call in Arabia and elsewhere.

There is nothing to positively identify Ophir, a place from which Jewish merchants returned with dazzling riches. Some have suggested it was India, though it is more likely to have been in or near Somalia, on the east coast of Africa.

In addition to fostering foreign commerce, Solomon oversaw a surge in the development of domestic industries. Large new areas of the land were opened to crop cultivation. Mines were dug and furnaces built south of the Dead Sea to expand copper production. Much of the newly created wealth remained in the king's coffers to finance royal expenditures and massive architectural projects designed to fortify and modernize cities across the land. Much of it also filtered down to his subjects, though people in the south of the land benefited most from the economic boom, an imbalance for which an accounting would have to be made.

Solomon vastly extended and altered the system David had devised for administering the land of Israel. It was divided into twelve districts for tax and administrative purposes. By substituting those districts for the preexisting tribal regions, Solomon hoped to weaken tenacious local loyalties and put an end to tribal divisiveness that might undermine his authority and administrative efficiency. The reorganization would also make it easier for the nation to integrate the many non-Jews who resided in the land and belonged to none of the ancestral tribes.

The system required great numbers of officials and civil servants of various kinds and ranks. A large bureaucracy was created, in addition to the small army of palace retainers and scribes. There were, for example, no less than 550 administrators for just the forced labor conscripted for Solomon's massive projects. The military—organized as a large standing army and garrisoned in various places across the country—was also intricately and expensively maintained.

An even more striking change under Solomon was the character of the royal court. During the last years of David's reign, the court in Jerusalem had begun to take on the trappings of luxury. But David had been a warrior, and his senior advisers and aides had gone through battle, intrigue, and exile with him. For much of the time, theirs had been a life of danger and excitement. David had required no vast army of officials, no battalions of courtiers, no bodyguard armed with golden weapons to provide a ceremonial escort wherever he went.

By the time Solomon ascended the throne, the rough edge of David's struggle for security had been worked smooth. The turbulent tone that had dominated the center of power and authority had been soothed and tempered. Now that center became the court of a securely established Middle Eastern potentate, more luxurious by far than anything the Jews had known before.

Solomon's harem was huge, swollen by the daughters of foreign kings and dignitaries whom he took as wives for diplomatic or commercial purposes. Among those in his seraglio were Ammonite, Moabite, Edomite, Tyranian, Hittite, and Sidonian women. Neither national identity nor religion was a bar. According to the Bible, Solomon took a total of seven hundred wives plus three hundred concubines. Many blamed the extravagant size of his harem for undermining his piety. The Bible says his foreign wives made him turn away from God.

For his Egyptian bride, who was accustomed to luxuries of the pharaoh's court, he imported vast amounts of gold and other precious construction materials to build her a palace where she could worship Egyptian gods. Egypt was far from the height of its powers at the time, but it was still a proud nation, one to be respected. That Solomon was permitted to marry an Egyptian royal princess testifies to his elevated personal status and the status of the land over which he reigned.

Some of Solomon's other foreign wives also practiced the rituals of their pagan religions, as did visitors from various lands who converged on Jerusalem for trade or to do homage to the king of the Jews.

By his orders, they were permitted to erect their idols and worship their gods in the holy city. Altars were erected there for the worship of the Sidonian god, Astarte; the Moabite god, Chemosh; and the Ammonite god, Milcom. Such pagan influences, as well as preexisting ones, would long continue to pose a challenge to the monotheism of the Jews.

Indignant priests of the Temple feared people would succumb to foreign idolatry, as they had at the foot of Mount Sinai while Moses was receiving the tablets of the law from God. The Bible says Solomon did "what was displeasing to the Lord"[19] by tolerating and even promoting pagan worship. The prophet Ahijah told him that his sinfulness would cost his offspring inheritance of the land of Israel. But, secure in his command of the nation and the religious centrality of the Jerusalem Temple, he was little troubled by such grim prognostications.

Solomon's harem and legion of servants, his courtiers and bodyguard, their multitude of military and ceremonial horses and camels all required considerable upkeep. This was provided by a regulated arrangement for the collection of royal tribute from the twelve districts into which the land was divided. The districts took turns providing the court with provisions, each for one month of each year. It was a severely taxing requirement. Just feeding the royal court was a major undertaking. Its kitchens had to be provided each day with thirty oxen, nine hundred bushels of flour, and one hundred sheep, as well as poultry and venison.

However, there was little to trouble Solomon, his court and his officials seriously during most of his thirty-seven-year reign. But in its closing years, neighboring tributary states, whose allegiance he had inherited from his father, grew restive.

Hadad (prince of Edom, south of the Dead Sea) sought belated vengeance for David's brutal suppression of an Edomite rebellion. He organized a troop of irregulars who engaged in hit-and-run attacks on Jewish outposts and on caravans carrying goods from the shores of the Red Sea.

Problems also developed with the Aramaean kingdom of Damascus, control of which was seized by Rezon, a survivor of the Aramaeans David had vanquished. Rezon crowned himself king of Damascus, and, like the Edomites, launched forays into Jewish territory. Solomon saw these as no more than nuisances with which his army could deal. But they chipped away at the fringes of his domain. He felt obliged to award friendly Tyre in Lebanon the gift of twenty towns in Galilee for its continuing fidelity.

That royal bestowal was not taken well by his subjects in the region. They objected to being made to pay the price for the king's generosity. But the seeds of decay for the nation Solomon had bureaucratized had already begun sprouting on home ground as well as beyond its borders.

Most Jews were still agrarians, living off the land. But increasing numbers of them had become city dwellers. Many were makers and sellers of goods or were artisans, merchants, and the providers of services. Solomon's commercial revolution, combined with the growth of urbanization which his projects accelerated, had made class stratification and class rivalries among the Jews much more pronounced than they had ever been before.

More people were rich. But countless more were poor, and the gaps between them grew ever larger, undermining national cohesion. The establishment of chariot units in the army had led to the creation of a corps of elite military officers whose privileged status undermined the egalitarian character of previous Jewish fighting forces. That was also resented, as was the conscription of Jews as well as foreigners for forced labor on Solomon's elaborate construction schemes. It conjured up images of slavery in Egypt before the Exodus.

The ostentatious luxury of the class of privileged nobles and aristocrats provoked much grumbling. Royal pomp and prodigal state expenditure could not sit well with people who had never been so heavily or methodically taxed by a well-organized central administration.

Before Saul had been crowned the first king of the Jews, the prophet Samuel had warned the people that their wish for a monarch of their own would lead to limits being placed on their freedom. That was now happening.

Solomon remained popular with the people of his own tribe, Judah, who continued to benefit most from the economic boom and whose men suffered less than others from forced labor requirements. They believed that he was fulfilling the prospect of glory that David's achievements had foretold and that God had promised through the agency of the Patriarchs and the prophets.

But alienation was rampant in parts of the land that did not do as well and was made worse by the reduced status of tribal elders. Having inherited the crown without having to seek the allegiance of those elders and, unlike David, never having had to solicit their support while on the run from enemies, Solomon had neither a sense of their importance nor interest in their future. Under him, regional administrators—who were answerable to the crown, and who were for the most part loathed by the people they governed on Solomon's behalf—expropriated their central role.

Disenchantment eventually led to a rising against him in the north. His army crushed it with little difficulty, and he remained incapable of recognizing the need to cultivate unity among a people which had been transformed from "an ancient tribal society into a sophisticated national state within less than a century,"[20] but for whom centrifugal forces were still very much in play.

The price the Jewish nation would have to pay for his shortcomings in that regard would be extracted immediately upon his death.

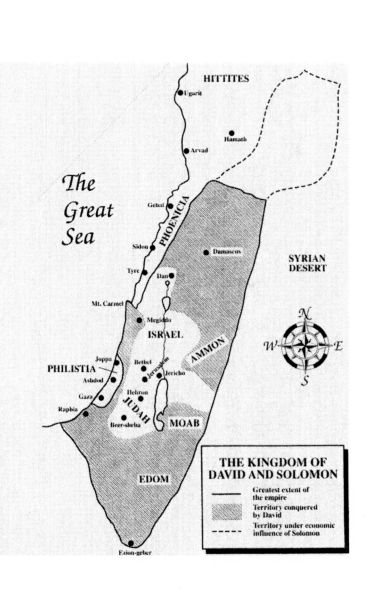

HITTITES

Ugarit

Hamath

Arvad

The
Great
Sea

Gebal

PHOENICIA

Sidon

Damascus

SYRIAN
DESERT

Tyre

Dan

Mt. Carmel

Megiddo

ISRAEL

AMMON

Joppa
Bethel
Jerusalem
Jericho

PHILISTIA

Ashdod

Gaza
Hebron

Raphia

JUDAH

MOAB

Beer-sheba

N

W   E

S

EDOM

Ezion-geber

THE KINGDOM OF DAVID AND SOLOMON

—— Greatest extent of
the empire

░ Territory conquered
by David

‑ ‑ ‑ Territory under economic
influence of Solomon

THE DIVIDED NATION

THE NEW KINGDOMS

The death of King Solomon opened a fresh chapter in the history of the Jewish people. Oppression by the instruments of the monarchy, sectional differences, and sharp disparities in living standards blunted their allegiance to the kingdom Saul had founded, David had united, and Solomon had turned into a bureaucratized state.

Most Jews had become alienated from the Jerusalem power center dominated by the tribe of Judah with which the smaller tribe of Benjamin had become closely affiliated. Feelings among the less privileged ten tribes had become so bitter that Solomon's kingdom was torn apart. The territories of Judah and Benjamin became the southern kingdom of Judah. The territories of the tribes occupying the center and north of the land merged to form the separate kingdom of Israel.

Each had its own king and army. Jerusalem remained Judah's national and religious center while Israel established its own centers of government and worship.

The peoples of both kingdoms continued to hold core values in common, including the belief that their God Yahweh had chosen them as His favored people and had made a covenant with them. They also shared tribal memories of the Patriarchs who founded their religion, of the escape from subjugation in Egypt, and of the long trek across the desert to the promised land.

Those were powerful linkages, undiluted by the differences that split their nation and kept the two kingdoms apart throughout their existences. Prophets and other holy men wandered across the barely defined dividing borders to promote the common Jewish identity of their people through observance of the laws God had handed down through Moses.

But despite having much in common, Israel and Judah were different in important ways. Territorially, the northern kingdom was much bigger. It had a significantly larger population and enjoyed greater agricultural and other natural resources. Israel was also strategically and lucratively situated astride the trade routes across the region and had access to the Mediterranean coast.

As a consequence, it played a more significant role than Judah in the international affairs of the region. The southern kingdom was, however, far less vulnerable than Israel to political upheaval and internal divisions. It benefited from almost uninterrupted rule by its religiously enshrined royal dynasty whose members were directly descended from David. With one brief exception, when Queen Athaliah seized the throne, all of Judah's monarchs were of that single dynasty.

The prophet Nathan had conveyed word from God to David that, "Your house and your kingship shall ever be secure.... Your throne shall be established forever."[21] Carried forward from generation to generation in Judah, that was a potent unifying symbol, assuring virtually uncontested royal continuity.

In contrast, struggles for power were a recurrent theme in Israel. Throughout its history, the northern kingdom could boast of only one monarchical dynasty able to survive more than three generations.

Judah also had an advantage over Israel in boasting Jerusalem as its capital. With its magnificent Temple housing the Ark of the Covenant, the holiest relic of the Jewish faith, the city enjoyed a distinctive mystique. As a popular national and religious center for all Jews, it could not be seriously rivaled by Samaria which would be founded to become Israel's capital city, or by religious shrines in the northern kingdom.

Israel's population included a large minority that did not worship Yahweh, or for whom He was only one of their deities. But paganism was a divisive element with which priests and prophets contended in Judah as well.

The two Jewish kingdoms alternated between hostility and collaboration. Divided, they were often exposed to harassment and invasion by people from neighboring lands, some of which had been reduced to vassal status during the reigns of David and Solomon.

Israel and Judah remained separate kingdoms until each was ultimately overrun by a foreign superpower. The Assyrians obliterated Israel in 722 BCE, two centuries after the two kingdoms were created. Judah fell to the Babylonians 135 years later, but the Jewish nation would subsequently be reborn.

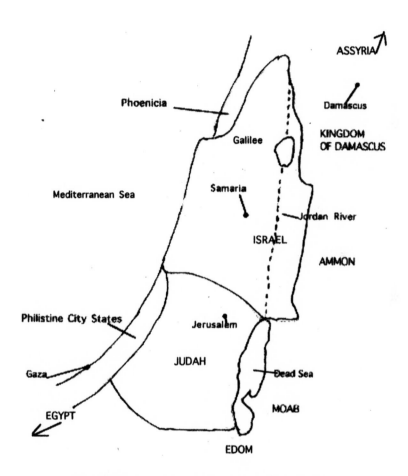

The Kingdoms of Israel and Judah

KINGS OF ISRAEL

JEROBOAM

931–910 BCE

As a young man, Jeroboam had been employed as a laborer on one of King Solomon's many construction projects. Judged worthy of greater responsibilities, he was made a regional supervisor of the forced labor engaged in some of those enterprises.

Despite his promotion, Jeroboam disapproved of fundamental aspects of how the land was being governed. He objected to the privileges awarded to the tribal region of Judah at the expense of the rest of the country and to generally heavy-handed rule from Jerusalem, as administered by regional civil servants like himself.

By Jeroboam's time, the kingdom of the Jews first established under King Saul had existed the better part of a century, more or less united during most of that time. But despite the attempt by Jerusalem to downgrade or discount tribal distinctions, they had become only marginally less significant to the people of the land, fueling enmity between the royally favored south and the less privileged territories of the other tribes.

Even as David had gone about unifying the land of Israel, those territories had often also been known collectively and separately as Israel, distinguishing them from the tribes of Judah and Simeon, the latter having been largely absorbed into Judah. It was a relic of the real, though less defined, relationships they had enjoyed during the time of the Judges, before the establishment of the monarchy.

Jeroboam's tribal affiliation was significant. His tribe of Ephraim occupied much of the center of the land. Because of its size and geographic position, it had been the most eminent of the tribes before being superceded by Judah under King David. It was from Ephraim that the great Joshua—who had led the Jews into the land of Canaan after their trans-Sinai trek—had sprung. It was the site of the most revered ancient shrines at Shiloh and Shechem, both now overshadowed by the Temple in Jerusalem.

During the closing years of Solomon's reign, Jeroboam, encouraged by the prophet Ahijah, organized a rebellion against the king's dictatorial rule. When it was crushed, he fled to Egypt, where he was given asylum by Pharaoh Shishak. When Solomon died and the future of the kingdom came into question, Jeroboam hurried back to claim leadership of the northern and central tribes.

By then, Solomon's son, Rehoboam, had inherited Solomon's crown and had assumed he would be his father's unchallenged successor. But the elders of the alienated tribes were enraged when the new king rejected their demand that he lighten "the heavy yoke"[22] his father had imposed on their people—the forced labor and steep taxes. Joining together to reject Rehoboam, they seceded from his kingdom and created one of their own, with Jeroboam as its ruler. Thus was the northern kingdom of Israel established, leaving Rehoboam to rule only what became the smaller southern kingdom of Judah.

On ascending his newly established throne, Jeroboam faced the enormous task of creating a nation where none had previously existed. There was no administrative center, no administration, and no army. Furthermore, the priesthood, loyal to the dynasty of David, was hostile, and he faced the danger that traditionally fractious northerners might be no more willing to be ruled by him than by Rehoboam. However, their tribal leaders recognized that this new kingdom had to be preserved under a central authority if Rehoboam's intention of reasserting rule over them from Jerusalem were to be frustrated.

Jeroboam was not totally without resources as he began his reign. He was able to gain the allegiance of elements of Solomon's army that had been garrisoned in his territory, and he salvaged some of the intricate administrative structure Solomon had set up across the land. But he also needed a geographic focus in Israel to reduce the attractions of Jerusalem, across the border in Judah.

For his capital, he first chose the ancient shrine city of Shechem in the hill country of Ephraim and fortified it against possible attack by the Judaeans. Shechem was imbued with much historical and religious symbolism. Abraham had built an altar there, the patriarch Jacob had lived there, Joseph had been buried there, and Joshua had held the first convocation of the tribes there. It was also the place where the gathering of the elders of the northern and central tribes had rejected Rehoboam's demand that they accept him as their king.

Nevertheless, Jerusalem continued to have a far stronger claim to be the center of the Jewish faith and worship, boasting as it did the Temple Solomon had built to house the Ark of the Covenant. At festival times, the Temple attracted great numbers of pilgrims from all over the land.

Such pilgrimages implied the pilgrims' acceptance of God's covenant with David and God's choice of David's descendants as the only rightful kings of the Jews, of whom the rejected Rehoboam was the most recent. That presented a threat to Jeroboam's royal legitimacy and even to his life. If the pilgrims "still go up to offer sacrifices at the House of the Lord in Jerusalem," he feared, "the heart of these people will turn back to their master, to King Rehoboam of Judah. They will kill me."[23]

To focus religious concentration of his subjects on sites within their own kingdom rather than on Jerusalem, Jeroboam rededicated holy shrines at Dan in the far north of the land, more accessible to his northernmost subjects, and at Bethel, not far from the frontier with Judah. Both had long been hallowed centers of Jewish cultic worship.

The golden calves he erected at those shrines proved controversial. Such images were said to serve as pedestals for the invisible presence of Yahweh and had not been unknown earlier in the ornamentation of Jewish places of worship. But priests at the Temple in Jerusalem, who objected to the existence of shrines anywhere else, condemned them as sacrilegious idolatry, not much different from the idol worship of Jeroboam's many non-Jewish subjects, descendants of the Canaanites.

Jeroboam dismissed their invective as Jerusalem's attempt to reestablish tyrannical control over the north. To consummate the rupture with the south, he established a separate priesthood in Israel, loyal to himself. To make a further distinction between the two Jewish kingdoms, he also changed the dates of religious holidays. *Rosh Hashanah*, marking each new year, was shifted from the fall to become a spring festival. *Sukkoth*, the Tabernacles holiday which commemorated the temporary shelters in which the Children of Israel lived in the desert after leaving oppression in Egypt, was moved to later in the year. He subsequently also shifted the first administrative center of his kingdom from Shechem, which was too close to Jerusalem for comfort, to Penuel in Transjordan and then, when he felt more secure, to Tirzah north of Shechem.

Inevitably, Jeroboam's innovations were controversial. Traditionalists among his subjects—including the prophet Ahijah, who had encouraged his original rebellion against Solomon—recoiled against some of the changes. They feared that his radical deviations from established practice would turn people away from proper religious observance and undermine their spiritual authority.

They said Yahweh was affronted by the turn of events and detected divine displeasure in signs and misfortunes. At a ceremony at one of the new shrines, when Jeroboam tried to seize a prophet who forecast disaster for the northern kingdom, his hand was said suddenly to have withered. Its strength was not restored until another prophet prayed for forgiveness on his behalf. However, that second prophet was said to have been subsequently eaten by a lion for presuming to exploit his holy prerogatives for unholy purposes. Lions were known to have existed in the region at the time.

*   *   *

The breakup of the Jewish nation and the difficulties associated with the creation of the new northern kingdom stripped it of the deference Solomon had been able to demand from other lands. Barely had Jeroboam consolidated his position on the throne when the Egyptians, under Pharaoh Shishak, invaded. They penetrated deep into Israel (as well as into Judah) and leveled dozens of its towns.

This was the same Shishak who had given Jeroboam sanctuary in Egypt years before, when his rebellion against Solomon had been crushed, and who had permitted him to return to the land of Israel after Solomon died. Shishak's motive in both earlier situations may have been to promote the breakup of the Jewish nation so that it would be more vulnerable to the conquest he now attempted.

But after their long period of decline, the Egyptians had not yet recovered their earlier might and self-assurance. Having to cope with other problems at the time, they stayed in Israel only long enough to plunder. But in demonstrating the young kingdom's military fragility, they prompted others to benefit from it. The Aramaean kingdom of Damascus in the northeast and the Philistines in the southwest, both of which had been submissive when Solomon was king, seized on the situation to encroach upon Israelite territory. There was trouble also with Judah to the south with which tension had been unremitting since the split in the Jewish nation. Its army made incursions northward, inflicting a major defeat on Jeroboam.

His series of military reverses stirred discontent among Israelite army commanders who were still coming to terms with the creation of their new nation and with their role in it. Nor was Jeroboam able to overcome vestigial regional and tribal rivalries in his fledgling kingdom. His entire reign was a struggle to hold it together. If his subjects had not dreaded the prospect of being reabsorbed into a state ruled from Jerusalem, he might not have been able to keep this newly established Israel from dissolving.

That he succeeded in doing so was nevertheless remarkable, as was his personal survival as king, in view of the radical changes he was required to oversee, the prickliness of his subjects, the pressures upon him from beyond his kingdom's borders, and the fact that, unlike the kings of Judah, he did not represent continuity of a royal line.

Upon his death, his son Nadab succeeded him on the throne.

NADAB

910–909 BCE

Little is known of Nadab, the second ruler of the northern kingdom of Israel. During his two-year reign, he was no more willing to recognize the long-established spiritual supremacy of Jerusalem and its Temple priests than his father, Jeroboam, the kingdom's founding monarch, had been. He also did just as little to try to stamp out pagan worship practiced by great numbers of his subjects, for which he earned condemnation in the Bible.

Jeroboam had ruled Israel for a score of years, but that had not been long enough for the principle of orderly royal succession, honored in Judah, to be firmly rooted among the Israelites, or for the sanctity of the royal person to be commonly respected by them. The elders of Israel and its people accepted Nadab's succession only on sufferance.

In addition to the crown, he had been bequeathed continuing friction with his kingdom's neighbors. During his brief time on the throne, Philistines, and others, still emboldened by the split in the Jewish nation, reclaimed territory they had previously lost to it. Israel's military commanders had not held his father in high regard and they now held Nadab also responsible for those losses.

He met his doom while exercising his royal prerogative in taking personal charge of his army. While he was with his army as it laid siege to the Philistine town of Gibbethon, near the Mediterranean coast, Baasha, one of his military commanders, brought Israel's short-lived first dynasty to an end. On duty with Nadab at Gibbethon, Baasha killed him and claimed the throne of Israel for himself.

BAASHA

909–886 BCE

During the closing years of Jeroboam's kingship, and especially during the abbreviated reign of his son Nadab, the army of Israel had grown bitter about their kingdom's weakness in the face of hostile neighbors and the loss of territory to them. In addition to the Philistines and the Aramaeans of Damascus[6], those neighbors included Judah, which had continued to challenge the legitimacy of Israel as a separate Jewish kingdom.

Baasha may have lusted for fame and power but like other of Israel's military commanders, he hungered also for a more vigorous national leadership than the northern kingdom had yet enjoyed. By assassinating Nadab, he intended to provide the required vigor and vitality. His seizure of the throne was the first serious intervention by the army in Israel's politics. There would be others.

Baasha also set another precedent for Israel, one that was consistent with practices not uncommon in the region. He had initially backed Jeroboam two decades earlier when he had established Israel as an independent state. Now, after killing Jeroboam's son and heir, he had all the remaining members of Jeroboam's family massacred to guard against an attempt by any of them to reclaim the throne on the basis of royal legitimacy.

Baasha was of the tribe of Issachar, whose home ground was on land near the Sea of Galilee. His seizure of power removed the larger tribe of Ephraim, to which Jeroboam and Nadab had belonged, from its position of preeminence in the kingdom. Whatever other difficulties Israel faced, that ensured the rivalry among the tribes would continue to be a destabilizing factor.

In addition to his aim of revitalizing his country, Baasha brought to his reign a determination to vanquish Judah and reunite the two kingdoms of the Jews under his own rule. With a larger population, greater natural resources, and being led by a fighting soldier, Israel was in a strong position to do so. But before mounting his attack on Judah, he took the precaution of negotiating peaceful relations with Damascus to the northeast, his most threatening neighbor.

That achieved, his army advanced deep into Judah and seized an elevated position a mere five miles from Jerusalem from which an attack on the holy city could be mounted. In desperation the Judaeans sought to outflank Baasha diplomati-

---

6.   The Aramaeans were a Semitic people to whom the Jews were racially related.

cally. Judah's King Asa ransacked his palace in Jerusalem and raided the Temple treasury for gold and silver with which to detach Ben-Hadad, king of Damascus, from his detente with Israel. With the prospect of appropriating Israelite territory and never averse to a bribe, Ben-Hadad happily accepted the inducement. Reneging on his pact with Baasha, he joined Judah in its war against the Israelite aggressors.

This Damascus-Judah alliance doomed Baasha's plans. When Ben-Hadad dispatched his army to ravage Israel's Galilee, Baasha was forced to withdraw the forces he had deployed to annex Judah and reposition them to defend his northern regions, including that of his own tribe of Issachar. Not only was the Israelite threat to Jerusalem lifted, but Judah's army advanced far enough into Israel to occupy some of the land of the tribe of Ephraim.

It was both a military and political humiliation for warrior-king Baasha. Unable to defend Ephraim, the tribal territory of Nadab whom he had assassinated, he could not sustain his claim to be the vigorous defender of Israel and promoter of its interests.

Of even greater significance was the conduct of Judah in this affair. For the first time, one of the two Jewish kingdoms had called for external assistance in its conflict with the other. In buying support from Damascus, Judah set a precedent that would lead both to grief.

The clash between Israel and Judah permitted Damascus to annex strips of Israelite territory, including land in Transjordan that had been part of Solomon's domain. Even after the cessation of hostilities, Ben-Hadad continued to play the two Jewish kingdoms against each other to assure neither would challenge his own growing influence in the region.

During virtually all of Baasha's twenty-three-year reign, Israel was either preparing for battle or already at war with Damascus, with Judah or with the revitalized Philistines along the coast. He scored no great victories against any of them.

But having been a senior military commander, Baasha retained the support of fellow officers who had acquired privileged status while he was on the throne. Their backing helped him sustain Israel's political stability despite territorial loss that, to its good fortune, was mostly in thinly populated areas.

ELAH

886–885 BCE

The reign of Elah, son of the soldier-king Baasha, was marked by the further mil-
itarization of political power in Israel. He was responsible, though it was not of
his doing. Given to drink but not to leadership, he lasted on the throne less than
two years. What little impact he had on developments was to the northern kingdom's disadvantage.

Baasha had died at a time when Israel was locked in hostilities with Judah
which he had tried and failed to conquer. The Israelite army was also engaged in
a stalemated campaign against the Philistines on the Mediterranean coastal plain,
and the kingdom of Damascus had already seized part of Galilee.

Elah showed little aptitude for confronting the difficult situations he had
inherited, much less for mastering them, and he displayed little interest in trying
to do so. Instead he handed over governance of the land to his courtiers.

His army commanders, who had come to form a privileged clique, despised
him as weak and incompetent. They engaged in a debilitating struggle among
themselves over which of them would replace him. In the atmosphere of schem-
ing that prevailed, anyone as unsuited as Elah to rule would have had little chance
of retaining the crown for long. His days as king were numbered from the start.

He was murdered while drunk at the home of his chief royal steward in the
Israelite capital of Tirzah. His assassin, Zimri, a senior officer in Israel's chariot
corps, proclaimed himself king in his place.

ZIMRI

885 BCE

By the time Zimri killed King Elah and seized the crown of Israel, the northern kingdom had been in existence almost half a century. Nevertheless, its survival as an independent state was still uncertain. The kingdom needed strong, assertive leadership to meet the challenges it continued to face from Judah, Damascus, and the Philistines. As a commander of its elite chariot corps, Zimri seemed well-suited to provide that leadership.

His first task was to secure his position as self-proclaimed king. To that end, he slaughtered all of Elah's male relatives and whichever partisans he could find of Elah's late father, Baasha. During Baasha's reign, the prophet Jehu had forecast that all of the king's descendants would be punished for his sinfulness. Now that appeared to be their fate.

In seizing the throne, Zimri compounded the antagonisms that had sprung up between the army's rival factions. Israelite troops laying siege to a Philistine city were bitter that Zimri, who had put himself out of harm's way far from the battle front, had presumed to seize the throne. They proclaimed Omri, their own general, the rightful king and marched on the capital of Tirzah to depose Zimri and formally present Omri with the crown.

Their forces were superior to those Zimri could deploy. Besieged in what passed for the royal palace he had occupied so briefly, and expecting little mercy from Omri, Zimri set fire to the structure and died in the flames. He had been king of Israel a mere seven days. His reign was quickly forgotten but his name became an epithet, symbolizing a servant who treacherously turns against his master.

Israel had by then been ruled for forty-six years by a succession of five kings, three of whom had met violent deaths. Wearing the crown of the northern kingdom had proved to be a hazardous calling.

Omri's Coup Against Zimri

OMRI

885–874 BCE

Since its creation as an independent kingdom, Israel had been a muddled, conspiracy-riven land, a place of uncertainty and foreboding. Its people had been given little reason for confidence or pride in their national identity. Their leaders had provided the kingdom with little stability. Their army had been repeatedly outmatched or stalemated in battle.

Omri, the sixth of Israel's kings, changed all that. During his reign Israel underwent sweeping transformation. Shedding its previous shakiness and vulnerability, it evolved into a strong, stable nation and was recognized as such beyond its borders. Omri's achievements were so striking that even after his death the kingdom of Israel would be known as "the House of Omri" to the rulers of the Assyrian regional superpower that had previously been given little reason to take much notice of it.

For many years, the shortcomings of the kingdom's nominal leadership had permitted senior military officers to become the arbiters of political power in the land. Omri was one of those officers and he ascended the throne by emerging triumphant from a struggle to the death among them.

Operational field commander in a deadlocked campaign against the Philistines, Omri was proclaimed king by his men after Israelite chariot corps officer Zimri assassinated the ineffectual King Elah at the capital of Tirzah. Informed that Zimri had claimed the crown for himself, Omri led his troops from the battlefront to Tirzah to eliminate him.

That achieved, Omri had to contend with Tibni, a commander of Israelite forces in the north of Israel who had been proclaimed ruler by the troops under his command there. Until Tibni died four years later, Israel was racked by civil war. The struggle between its generals had been sapping its resistance to territorial incursions by its neighbors. The Aramaeans of Damascus had already exploited the rivalry between Israel and Judah to seize a strip of Galilee from the northern kingdom, as well as cities in Transjordan that had been under Jewish dominion.

But after eliminating his rivals for the throne, Omri began forging a new reality for his trouble-scarred kingdom. Recognizing how seriously regional and tribal squabbles had undermined the national unity of his subjects, he sought to give Israel a proud new identity. He shifted his court from vulnerable Tirzah to an elevated location easily defendable from attack and founded a city there which was called Samaria. His palace was built on land he purchased from a resident Canaanite named Shemer, from which the name Samaria may have been derived.

Defensive walls were erected around the city. Granaries and a reservoir were built within them so that it might withstand lengthy sieges. Securely positioned and fortified, Samaria was to remain Israel's capital for the reminder of the kingdom's existence. The entire region later came to be known as Samaria, a name and place that has retained its geopolitical resonance with the passage of time.

While striving to reconcile diverse and conflicting elements within his realm, Omri also dealt energetically with external issues. He cultivated friendly relations with Judah, badly soured by decades of mutually destructive hostility and conflict. Though no effort was made to reunite the two Jewish kingdoms, as a soldier by training and experience Omri fully recognized the vulnerability of both to aggressive foreign forces if the Jews remained at odds among themselves. Damascus, the most assertive of Israel's neighbors, was of particular concern to him. Its power and influence had become so formidable that Damascene merchants who bought and sold goods in the newly established bazaar of Samaria were able to demand and receive special concessions and privileges there.

That would not last long. Having overcome strife between Israelite military commanders, Omri was able to reorganize and revitalize his army. Damascus was to remain a threat but he retook territory in Transjordan which his previously shaky kingdom had been forced to surrender to it. Mastery was similarly reestablished over the desert land of Moab, east of the Dead Sea, which had been lost during Baasha's troubled reign.

Omri also maneuvered diplomatically to promote Israel's recovery and to enhance its image. His friendly overtures to the Phoenician city-states on the coast of Lebanon were greatly welcomed by them. They hoped the understandings they reached with him would deter Damascus which was eager to gobble them up.

The maritime skills and adventurous seaborne exploits of the Phoenicians engaged them in far-reaching commercial activity and brought them much wealth—now increased by access to the increasingly secure overland trade routes to Egypt and Arabia through territory either ruled by Omri or controlled by him. The commercial links he established with the Phoenicians, similar to those enjoyed by Solomon, significantly assisted the revival of Israel's stunted economy.

The alliance between Israel and Tyre, the most prominent of the Phoenician city-states, was sealed by the marriage of Jezebel, daughter of the king of Tyre, to

Ahab, Omri's son and heir. It was a coupling that would have tumultuous consequences.

Under Omri, Israel became a different place than it had ever been before. But not all his subjects were able to benefit from the greater security, expanded territorial domain, and enhanced commercial activity the kingdom came to enjoy during his rule. Prices rose and imported goods competed with those produced by Israelites working the land. For many of them, the rewards of peace had to be weighed against gradual impoverishment.

Despite the transformation of conditions in the kingdom, and despite greater unity of purpose between Israel and Judah than at any time since the death of Solomon, the reign of Omri is only briefly noted in the Bible—and he is severely admonished. He is said to have been "worse than all [kings] who preceded him,"[24] probably because he made no attempt to ban heathen practices[7] among his subjects. They included a large non-Jewish minority, mostly descended from pre-Exodus Canaanite peoples who built their own shrines, worshipped idols, and performed pagan rites. The alliance with Phoenicia further exposed Israelite Jews to non-Jewish religious influences. The cult of Baal had a particularly wide following, notably at Omri's court in Samaria where Baal worship became fashionable. Some Israelites worshipped both Yahweh and other deities.

Such promiscuous devotions and the toleration of paganism provoked the ire of those in both Israel and Judah who remained faithful to traditional Jewish religious observance. Many had never been reconciled to the golden statues of calves Jeroboam had erected at the shrines at Dan and Bethel when the northern kingdom was founded, though both places remained centers of worship for Israel's Jews.

Seeds of religious conflict sprouted during the final period of Omri's reign. But on his death he handed on to his son Ahab a kingdom far less troubled than before. Ahab was able to mount the throne without challenge and to make an even greater impact than his father on the fortunes of the northern kingdom of the Jews.

---

7.   Omri is identifiable neither by tribal affiliation nor by the name of his father. That may indicate he was a convert to Judaism.

AHAB

873–853 BCE

Until the reign of Omri, no royal heir to the kingdom of Israel had come close to matching his father in notable achievement. Jeroboam, its founding monarch after the split in the Jewish nation, had bequeathed Israel to Nadab, who proved to be no more than a cipher and who reigned briefly. Elah, who had inherited the crown from his soldier father, Baasha, was a drunk and incompetent whose tenure was equally abbreviated. But in succeeding the able and enterprising Omri, his son Ahab changed that pattern and proved to be even more accomplished than his eminent father.

Omri handed on to Ahab a revitalized Israel, one that was no longer the intrigue-ridden, emasculated state it had earlier been. Under Ahab, the kingdom was to play an important international role, growing ever stronger and more prosperous.

Extensive commercial activity, stimulated by diplomatic and economic collaboration with both Judah and Tyre, had filled the royal coffers and continued to do so. With substantial resources at his disposal, Ahab continued furbishing the new Israelite capital city of Samaria his father had founded, turning it into a place of notable character and splendor. Extensive modernizing construction projects were also undertaken at other of Israel's cities. Samaria would never match the grandeur or spiritual impact of Jerusalem but it served well enough as the center of the northern kingdom's political and cultural life. Ahab turned Israel into an even more robust military power than it had become under Omri, especially enlarging its corps of charioteers and greatly improving facilities for them at strategic locations in the land from which to defend the nation or embark on offensive operations.

A focus of regal favor and no longer hobbled by internal rivalries, the military was able to consolidate the position it had earlier enjoyed as a political force in the kingdom. It came to wield greater influence in Samaria than the increasingly impotent tribal elders and the mostly agrarian population those elders represented.

During the early years of Ahab's reign, King Ben-Hadad of Damascus posed a major threat to Israel's independence. Dominating several of the smaller states in the region, he sought to extend his mastery to Israel as well, and almost succeeded.

His army unexpectedly launched an invasion and penetrated deep enough into Israelite territory to lay siege to Samaria. Though outmatched in numbers, Ahab's warriors surged out of their elevated, fortified capital in a surprise onslaught that scattered Ben-Hadad's army. He himself had to flee on horseback, barely managing to escape capture by Ahab's men.

Still intent on conquering Israel, he took advice from his counselors who urged him to draw the Israelites into combat on level ground rather than in the hills where they had proved superior. But before he could launch this second attack, Ahab's army, anticipating his move, devastated his forces in the Golan Heights border area, a portent of what was to happen there almost three thousand years later.

The Israelite victory was so thorough that Ben-Hadad was compelled to surrender personally and plead for his life. Against the advice of his counselors, Ahab freed his royal prisoner and permitted him safe passage back to Damascus.

His leniency was not without motive. Neither did he overlook the spoils of war. Ben-Hadad was made to surrender territory Israel had previously been obliged to hand over to Damascus in Galilee and east of the Jordan River. While Damascene merchants had demanded special privileges in the bazaar of Samaria during Omri's reign, now Israelite merchants were awarded special concessions in the bazaars of Damascus.

But Ahab realized he and Ben-Hadad had a common interest of far greater importance than their differences. Looming in the near distance was a grave danger to both: the armies of Assyria were on the march from the east, overwhelming all resistance they met.

To confront the Assyrian threat, Ahab promoted the formation of a military alliance of regional states, including his arch-rival, Damascus. As a matter of general policy, as well as to meet the needs of the moment, he also cemented relations with Judah, marrying off his daughter Athaliah to Jehoram, son of Judaean King Jehoshaphat. (Judah's Jehoram had the same name as one of Ahab's sons, who would later succeed his father as king of Israel.)

According to the inscription on an Assyrian relic, Israel was by then recognized as a military power. "Ahab the Israelite" was described as contributing two thousand chariots and ten thousand men to the anti-Assyrian defensive coalition. That was a greater number of chariots than any other member of the alliance provided, and more soldiers than most.

Battle between the forces of the alliance and the Assyrians was joined at Qarqar in northern Syria. It ended inconclusively but, having to cope with difficulties elsewhere in their empire, the Assyrians received enough of a mauling for their advance deeper into the region to be halted for the moment and Israel's army returned home in triumph.

Despite the wealth, security, and power that the northern kingdom attained during Ahab's reign, he is popularly remembered more for the actions and reputation of his wife, as recounted in the Bible. For diplomatic reasons, their respective fathers had arranged his marriage to Jezebel, daughter of the king of Tyre, when he was a young man.

The marriage did more than firm up the alliance between Israel and the Phoenicians. When moving from Tyre to Samaria and taking up residence there, Jezebel entered a milieu completely different from the one she had previously known. Before his enthronement, her father Ethbaal had been a priest of Astarte, goddess of love and fertility, whose worship involved orgiastic rites. These were considered both obscene and blasphemous by worshipers of Yahweh, the God of Israel, whose queen Jezebel became when Ahab succeeded his father on the throne.

Also, in sharp contrast to the comparative austerity of the Israelite capital of Samaria, Tyre, the Phoenician commercial hub in which she had been raised, was a cosmopolitan center. It was a crossroads of the eastern Mediterranean, a place of great diversity and activity. Refusing to adapt to the different setting in which she found herself when she married, Jezebel intended instead to make major changes to her new homeland.

As a royal princess, she had not traveled alone when coming to Israel to marry Ahab. A retinue of servants and an entourage of friends had accompanied her to Samaria. They brought with them their ways and their beliefs. Because she was a princess and because religious diversity already existed widely in Israel, these were tolerated. But when Ahab became king, Jezebel went further than merely adhering to the religious observances of her upbringing.

She had her husband build a pagan temple in Samaria and she filled it with idols and altars dedicated to the worship of Moloch, the god of fire and destruction, Baal and Astarte. She also imported hundreds of Phoenician priests for those deities. Some became part of the royal household. Others traveled across Israel preaching their pagan faith. Their rituals aroused much attention. In some cases, those priests donned women's clothes and painted their faces like female prostitutes. Some indulged in orgiastic dancing and fearsome wailing and sometimes mutilated themselves with whips, knives, and scourges.

Not all Israelites were dismayed or offended by such conduct. Many of Canaanite descent also worshipped pagan deities. Many who had converted to Judaism not long before clung to old habits and traditions while worshipping Yahweh, nurturing a lingering reverence for pagan rituals. Many Jews were attracted to exciting and colorful religious rites linked to the weather, harvest, and procreation.

Such displays were in contrast to the more ascetic devotions of their own faith. Some were drawn to pagan rituals after being denied facilities for their traditional Jewish observances by priests of Baal who, acting with the authority of Queen Jezebel, replaced their altars with others dedicated to their own gods.

Ahab's court was largely paganized through the efforts of his queen. Angered by any resistance to her paganization of the kingdom, Jezebel used her royal authority to initiate a campaign to persecute worshipers of Yahweh. Their shrines were destroyed. Their priests were driven into hiding. Many were executed. Others, like Obadiah, head of the royal household, felt constrained to conceal their attachment to Yahweh, though he protected many who remained true to their faith, hiding them in caves to protect them from Jezebel's wrath.

Israel faced a religious crisis. For the first time, Jews were persecuted because of their beliefs, and in their own land. As the situation came to a head, the prophet Elijah appeared from across the Jordan. Long-haired Elijah was a striking figure, wearing a cloak of black animal skin.

Like other prophets who appeared in biblical times to affirm that Yahweh was the one true God and warn about sinning against Him, Elijah was not identifiable by tribe—he seemed to spring from the people at large to sustain the centrality of Jewish worship in Israel and Judah despite the inroads of paganism. Though he was persecuted by Jezebel, she could not go so far as to kill him or limit the effect his presence and pronouncements had on the people. The Bible describes how he frustrated her efforts to root out Jewish worship and emerged triumphant from a dramatic showdown with pagan priests on whether Yahweh or Baal was the true God. (Jezebel was to meet her fate several years later, killed by command of King Jehu when he seized the crown of Israel from her son, Jehoram.)

Little concerned with religious belief or observance, Ahab devoted himself largely to matters of state. Hostilities between Israel and Damascus had been discontinued when the threat to both kingdoms from Assyria had materialized. But their mutual enmity reasserted itself when the Assyrians, distracted elsewhere, suspended their march of conquest in their direction. War again with Damascus soon followed.

Ahab went to the front to lead his forces in a bid to recapture Ramoth-Gilead in Transjordan which the Damascenes had earlier agreed to hand back to Israel. Expecting to be made a special target by the enemy, Ahab disguised himself by donning the attire of an ordinary soldier before entering the fray. It did not save him. Struck by a stray arrow, he died at sunset that day.

Having lost their commander and king, the Israelite forces withdrew from the battle and scattered. What started with confidence ended with despair. Nevertheless, during his reign Ahab had consolidated and enhanced the security and image of his kingdom and had formed an alliance between Israel and Judah that was closer than any since Solomon's kingdom had split in two.

King Ahab Mortally Wounded in Combat With the Syrians

AHAZIAH

853–852 BCE

King Ahab's death in battle while fighting with his soldiers against Damascus, and the defeat his army suffered in that clash, had a devastating impact on his kingdom, especially in view of the character of Ahab's eldest son, Ahaziah, who succeeded him on the throne. Ahaziah was a shadow of his dynamic father and his redoubtable grandfather, Omri.

Incapable of providing Israel with the resounding leadership it needed at a time of despair and confusion, Ahaziah was obliged to suffer the disaffection of Moab and other neighboring territories over which Omri and Ahab had maintained mastery.

Israel also lost ground diplomatically and economically. Judah, with whom Ahaziah's familial predecessors had established close ties, saw no reason for an alliance with a partner whose ruler was of questionable capabilities. It also declined to participate in joint commercial ventures that would have contributed to Israel's continuing prosperity.

Ahaziah was given little time to recover from such reverses. He reigned for little more than a single year. Aside from his setbacks, he is known primarily for having injured himself badly in a fall from a window of his palace in Samaria. Influenced by the pagan devotions of his mother, Jezebel, he sent to the shrine of the Philistine god Baal-Zebub at the Philistine city-state of Ekron for forecasts on his chances of recovery. For seeking the comfort of a pagan deity rather than Yahweh, he was denounced by the prophet Elijah who prophesied that for his act of blasphemy, the king would not rise from his sick bed.

He did not.

JEHORAM

852–841 BCE

Ahab's son, Jehoram, could not have relished succeeding to the throne upon the death of his brother, Ahaziah. Israel was locked in a losing war with Damascus at the time and its people were shrouded in gloom and foreboding. Not long into Jehoram's reign, the Damascenes came close to conquering his kingdom and absorbing it into their own.

Their army penetrated deep enough into Israel to lay siege to Samaria and threaten a final assault as hunger raged through Israel's isolated hilltop capital city. Remote from the needs and difficulties of his subjects, Jehoram did not realize how desperate the situation had become until he encountered two women quarreling on the city wall because one of them was reneging on an agreement to save themselves from starvation by eating their children.

For unknown reasons, possibly plague in their camp, the Damascenes suddenly abandoned the siege and withdrew, saving Samaria from having to choose between starvation and surrender. Nevertheless, morale in Israel's army was blighted by its failure to prevent the enemy from coming so close to subjugating the kingdom. Jehoram's senior military commanders held him responsible and it strained their loyalty.

Jehoram's standing was tarnished among his subjects by the apparent fulfillment of prophetic warnings that Yahweh would punish Israel because of widespread pagan practices in the kingdom which had been promoted by his mother, Jezebel, and tolerated by him. Prophets and other holy men, recognizable by their hair shirts donned in penance for the transgressions of the Jews, wandered through the country uttering forebodings of divine retribution. A series of droughts and poor harvests seemed to bear out their prophecies.

Jehoram (also known as Joram) did gain some favor among his subjects by ordering the removal of pillars in Samaria dedicated to a pagan deity. But enough of Jezebel's domineering influence persisted to keep him from destroying the more prominent temple of Baal that had been built for her, or from launching a wider campaign against paganism.

Jehoram's downfall came after a battle with Damascus in Transjordan in which he was present with his army at the battlefront. Wounded, he withdrew to his winter capital at Jezreel to recover, leaving his general, Jehu, in command.

While he was at Jezreel, Jehu declared him deposed and raced there by chariot to eliminate him and mount the throne in his place. Informed of his approach and unaware of his intentions, Jehoram rode out in his chariot for news from his general of what was happening at the front.

It was a fatal ride. Jehu cut him down, ingloriously ending the Israelite dynasty that had been founded by his grandfather, the formidable Omri.

Syrians Abondoning Their Siege of Samaria

JEHU

841–813 BCE

Conveying the words and commands of Yahweh to the Jewish people was the role of the prophets of ancient Israel. They transmitted His promises of divine favor if they remained true to Him and issued His warnings of severe retribution for sinfulness. The sacred duty of those holy men included fearless condemnation of injustice, corruption, oppression, and poverty. Living and preaching in times when unprincipled behavior by those in power was not uncommon, they wove an indelible ethical thread through the fabric of Judaism that has endured to the present day.

However, some prophets sought to exploit their venerable status to advance political objectives not necessarily within their holy writ, or only marginally associated with it. Samuel attempted to prevent the establishment of a Jewish monarchy that would weld the nation together but would also undermine his spiritual authority. The prophet Nathan influenced David to pick Solomon as his royal successor rather than his older son, Adonijah, and falsely convinced the elderly king that he had earlier promised to do so. Ahijah encouraged Jeroboam to lead an uprising against Solomon who had downgraded the priesthood.

The prophet Elisha was active at a time when those dedicated to Jewish religious traditions were particularly dismayed by the extent of pagan worship in Israel, and by their own diminished influence. With the Israelite royal court in Samaria heavily heathenized through neglect by King Jehoram and by the influence of his mother, Jezebel, Elisha saw the army, long a breeding ground of political plotting, as the only force capable of producing a Judaic resurgence. He wanted Jehoram overthrown and vengeance for the prophets who had been killed in Jezebel's campaign to stamp out Jewish worship.

Elisha acted while Jehoram was at his winter capital of Jezreel, recuperating from a wound sustained while fighting against the forces of Damascus for territory in Transjordan. With him out of the way, Elisha sent a priestly emissary to meet with Israelite army commander Jehu at his battle headquarters and urge him to take action against the king's failure to fulfill his religious obligations.

Subsequently asked by his brother officers about his audience with the "madman"—as the long-haired visitor had seemed in his animal skin attire—Jehu told them the prophet's envoy had anointed him king of Israel in place of Jehoram and also told them about the task with which he had been entrusted. The officers received the news of their commander's coronation with cheers and symbolically spread their cloaks for Jehu to walk on as trumpets blew in celebration. The army's backing for the coup assured, the hot-tempered Jehu raced by chariot to Jezreel where he slew the king and mortally wounded his cousin, King Ahaziah of Judah, who had been visiting him at the time.

Jehu's next victim was the hated Jezebel who was also in Jezreel. Having heard what had happened to her son and knowing what to expect, the proud Jezebel prepared to meet her doom looking her best. She arranged her hair and applied makeup to her face. But she was denied a dignified end to her life. Arriving at the royal palace, Jehu commanded her eunuch servants to throw her from a palace window. Terrified, they did as they were told, and Jehu rode over her body with his chariot. Her blood was splattered over the palace walls and the legs of his horses, and her body was left for stray dogs to devour.

Then, rather than proceeding to Samaria to put the finishing touches to his coup, Jehu sent a command to the elders of the capital city. They were to kill all surviving sons and grandsons of Ahab, Jehoram's deceased father, to eliminate any possible future revival of the dynasty founded by Omri. Collaboration in the slaughter by senior figures in the land, no matter how reluctantly tendered, would ensure that responsibility would not be his alone while his claim to the throne remained tenuous.

Word of what Jehu had perpetrated at Jezreel having already reached the terrified elders in the capital, they quickly complied with his instructions. Members of Jehoram's family and their servants were killed, as were friends of the murdered king, his personal priests, and ranking officials of the kingdom. When Jehu finally reached Samaria, he continued the massacre, wiping out whatever surviving relatives of Jehoram he could track down.

Pretending to offer a sacrifice of thanksgiving at the pagan temple of Baal that Jezebel had built, Jehu invited all prophets, priests, and worshippers of Baal in Israel to attend. When many had gathered there, he turned loose his soldiers to slaughter them and he destroyed the temple.

Though meant to purify and strengthen the kingdom of Israel, Jehu's coup had the opposite effect. The slaughter of its officials left the kingdom without experienced administrative leadership. The foreign pagan worship Jezebel had promoted was greatly eradicated but indigenous heathen practices, which predated the return of the Israelites from oppression in Egypt, remained largely unaffected. Many in Israel continued to worship other deities, as they had before, often at the same time as they worshipped Yahweh. Religiously, Jehu's coup proved little more than a xenophobic rebellion against foreign influences rather than a campaign of spiritual purification.

In foreign affairs, Jehu's assumption of power was a catastrophe. His murder of visiting King Ahaziah of Judah at Jezreel, as well as Ahaziah's brothers whom he happened by chance to capture, immediately soured relations with the Judaeans. And the killing of Jezebel, who was from the royal family of Tyre in Lebanon, destroyed those close links. Thus, what remained of the triple Judah-Israel-Lebanon alliance, which had been diplomatically and commercially fruitful for the Israelites, was abruptly nullified. It left Israel isolated and vulnerable to renewed aggression by Damascus.

Having led Israel into dire straits, Jehu was required to seek the protection of the increasingly assertive Assyrian superpower and obliged to pay tribute to it. An image on an Assyrian obelisk at the British Museum in London shows a figure identified as "Jehu, Son of Omri" (though Jehu had destroyed the dynasty of Omri) prostrate at the feet of the Assyrian king, Shalmaneser III.

His obeisance did neither him nor Israel much good. The Assyrians were momentarily occupied with other pressing matters and could offer him little help against Damascus. Its army drove the Israelites out of most of the territory they still held in Transjordan—probably assisted by Jehu's impetuous abandonment of his military command there—and out of much of Galilee too. It seized land on the west bank as well, forcing the people who lived there, small farmers mostly, into semi-slavery.

No longer enjoying cordial relations with Israel, Judah and Tyre also encroached on the territory of Israel so that Jehu, though he reigned for twenty-eight years, ruled an ever-smaller domain.

Nevertheless, the dynasty he founded was to last a century. Despite mixed fortunes, it was to prove the most enduring in the history of the northern kingdom.

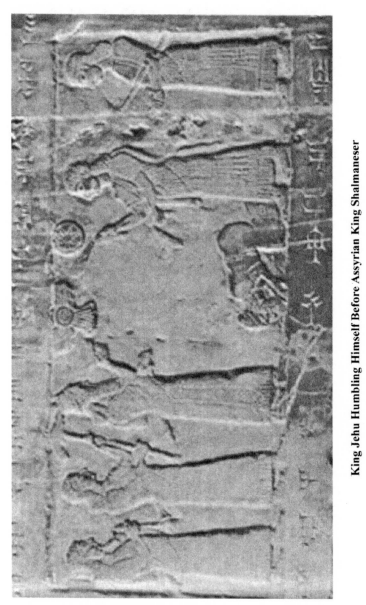

King Jehu Humbling Himself Before Assyrian King Shalmaneser

JEHOAHAZ

813–797 BCE

Despite his crusading zeal—though more likely because of it—the warrior king Jehu had inflicted such damage to the fortunes of Israel that the kingdom was doomed to further decline when he died and was succeeded on the throne by his son, Jehoahaz.

In the climate of unrest and land grabbing that blanketed the entire region at the time, a strong, well-equipped army was essential for a nation's security. But the once-formidable Israelite army, having been thrashed by the forces of Damascus, dwindled to a size capable only of repelling raiders who attempted to seize Samaria. Had the capital been situated in a less impregnable, less elevated position, it probably would have been conquered, and Israel would have been extinguished as an independent state.

Six decades earlier, it had sent two thousand chariots to help challenge the might of the rampaging Assyrians. Now it could field only ten chariots in an armed force limited to ten thousand foot soldiers and fifty horsemen—more a police force than an army.

Only when it became necessary for Damascus to divert occupying forces to resist Assyrian aggression against its own territory was the pressure relaxed on the Israelites, though not sufficiently to permit more than a marginal respite from Israel's misfortune. Damascus had already annexed most of the northern kingdom and was still in a position to demand tribute from the rest.

During Jehoahaz's reign, Israel was a weak, virtually defenseless, impoverished rump of a nation, most of whose people were subjected to foreign oppression. Its king displayed none of his father's zeal for religious purification, nor it seems for anything else. He made little personal impact on the land or his subjects.

JEHOASH

797–782 BCE

External events often have a critical bearing on the fate of small states. Such was the situation for Israel during the reign of Jehoash, son of hapless King Jehoahaz. The fortunes of the kingdom, at low ebb when Jehoash ascended its throne, dramatically improved during his reign. But that was solely because of happenings beyond Israel's borders, and one development in particular to which its fate would be inextricably harnessed from then on.

The Assyrians had resolved distracting difficulties elsewhere in their empire and their armies were on the move again in the region. The Aramaeans of Damascus, who had humbled Israel during the reign of Jehoash's grandfather Jehu and his father Jehoahaz, were now themselves humbled by the Assyrians. The threat from Damascus had been so thoroughly reduced that Israel was able to reclaim all the territory on both sides of the Jordan River it had previously lost to its now-battered nemesis.

Territorial recovery was accompanied by the strengthening of Israel's emasculated army and renewed control of trade routes through the region. The stage was set for the kingdom's economic revival.

But a price had to be paid. Jehoash was required to acknowledge the mastery of the menacing Assyrians over the horizon and had to bribe them copiously to keep them at bay.

It was not only the Assyrians who were creating difficulties for Israel. Hostility with Judah had been smoldering for more than three decades, ever since Judah's King Ahaziah, visiting the northern kingdom, had been killed by Israel's usurping King Jehu simply because he was on the spot during his bloody coup. Now Amaziah, grandson of the luckless Ahaziah, was bent on revenge for his family and for Judah.

But his objectives were wider than mere vengeance. He intended to conquer and subjugate Israel and force the divided Jewish nation to come together again under his own rule. Seizing on a comparatively trivial incident, he provoked hostilities with his northern neighbor.

He had recruited mercenaries in Israel to help his army conquer the kingdom of Edom in the southern desert now that it no longer enjoyed the protection of enfeebled Damascus. When he subsequently decided he did not need those mercenaries and sent them back to Israel, they reacted angrily and rampaged through towns in Judah on their way home. Amaziah decided to hold Jehoash and Israel responsible for the damage done.

Jehoash tried to calm the situation, but Amaziah used the incident as an excuse for an expansionist war against Israel. However, he badly miscalculated the comparative military prowess of the two Jewish states. In the ensuing struggle, Israel's newly reconstituted army decisively thrashed the aggressive Judaeans and marched on Jerusalem. Seizing the holy city, it looted its royal palace and Temple treasures, tore down part of its protective wall, and took the reckless Amaziah prisoner.

Judah was left at Jehoash's mercy. The Jewish kingdoms could have been reunited under Israel's dominance at the time, rather than under Judah's as Amaziah had intended. But Jehoash chose instead to free his royal prisoner and withdraw from Judah, taking hostages from among Judaean dignitaries to guarantee no further trouble from the south.

He may have believed the division of the Jewish nation was by then too firmly established to be easily undone. More likely, he feared renewed trouble from Damascus and did not want his defensive forces to be too greatly stretched.

Despite the looming threat from Assyria, Israel recovered its self-assurance and stature in the region under Jehoash. Its people grew less fearful of invaders, occupiers, and marauders. Religious chroniclers attributed the turn-around in its circumstances to the king's piety.

Upon his death, Jehoash was succeeded by his son Jeroboam II who would rule the northern kingdom during its most glorious period.

JEROBOAM II

782–747 BCE

If there is a single period in the history of the northern kingdom of the Jews in which it best showed its potential for greatness, it was during the reign of Jeroboam II. Under him, Israel was more confident and more secure than it had ever been before or would ever be again.

During the reign of his father, Jehoash, Israel had begun to recover from the consequences of a long period of disarray and weakness. Jeroboam built on that revival. Under him, Samaria once again became a thriving city. The Israelite capital was adorned with ornate buildings, graced with extensive cultural activity and alive with bustling markets. With vigorous leadership and a strengthened army, Jeroboam recovered all the land on both sides of the Jordan River that Israel had lost since the Jewish nation had fractured in two. His rule soon stretched from deep in Syria to the borders of Judah, and from a line well east of the Jordan to the Mediterranean coast. No previous Israelite king had exercised authority over so extensive a dominion. Chronic adversary Damascus, which had earlier occupied much of Israel, was reduced to the status of Israel's vassal state.

Its resurgence coincided with improved circumstances as well for Judah under King Uzziah. The lapsed alliance between the two now-flourishing Jewish nations was renewed and strengthened. Together Jeroboam and Uzziah controlled territory almost as extensive as that ruled by Solomon at the height of his powers. With that revival came prosperity from commerce, stimulated through cooperation with the enterprising Phoenicians who were also doing particularly well at the time. To that was added the development of domestic industry and agriculture as well as control of major regional trade routes.

Inevitably there was a downside. Great wealth poured into Israel and was generated within it. Nevertheless, the gap between rich and poor in the kingdom grew ever wider. The aristocracy, merchant and administrative classes and large landowners did extremely well while poor agrarians, who made up the bulk of the population, did not.

In recurring periods of drought, great numbers of them fell deeply in debt. Many were reduced to a semi-feudal relationship with large landowners and moneylenders and often found little sympathy from corrupt magistrates and state officials. The rich built "ivory palaces"[25] and "great houses" in Samaria and exploited their wealth to become even richer and more powerful, while the poor were often denied simple justice.

The widening differences between social and economic classes over the previous decades had diluted tribal solidarity. Though tribal distinctions had earlier often militated against the unity of the state, they had provided an instrument of social cohesion that was now increasingly undermined. Even when they shared tribal identity, people of privileged class and station had little in common with the poor and dispossessed. Though Israel prospered during Jeroboam's long reign, its social fabric decayed.

As before, great numbers of people, both rich and poor, strayed from the religion and laws of Yahweh. Paganism was renascent. The campaign of religious purification undertaken by Jehu, Jeroboam's great-grandfather, proved to have had meager longterm impact. With some Israelites worshipping both Yahweh and pagan deities, many local shrines became ecumenical, as did many priests who saw no reason to fear the anger of Yahweh when their king vanquished all enemies and inaugurated a golden age for Israel. Nor did the brotherhood of prophets offer much in the way of censure or foreboding, dazed as its members were by the kingdom's remarkable renaissance

An exception was Hosea who condemned Israelites for supposing their good fortune resulted from pagan worship. He warned that because Jews had not obeyed God, "they shall go wandering among the nations."[26] The prophet Amos was similarly appalled by what had been happening. Originally a shepherd from Judah, Amos did not hesitate to convey God's judgment on the effect social transformation was having on the Israelites.

> *They have sold for silver*
> *Those whose cause was just,*
> *And the needy for a pair of sandals.*
> *You who trample the heads of the poor*
> *Into the dust of the ground,*
> *And make the humble walk a twisted course!*
> *Father and son go to the same girl,*
> *And thereby profane My holy name.*
> *They recline by every altar*
> *On garments taken in pledge,*
> *And drink in the House of their God*
> *Wine bought with fines they imposed....*
> *You have turned justice into poison weed*

And the fruit of righteousness to wormwood....
I, O House of Israel,
Will raise up a nation against you....
I will make the sun set at noon,
I will darken the earth on a sunny day.
I will turn your festivals into mourning
And all your songs into dirges.[27]

Amos's warnings of doom outraged Israelite priests who had long been held in disdain by the Jerusalem priesthood. At the shrine at Bethel, the priest Amaziah urged the prophet to leave Israel and return to Judah. He told Jeroboam that Amos was plotting against him and that his pronouncements would destroy the kingdom.

Riding a crest of success and acclaim, Jeroboam was unruffled by forecasts of disaster, or evidence that it was menacingly close. But he would prove to be last king of Israel before its terminal decline set in.

The Prophet Amos

ZECHARIAH, SHALLUM, MENAHEM, PEKAHIAH, PEKAH, HOSHEA

747–724 BCE

During the quarter century before its final destruction, the northern Jewish kingdom came to be overwhelmed by crisis and existential anxiety. None of those who would be Israel's last six kings was of exceptional character or significant achievement. The prophet Hosea conveyed God's lament that Israel had made kings, "but not with My sanction; they have made officers, but not of My choice."[28]

But divine intercession would have been required for any ruler, no matter how gifted, to hold back the tide that was about to engulf the land or to have exercised much control over its people and their fate. While Judah to the south repeatedly bounced back from recurring difficulties, the time of even a semblance of self-determination for the Israelites was drawing to a turbulent conclusion.

The Assyrians deployed armies more powerful by far than any other in the region and they were casting an ever-more-ominous shadow. Straddling the landbridge between them and the treasures and wonders of Egypt, Israel became a primary Assyrian target. Its subjugation had become inevitable.

The widened gap and growing hostility between rich and poor stoked domestic ferment, compounding the external threat. The territorial conquests and general sense of good times during the reign of Jeroboam II had done much to paper over unrest. But upon his death, Israel's cohesion began to dissolve. It became plagued by open discord at a time when the Assyrian menace loomed largest.

Jeroboam's son, Zechariah, was allowed little time to influence the situation in any way. He wore Israel's crown a mere six months, long enough only to recognize the dimensions of his difficulties. The most notable aspect of his reign was his assassination. His death snuffed out the longest lasting dynasty in Israel's mercurial history, established by Jehu a century earlier.

The prophet Micah brought word from God that He had given up on Israel because of its sinfulness.

> *I will turn Samaria into a ruin in open country, into grounds for planting vineyards.... I will tumble her stones into the valley and lay her foundations bare. All her sculptured images shall be smashed and all her harlot's wealth will be burned.*

And I will make a waste heap of her idols.... I will lament and wail; I will go stripped and naked.... For her wound is incurable.[29]

∗   ∗   ∗

Only four things are known about Shallum who succeeded Zechariah as king of Israel, and none of those are known in any detail. He was probably a senior Israelite military commander; he assassinated Zechariah; he then seized the throne of Israel for himself; and he was in turn killed a month later by Menahem who then succeeded him as king.

Rival figures competed for power as Assyria's expansionist pressures grew ever more menacing. How to deal with the situation became a subject of raging controversy among Samaria's leading figures—its officials, aristocrats, and plutocrats—and a source of anguish among its people.

Shallum may have assassinated Zechariah because he responded too timidly to the Assyrian menace. Menahem, Shallum's own assassin and successor as king, may have killed him for fear that his defiance of the Assyrians exposed Israel to immediate military devastation. That Menahem had marched on the capital of Samaria from the former capital of Tirzah to seize the crown suggests he had been a figure of authority there and that fragmentation of the kingdom was well under way by then.

∗   ∗   ∗

Caught up in a frenzy of factional and regional rivalries, Israel's central administrative control had largely broken down. To establish and maintain his authority as ruler after eliminating his predecessor, Menahem resorted to brutal suppression. The Bible tells of his massacre of all inhabitants of the town of Tappuah who had scorned his claim to be their ruler. But the breakdown of law and order was well beyond repair and his ruthless insistence on obedience failed to restore the cohesion of a society in the process of breakdown. Even Samaria, the capital, was in a state of social disintegration. The prophet Hosea told of the Lord's despair over the behavior of the people.

There is no honesty and no goodness
And no obedience to God in the land.
[False] swearing, dishonesty, and murder,

And theft and adultery are rife.
Crime follows upon crime.[30]

When the Assyrians seized Galilee after overrunning neighboring territory, Menahem gave up even the pretense that Israel was an independent land and hurried to pledge unqualified allegiance to their ruler. "As for Menahem," King Tiglathpileser III noted in an Assyrian inscription, "I overwhelmed him … and he fled like a bird and [submitted]."[31]

To retain his crown and persuade the Assyrians to withdraw from the parts of Israel they had occupied, Menahem paid a huge tribute funded by a steep tax on his property-owning subjects. That burden aggravated discontent among the privileged classes and sharpened the conspiratorial plotting which had become a feature of political life in Samaria. Nevertheless, Menahem managed to cling to the throne for five precarious years and to pass the crown on to his son, Pekahiah, when he died.

Whatever abilities Pekahiah might have brought to the throne, the northern kingdom was slipping inexorably toward oblivion. Like his father, he swore obeisance to the Assyrians to keep them from occupying the land. But anarchy reigned in Israel, rather than Pekahiah. Only the army could exercise any element of control, but it was limited in size and strength and riddled with rivalries.

Burning resentment built up among Israelites who had not already been alienated by impoverishment and who were heavily taxed to fund the extortionate tribute payments demanded by the Assyrians. An underground movement, objecting to Pekahiah's craven submission to the despotic foreign power, challenged his authority.

Its members realized that if Israel stood alone, its defiance of mighty Assyria would be futile. They looked to Egypt, the rival superpower in the region, for assistance. With problems of their own to resolve, the Egyptians could offer only moral support. Nevertheless, Pekahiah's policy of obeisance to Assyria remained the target of vigorous dissent in Samaria. After two jittery years on the throne, he was relieved of his burden when he was assassinated by Pekah, the chariot commander of his army, who took the crown for himself and immediately made it clear he would not submit to rule by the Assyrians.

He did not stand alone in assuming such an audacious stance. Defiance had also unfolded in neighboring lands similarly menaced by the great power to the east. Together with the kings of Damascus, Ammon, Moab, and Philistine city-states, Pekah formed an alliance to resist Assyrian subjugation. He also tried to recruit King Ahaz of Judah to this alliance. But Ahaz considered the formation of the anti-Assyrian coalition hopeless and provocative and declined to be drawn in.

His snub was not to be tolerated by the newly formed alliance. Fearing the presence of a potentially hostile nation at their rear when the Assyrian campaign against them was likely to be launched, Israel and Damascus reacted by attacking recalcitrant Judah. Defeating the outmatched Judaean army, they overran much of the southern kingdom, looted its treasures, and took hostages.

But despite Pekah's boldness, Israel's domestic problems remained unresolved. Insurrections and conspiracies abounded. Civil order could not be resuscitated. Neither life nor property could be protected by what remained of the instruments of the state.

In the deepening climate of fear, increasing numbers of Israelites turned to the worship of gods other than Yahweh to escape despair and seek the emotional security which Yahweh seemed no longer willing to offer them.

Meantime, resistance to the Assyrians was doomed to failure. Their empire was at the height of its power and a grouping of mini-states stitched together to stop their march of conquest did not much worry them. They considered Pekah's insubordination perfidious in view of Israel's previous servility and sent an army to deal with it.

The Israelites could offer little effective resistance. Except for Samaria and the countryside around the capital, the territory of the northern kingdom was quickly annexed outright and turned into three Assyrian provinces: Gilead in Transjordan, Megiddo (which included Galilee), and Dor on the coastal plain. Great numbers of Israelites were forced from their homes and expelled to other parts of the Assyrian empire.

Only the assassination of Pekah and the seizure of the throne by Israelites prepared to renew Israel's submission to Assyria's Tiglathpileser delayed its complete obliteration.

*   *   *

Pekah's assassin, Hoshea, his successor as king, was the last to wear the crown of the northern kingdom. He was probably an Israelite army commander like his immediate predecessors. In usurping the throne, he may have been acting as an instrument of the Assyrians in the atmosphere of confusion and discord that now blanketed Samaria.

By resuming tribute payments to Assyria which Pekah had suspended, Hoshea was at first able to keep what little remained of his realm from being absorbed into its empire. However, even his small bit of territory became little more than an Assyrian appendage.

When Tiglathpileser died, Hoshea sought benefit from the distracting power struggle that usually attended the death of an absolute ruler. Encouraged by Egypt, he tried to throw off the yoke of the Assyrians. Once more, Israel ceased its tribute payments to them.

It was an act of national suicide. The Egyptians again proved incapable of providing promised military support and a new ruler, Shalmaneser V, ascended the Assyrian throne without having to contend overly much with a struggle for power at home of the kind from which Hoshea hoped to extract advantage. Shalmaneser reacted furiously to Hoshea's insubordination, attacked in force, took Hoshea prisoner, and sent him off into exile. Nothing more is known of his fate.

The city of Samaria, to which refugees from elsewhere in Israel had fled for sanctuary, managed to hold out for another two years. Its fortifications had been strengthened. Food and water had been stored in granaries and reservoirs, permitting its inhabitants to survive a lengthy siege. But the Assyrians knew a lot about overwhelming fortified cities.

When Samaria ultimately fell to them, much of it was leveled. Other Israelite cities were also wholly or partially destroyed. A large part of the population, including the elite and skilled of the kingdom—administrators, military officers, merchants, scribes, and craftsmen—were rounded up and deported to various regions of the Assyrian empire. The land was resettled with people brought in from other lands that had been subjected to Assyrian rule. It was to be a new place, its links with its past expunged.

Many Jews remained. But in due course the preponderance of non-Jewish influences and intermarriage with the newcomers resulted in a vastly reduced Jewish presence in what had been the northern kingdom.

Some there still clung to forms of worship of Yahweh. But they were not recognized as true Jews by the priests in Jerusalem whose claim to be the only custodians of the Mosaic heritage carried even greater weight now that Israel was no more, having been transformed into the Assyrian province of Samarina. Those northerners would later form the core of the community of Yahweh-worshipping, Torah-venerating Samaritans of whom small enclaves survive to the present-day in modern Israel and Palestine.

The northern kingdom of the Jews had existed for two centuries during which it had been ruled by a succession of nineteen kings.

Little is known of the fate of the great numbers of Israelites who were deported by the Assyrians when they conquered the land. No credible confirmation has ever been found for often-fanciful reports over the ages from adventurous travelers who told of sightings of one or more of the "Lost Tribes" in far-off parts of the world.

THE LOST TRIBES OF ISRAEL

When the Assyrians stormed the city of Samaria in 722 BCE, they did more than overrun Israel's last remaining bastion. In seizing its capital, they completed the process of obliterating the northern kingdom of the Jews as a political, geographic, ethnic, and religious entity. New inhabitants brought in by the conquerors to settle on the land were from various other parts of the Assyrian empire. They had different ways and worshipped different deities.

Little is known of the fate of the Israelites who were deported to Mesopotamia, Media, and elsewhere in the sprawling Assyrian realm. Their dispersal later intrigued scholars, travelers, and fantasists, both Jews and gentiles, sometimes giving rise to bizarre accounts of where they ended up.

Their return to the homeland of the Jews had been forecast by the prophet Ezekiel, through whom God had said, "I will gather you from the peoples and assemble you out of the countries where you have been scattered, and I will give you the Land of Israel."[32]

For many Jews, during long centuries of dispersal and persecution in Europe and Moslem countries, the idea of the lost tribes took on a mythology of hope. They were imagined to have become a mighty nation of holy warriors who would one day be unleashed by God to journey from the remote regions where they had come to rest and would rescue the Jewish people from their tormentors.

The historian Josephus claimed that the lost tribes had grown to be a vast multitude of people and were to be found beyond the Euphrates River. The third-century Christian poet Commodianus wrote of a place where the lost Jews lived, where their bodies suffered no pain, and from which they would return to rescue their "mother," Jerusalem.

> *Almighty God ... will bring forth a people hidden for a long time. They are the Jews who were cut off by the river beyond Persia whom God willed to remain there until the end.... There is no lying nor any hatred [among them], therefore no son dies before his parents.... [T]hey look for a resurrection still to come.... [T]hey purely obey all the laws.... This people ... will return to the land of Judah, the river being dried up. And with them God will come to fulfill [His] promises.[33]*

In the ninth century, a traveler named Eldad ha-Dani appeared at the Jewish community in Kairouan in present-day Tunisia, claiming to be of the lost tribe of

Dan. He said that it and other lost tribes were gathered as a nation that had settled in East Africa, near Ethiopia.

The twelfth-century Spanish Jewish traveler Benjamin of Tudela wrote of people he had met on his journeys who told him of having encountered Jews of the
lost tribes of Dan, Asher, Naphtali, and Zebulun in the Nishapur Mountains of
Persia. Other accounts said a corps of Genghis Khan's warriors was composed of
Jews from the lost tribes, that people of Afghanistan were descendants of the lost
tribe of Asher, and that communities of Jews in India were descended from the
tribes of Ephraim and Manasseh.

The Jews of the city of Kaifeng, in China, were said to have been from a lost
tribe that had migrated from its earlier settlement in India. The Lembas of South
Africa were said to have been descended from a lost tribe that had originally made
Yemen its home. Western travelers claimed to detect cultural practices similar to
those of Jews in many remote regions, including their dietary observances and
male circumcision.

In the sixteenth century, David Reubeni arrived in southern Europe claiming
to be the brother of King Joseph who, he said, ruled the lost tribes. Reubeni is
believed to have been born either in a Jewish community in India or among the
black Falasha Jews of Ethiopia. So impressive and persuasive a figure was he that
he was received by Pope Clement VII in Rome, to whom he proposed an alliance
with the lost tribes against the Islamic Ottoman Empire. He was also permitted
an audience with the king of Portugal. In due course, Reubeni's pretensions wore
thin. He was accused of criminally persuading Jews who had converted to Christianity to revert to their original faith, was imprisoned, and died in captivity.

According to one legend, the lost tribes of Israel were exiled beyond a river
called Sambatyon, the location of which was a mystery. This remarkable stream, a
violent torrent that swept along an avalanche of boulders and stones, was said to
be impassable on six days of the week. In accordance with the laws of Moses, the
river rested on the seventh day and could then be forded. But members of the lost
tribes were obliged to rest on the Sabbath as well and therefore could not make
their way back to the Holy Land from exile. Their return across the Sambatyon
was said to await the coming of the Messiah when the turbulence of the river
would be calmed to mark the occasion.

In the seventeenth century, a letter surfaced in Jerusalem, allegedly delivered
to a Jewish traveler in Persia by a warrior of the tribe of Nephtali. It offered assur-
ance from the lost tribes to "our brethren" that salvation would ultimately come.
"Do not ask why we wage no war against the nations [to liberate you], for you

should know that we ... cannot cross the river [Sambatyon] until the end be, when the Lord will say to the prisoners 'Go forth.' ..."[34]

At about the same time, Sabbatai Sevi of Smyrna (Izmir in present-day Turkey) gathered large numbers of followers and caused a great stir by claiming to be the living Messiah. Belief in Sabbatai convulsed Jewish communities in Europe, the Middle East, and North Africa with a frenzy of end-of-the-world speculation. After his forced conversion to Islam and subsequent death, he was said to have gone to live among the lost tribes on the far side of the Sambatyon. It was said he would return, with his bride, the daughter of Moses, to lead the tribes when the world was ready for redemption.

As for the geographic location of the tribes-in-waiting, the scholar Gershom Scholem wrote, "The Egyptian Jews preferred the Arabian desert, which was nearest to them, and peopled it with the army of the Ten Tribes.... [This] 'Arabian' army became the vanguard of an even larger Jewish army advancing from Africa.... The [Ottoman] Turks [would be] unable to fight them, their own swords and muskets turning against themselves and striking them down."[35]

During the age of European exploration, conquistadors and explorers claimed to have made contact with the lost tribes in Peru and elsewhere in South America. A Marrano traveler named Aaron ha-Levi claimed in 1644 that he had met members of the tribe of Reuben in Ecuador.

In his *History of New Spain*, Father Duran, a missionary, wrote that he was convinced the Mexican Indians, whose religious rites he had observed, "are of the ten tribes of Israel that Salmanasar, king of the Assyrians, made prisoners and carried to Assyria in the time of Hoshea, king of Israel." The seventeenth-century English explorer Charles Beatty claimed to have found Jews of the lost tribes among the Delaware Indians. Others identified them as the forebears of other North American Indian tribes. Indeed, it was suggested by some that members of lost tribes discovered America and were the ancestors of all the American Indians.

Many of the sightings in various remote parts of the world can be attributed to the attractions of romantic tales of remarkable survival and to lack of knowledge of Jewish customs by non-Jewish explorers over the centuries.

Those men had heard tales of the scattered tribes of the ancient kingdom of Israel awaiting discovery. It was not difficult for them to imagine that exotic and otherwise incomprehensible ways of peoples they encountered on their travels matched legends they had heard about the Jews of biblical times. There was also the eternal hope of Jewish travelers and scholars that a great Jewish nation did actually exist somewhere, one with which the dispersed and oppressed Jews of the Diaspora could identify.

Many who wrote or told of having found lost tribes did in fact come across communities of Jews in far-off places—including Ethiopia, India, and China. It is not totally inconceivable that some were descendants of Jews who had been driven from the fallen kingdom of Israel by the Assyrians.

In his *Pictorial History of the Jewish People*, the historian Nathan Ausubel has observed, "There are quite a number of peoples today who cling to the ancient tradition that they are descended from the Jewish Lost Tribes: the tribesmen of Afghanistan, the Mohammedan Berbers of West Africa, and the six million Christian Igbo people of Nigeria. Unquestionably, they all practice certain ancient Hebraic customs and beliefs, which lends some credibility to their fantastic-sounding claims."[36]

A prominent Israeli rabbi recently declared that people of the Bnei Menashe community of northeastern India are descendants of a lost Jewish tribe that has lived in exile for twenty-seven centuries, ever since the Assyrian expulsion. Many of its members have been assisted in migrating to Israel by the Israeli government.

But the origin of most rediscovered "lost tribes" is generally explained differently. Some—the community of Falasha Jews of Ethiopia, perhaps—could date as far back as the days of Solomon and his far-flung commercial enterprises. Others date from the Diaspora that took root in the Babylonian exile after the fall of the kingdom of Judah. And many Jewish communities were established in remote parts of the ancient world during the time of the ancient Greeks and Romans. The Khazar people of the Caucasus were converts to Judaism much later.

Despite the advent of aerial photography and other modern technological tools, the remarkable River Sambatyon has yet to be found.

KINGS OF JUDAH

REHOBOAM

931–914 BCE

As with the creation of the northern kingdom, when the Jewish nation split in two after Solomon died, the foundation of the southern kingdom was a watershed in the history of the Jewish people.

It did not come about immediately. Solomon's son, Rehoboam, inherited a strong, undivided nation to which neighboring states had sworn allegiance and paid tribute. Crowned at the age of forty-one, Rehoboam also inherited the allegiance of the people of his tribal territory of Judah who had been favored by his father and who had benefited more than those in the other parts of the land from the kingdom's prosperity during Solomon's reign.

However, mistrust of central authority had long been a feature of the mood in the tribal territories in the central and northern regions. Even under the acclaimed David, people there had been less than enthusiastic about being part of a nation ruled from Jerusalem by a king from the southern tribe of Judah, the people of whom were held in special regard by the crown. They had gratefully welcomed David's elimination of Philistine and other external threats to the Jewish nation. But the beginnings of administrative centralization during his reign had been received with suspicion, as had his national census taking. Solomon's heavy taxes and forced labor schemes had deepened their discontent, as had the downgrading of their tribal elders by the royal functionaries appointed by Jerusalem to govern the land.

Through administrative control, oppressive policing, protection against foreign incursion, and distribution of favors, Solomon had maintained the nominal allegiance of the people throughout the land during most of his reign. But when he died and Rehoboam mounted the throne, the new king was made to understand that the loyalty of the disgruntled tribes could not be taken for granted.

Confident of support for his leadership in the south, Rehoboam journeyed to Shechem, in the territory of the tribe of Ephraim, to confer with elders of the rest of the land and extract their vows of allegiance. Shechem was the site of an historic shrine where, long before, Joshua had gathered tribal leaders of the Jews to renew the covenant God had made with their Patriarch ancestors. Rehoboam expected that the symbolism of the place would help him establish a new covenant, one between him and the alienated tribes.

The Elders Of The Northern Tribes Rebel Against King Rehoboam

His journey was a concession, an acceptance that the disaffected elders would have ignored a summons to Jerusalem to have their vows of loyalty extracted from them. But though their discontent had festered and their mood was rebellious, they were prepared to make concessions too.

"Your father made our yoke heavy," they told Rehoboam at Shechem. "Now lighten the harsh labor and the heavy yoke which your father laid on us, and we will serve you."[37]

Rehoboam was faced with a dilemma. To accede to those demands might encourage the northerners to demand more. Even if they did not, his royal authority would have been successfully challenged and undermined. However, the alternative might be worse. If he rejected the demands, he might be confronted with open insurrection far from the safety of Jerusalem and the protection of his army.

He told the assembled elders he would reply to their requests in three days' time and summoned his advisers. They provided him with conflicting counsel.

Older advisers, whom he had inherited from his father, advised him to give the northerners what they wanted. He would thereby assure their allegiance at a crucial time, before he had made his mark as their king. The implication was that once he had extracted himself from this difficult encounter and firmly established himself on the throne, he could follow whatever course he wished.

But Rehoboam's younger counselors, aristocrats with whom he had grown up at Solomon's court, urged a different course of action. They urged him not even to pretend to give in. They warned that to show any weakness at the beginning of his reign would seriously weaken his position and tarnish his reputation.

Recalling Solomon's uncompromising treatment of dissidents and potential rivals, Rehoboam decided to follow the course suggested by those advocating firmness. Accordingly, at the end of the three days he had requested to consider easing tax and other burdens, he responded to the assembled elders with threats of still harder times to come for the people of their tribes. "My father made your yoke heavy, but I will add to your yoke; my father flogged you with whips, but I will flog you with scorpions [whips studded with barbs]."[38]

If Rehoboam expected the elders to cringe in terror and beg forgiveness, he was quickly disabused of that notion. They reacted furiously. Their loathing of the king and resentment of the favored south was now undisguised. A call for rebellion rose among them with a cry that revealed how, for all their achievements, David and Solomon had failed to heal the breach between the south and rest of the land. "We have no portion in David," the elders announced, signaling rejection, not only of Rehoboam, but also of general submission to Jerusalem. "To your tents, O Israel!"[39]

Having taken a stand, Rehoboam could not back down. Committed to a policy of unwavering firmness, he sent Adoram, his administrator of forced labor—a provocative choice—to respond to this challenge by the incensed northerners. Adoram was to warn them of the risks they ran if they refused to swear allegiance to the king and obey him in all things. It was a mistake. Reacting in fury, the northerners stoned the king's emissary to death.

Believing the same fate awaited him if he tarried in Shechem, Rehoboam mounted his chariot and fled back to Jerusalem with his entourage. But the assembled elders were now bent on doing more than merely proclaiming their dissatisfaction and demanding concessions. They were determined their tribes would never again be governed by the south. Instead, they would have a kingdom of their own. It would be called Israel and be independent of rule from Jerusalem. For their king they chose Jeroboam of the tribe of Ephraim, which inhabited a large swathe of the center of the land. Ephraim had long been particularly resentful of Judah's preeminence among the tribes, which had once been its own.

Safely back in Jerusalem, Rehoboam proceeded to draw up plans to restore the unity of the shattered Jewish nation and his own mastery of it. He organized a force of picked warriors for a campaign to crush Jeroboam and the rebellion.

But the prophet Shemiah warned against such action. He told Rehoboam it had been God's will for the kingdom of Solomon to be divided. The Lord, said Shemiah, commanded him not to send his army against the Israelites who were his kinsmen. Possibly fearing an attack from newly resurgent Egypt while his forces were locked in battle to the north, Rehoboam held back.

Thus the two separate kingdoms of the Jews, with Rehoboam as king of Judah and Jeroboam as king of Israel, came into existence without armed conflict. A truce was established between them, punctuated by no more than minor skirmishes from time to time during the remainder of Rehoboam's reign.

The consequences of the division of Solomon's empire were enormous. Judah had been the administrative heart of the nation but was now left with only its own tribal territory and that of the adjoining smaller tribe of Benjamin. Of the rest of the realm Solomon had dominated, Judah retained only the desert kingdom of Edom as a tributary. Other neighboring peoples seized the opportunity to relieve themselves of Jerusalem's dominance. Among them, the kingdom of Damascus exploited the situation by seizing territories in Transjordan that had been part of Rehoboam's legacy from Solomon.

However, Jerusalem's, and therefore Judah's, position as center of the Jewish faith was enhanced by the migration southward of priestly Levites from Israel. They believed their place was with Rehoboam, descended from David and guardian of the Ark of the Covenant which was sheltered in the Jerusalem Temple. The Levites were, in any case, being deprived of their priestly functions by Jeroboam who appointed a new Israelite priesthood, loyal to himself and Israel, men who would not look to Jerusalem for spiritual guidance.

However, the hopes of the Temple priests for a religious revival in the south proved futile. Despite their hopes, Rehoboam initiated no crackdown on pagan worship there. Though not as widespread as in the north, altars for the worship of Baal remained in place at various sites in Judah, as did idols for the worship of Astarte and other pagan deities. In some cases, public worship involved the services of female and male prostitutes and included fertility rites which worshippers of Yahweh abominated as obscene and blasphemous.

Shorn of the larger territory that constituted the new kingdom of Israel (and the taxes it had provided), Judah was so weakened that, five years after Solomon died, the Egyptian pharaoh, Shishak, seeking to recapture the lost glory of ancient Egypt, felt free to invade the southern kingdom (and Israel as well). His army of sixty thousand horsemen, more than one thousand chariots, and Libyan, Ethiopian, and Sudanese auxiliary units easily vanquished the Judaeans as it swept toward Jerusalem. Only by paying a heavy tribute did Rehoboam persuade the Egyptians not to storm the capital.

He handed over many of the treasures accumulated during Solomon's reign, even the gold shields and spears of the royal bodyguard. Judah's elite troops were to be reduced to parading with less splendid bronze weapons. Egypt laid waste to several of the fortress cities Solomon had built. But it was not the power it had once been and would later again become, and it had other pressing concerns. Its army soon had to withdraw.

Nevertheless, Rehoboam was badly shaken by the losses he incurred and the damage to his image. To salvage what was left of his position, as well as the standing of his kingdom, he embarked on a program of bolstering Judah's defenses. He rebuilt fortress cities the Egyptians had ravaged and built new ones for his shrunken land. Instead of spreading his forces thinly, as his father had done while guardian of what had been a large commercial empire, he concentrated on assuring the security of Judah's heartland in the event of another foreign assault.

To guard against the emergence of potentially rebellious local warlords, he placed his sons—he had twenty-eight of them and sixty daughters from his eighteen wives and sixty concubines—in command of his fortress cities and supplied them well to withstand sieges. This chain of defenses proved so well designed that it continued to function effectively against Judah's enemies long after Rehoboam had passed into history.

He was succeeded by his son Abijah to whom he bequeathed a kingdom far smaller, weaker, and poorer than the one he had inherited from Solomon.

ABIJAH

914–911 BCE

Hostility was the keynote of relations between Judah and Israel from the moment of their establishment as separate states. But Abijah has the distinction of having launched the first major war between Jews. He was the second to wear the crown of Judah after Solomon's kingdom split in two, and his legacy from his father, Rehoboam, included his claim to be king of Israel as well as Judah by virtue of descent from his great-grandfather, David. Immediately after ascending the throne, he embarked on a military campaign to press that claim.

Jeroboam, first ruler of Israel, was at the time still trying to consolidate his authority over his newly established kingdom and his military resources had been stretched fighting off plundering raids by the Egyptians. Nevertheless, he dispatched an army to confront the Judaeans when Abijah led them north on his mission of conquest.

Before combat commenced, Abijah urged the northerners not to resist him and their southern brethren. He reminded them that God had made an unbreakable covenant with David, assigning to him and his descendants kingship over all Jews for all eternity. He said Jeroboam's Israelite subjects had been led along a road of impiety and blasphemy and that to fight against Judah would be to fight against God.

His exhortation was received with contempt by the Israelites and the two Jewish armies joined in combat. The battle cries of warriors rang out over the battlefield and priests on both sides blew ceremonial ram horns to summon divine assistance.

Despite a numerical advantage, the Israelite army was driven back by the Judaeans who overran territory in the hills of Ephraim. Among their conquests was the site of the historic Israelite shrine at Bethel, an achievement of symbolic significance, though far short of Abijah's hopes of conquering all of Israel.

Accounts in the Bible and in the writings of the historian Josephus say the Israelites lost a half million men in the conflict, no doubt a hugely inflated figure. Nevertheless, Abijah's victory was a serious setback for Israel from which Jeroboam did not fully recover during the few years still remaining to his reign.

Judah's victory was partly the result of assistance it received from the Aramaeans of Damascus with whom Abijah had formed an alliance. Having long before been trounced by the armies of David and Solomon, the Aramaeans did not hesitate to take advantage of the rift between the Jewish kingdoms.

Abijah did not long enjoy his military and diplomatic successes. He died after ruling over Judah a mere three years and was buried in the royal tomb in Jerusalem.

ASA

911–871 BCE

Though Judah and Israel shared a spiritual and historical heritage, their separate perceived national interests rather than what they held in common dominated their policies and actions. When in dispute, as they often were, each was prepared to form an alliance with a non-Jewish third state to be used as an instrument against the other.

Nevertheless, their Jewish faith and religious observance was at times a matter of state policy. Asa was the first ruler of either of the two kingdoms to make it so.

He was still a youth when his father died. Ruling in his name, his idol-worshipping mother, Maacah, installed men from among her own courtiers in positions of authority. When Asa came of age to exercise his royal prerogatives, he removed them in favor of his own appointees.

He had spent his boyhood years under Maacah's control and care but proved to be a forceful and assertive king. Despite his mother's pagan beliefs and the previous tolerance of pagan religious practices in Judah, he ordered heathen worship to be rooted out and the destruction of pagan religious centers. Asa even banned his mother from worshipping her Canaanite fertility goddess Asherah and destroyed the lascivious statue of the deity she had built, an act which certified her dismissal as a figure of influence. The practice of religious prostitution that accompanied some forms of pagan worship was prohibited.

Also outlawed were vestiges of what Asa deemed to be idolatrous worship among Jews. Statuary was removed from Jewish shrines wherever such "high places" continued to exist in Judah despite the centrality of the holy Temple in Jerusalem.

Asa well understood the political implications of his policies. So closely linked were religious and national feelings among Judaeans that his campaign of spiritual purification stirred national pride and ardor. His actions may also have been motivated by expectations of support for Judah from those within neighboring Israel offended by far more prevalent pagan practices there. The hope of eventual reunification of the Jewish nation, with Jerusalem at its heart, remained undiluted.

A period of comparative peace after Asa had become king in fact as well as name permitted him to tighten Judah's national security. Adding to the chain of fortified cities designed to guard the kingdom from external aggression earned him a reputation as military leader and national guardian, as did his handling of a threat from Egypt

The forces he mustered at the fortified city of Mareshah, west of the Dead Sea, repelled a powerful thrust by Zerah, the Nubian commander of mercenaries garrisoned at an Egyptian outpost on Judah's southern flank. His army scattered Zerah's attackers and pursued the survivors beyond Gaza. It was a surprising but resounding victory and kept the Egyptians at bay for many years.

Antagonism between Judah and Israel proved more difficult to resolve. Increasingly bitter, it persisted for most of Asa's long reign, during part of which the throne of Israel was occupied by the soldier-king Baasha. Baasha sent his much stronger army south to reclaim border territory that had been annexed by the Judaeans during the reign of Asa's father. Succeeding in that objective, the Israelites went on to invade Judah proper and even secured positions within striking distance of Jerusalem.

With his crown, capital city, and kingdom at stake, Asa bought the help of King Ben-Hadad of Damascus with extravagant gifts. Unable to fight a two-front war, the Israelites had to withdraw from Judah.

However strife between the two Jewish states continued unabated. Fearing a resumption of attacks from Israel, Asa seized upon its difficulties with Damascus to resecure the disputed border area between them, conscripting an army of laborers to fortify his positions there. The situation became stalemated and armed confrontation between the two kingdoms gradually petered out.

In his last years, Asa suffered a crippling foot disease. Priests attributed it to his having drafted even religious students for military service.

JEHOSHAPHAT

871–848 BCE

It was difficult for the nation ruled from Jerusalem to reconcile itself to transformation from the regional power it had been under Solomon to the shrunken state it became as the kingdom of Judah after he died. It took Judah six decades to adjust to the change.

Being ruled by a succession of David's divinely ordained blood descendants spared Judah the sequence of violent royal usurpations and upheavals that plagued Israel. But not until the reign of Jehoshaphat, its fourth king, did the southern kingdom of the Jews truly achieve self-assurance and sense of purpose. Under him, it came to enjoy greater economic stability and domestic tranquility than at any time since its establishment. His comprehensive reforms included a revision of the system for administering justice. Formerly under the direct, haphazard control of the royal court, it was now made far more accessible to the king's subjects with courts set up in major population centers so that justice could be more quickly dispensed. What was in effect a court of appeals, presiding over by both religious and secular authorities, was also established.

Officials and priests were commanded to deal honestly in matters of civil law. Bribery was prohibited and judges were warned against being influenced by the rank, wealth, and social positions of those upon whom they were called to pass judgment.

Jehoshaphat was thirty-five years old when he ascended the throne after his father, Asa, died. He had already been made sensitive to the superior military strength of Israel, the territorial ambitions of the Aramaeans of Damascus, and the rising menace of the Assyrians beyond them.

Of the last two, there was little he could do except strengthen his kingdom's defenses. But he recognized that other possibilities existed with regard to his nation's destructive long-standing rivalry with the Israelites. Accordingly, he sought reconciliation with Israel, the first such move since the two kingdoms had gone their separate ways.

Firmly in command in Judah, Jehoshaphat was aided in his search for rapprochement by the fact that his reign coincided with that of a strong, receptive monarch in the north. King Ahab there shared his wish for reconciliation and responded warmly to his overtures. His authority similarly unchallenged in his own previously unstable nation, Ahab was able to do so without arousing disruptive popular agitation among his normally wary northern tribes.

The alliance was sealed when Jehoshaphat dispatched Judaean troops to reinforce Ahab's army during Israel's war with Damascus. He also sent his army to support the Israelites when they clashed with the Moabites.

He was the first Judaean ruler to cross into Israel as a royal guest and was received there with much pomp and ceremony. To further cement relations, he arranged for his son and heir, Jehoram, to marry Athaliah, Ahab's daughter.

Reconciliation notwithstanding, the reestablishment of a single Jewish state remained out of the question. The Israelites still did not want to be ruled and taxed by Jerusalem as their forebears had been. And the Judaeans, occupying a much smaller land with a smaller population, had no wish to surrender their well-ordered insularity, their Davidic dynasty, or their belief that they, rather than the Israelites, were the beneficiaries of the covenant with God.

To protect their new accord from dissent, it was understood by all concerned that their reconciliation was not a prelude to reunification (though it may be that Israel had by then grown so strong under Ahab that Judah had virtually become his vassal.)

The new alliance extended to commerce in the region. Their friendship with the seafaring Phoenicians significantly increased lucrative trade for all concerned. Vessels were built at Ezion Geber on the Gulf of Aqaba to facilitate seaborne commerce through the Red Sea. Though indicative of the high level of cooperative endeavor, that project went awry. The ships proved unwieldy and foundered in rough waters soon after leaving port. Nevertheless, Judah, under Jehoshaphat, was increasingly engaged in economically and diplomatically productive commercial activity.

For the security of his kingdom, he reorganized and streamlined the Judaean army. In addition to a standing force, arrangements were made for reserves to be quickly called to the colors when needed. To neutralize potential external threat, chariots were garrisoned in positions guarding access to the Judaean heartland and to its major cities, and military operations were launched against external marauders. Nomadic Arab tribes and the now-enfeebled Philistines on the coastal plain were made to pay tribute.

To challenge Jehoshaphat's increasing assertiveness, the Ammonites, Moabites, and their allies organized a campaign against him. A combined army penetrated into the Hebron hills from beyond the Dead Sea. But the attack misfired when dissension and armed clashes erupted within the invading force. A

Judaean force sent to deal with the incursion was required to do no more than collect the spoils in the abandoned camps of the invaders.

Unlike some of his predecessors, Jehoshaphat was deemed above reproach by the senior priests in Jerusalem to whom he granted authority to enforce religious observance and some of whom he numbered among his advisers. He adhered to traditional religious law and continued with his father's policy of banning pagan worship. He dispatched religious instructors to teach the law throughout the land. Regional Jewish shrines, which had survived his father's campaign against them, were shut down as still divisive. Deprived of them, larger crowds of worshipper converged on the Temple in Jerusalem at festival times and holy days. Pilgrims came the year round.

However, Jehoshaphat did not completely escape priestly censure. He was rebuked for promoting Judah's alliance with Israel. Pagan practices tolerated in the northern kingdom drew bitter criticism in the south, as did the continued refusal of the Israelites, with shrines of their own, to accept the Jerusalem Temple as the center of Jewish worship. The prophet Jehu demanded of Jehoshaphat, "Should one give aid to the wicked and befriend those who hate the Lord?[40]"

In contrast to most of his predecessors, Jehoshaphat was a man of few personal pretensions. When he changed out of his royal robes into ordinary attire when calling on the prophet Elisha, it was considered characteristic of his modesty. He was a popular monarch, a description that would not be applied to his son Jehoram when he succeeded to the throne upon his father's death.

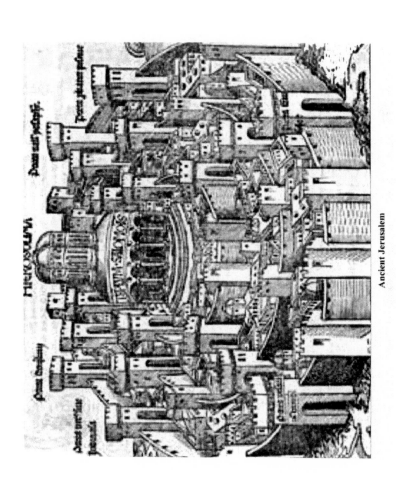

Ancient Jerusalem

JEHORAM

848–841 BCE

For a small state in a turbulent region subjected to rapidly shifting conditions, stability can never be guaranteed. The situation is even more difficult when the actions of the ruler of that small state compound the attending perils. Upon his death, Jehoshaphat bequeathed his oldest son Jehoram a secure, self-assured Judah. But Jehoram quickly tipped Judah into decline.

Jehoshaphat had attempted to maintain the nation's security and cohesion by giving each of his sons command of one of the kingdom's fortified cities. Having named Jehoram (also called Joram) his successor on the throne, he had left some of his royal treasure to his six younger sons: Azariah, Jehiel, Zechariah, Azariahu, Michael, and Shephatiah.

But Jehoram, a vain, paranoid figure, saw that as a threat to himself, which it may well have been in the atmosphere of intrigue that had developed at Jehoshaphat's court despite the kingdom's well-being during his reign and his laudable character. Upon donning the crown at the age of thirty-two, Jehoram quickly secured his position against possible challenge from his brothers by having them killed. Court officials who had served his father, but whose loyalty to himself he questioned, were also disposed of.

Such measures may have shielded Jehoram from overthrow. But his actions undermined Judah's unity and exposed it to external threat. The tributary kingdom of Edom declared its defiance and proclaimed allegiance to a king of its own. When Jehoram sent his army to deal with such insubordination, demoralized by Judah's domestic convulsions, it was easily overwhelmed by the Edomites.

The loss of Edom had serious security and economic implications for Judah. It cost the kingdom control of a profitable trading route to Arabia which Jehoshaphat had maintained through diplomatic ingenuity and guarded with military muscle.

Emboldened by the evident weakness of the southern kingdom under its new ruler, nomadic Arab tribes to the south and the Philistines along the Mediterranean coast, both of whom had been cowed by Jehoshaphat, embarked on plundering raids into Judaean territory. Those raids grew more daring when Jehoram and the bulk of his army were away in the north attempting with Israel and other northern states to deal with the more worrying, looming menace of expansionist

Assyria. Judah's army was so fully stretched that Philistine marauders were able to mount a successful raid on Jerusalem where they slaughtered most of the royal family and carried off much treasure. The only male survivor among the royals, other than the absent king, was Jehoram's son Ahaziah.

A crisis in matters of Jewish worship, the bedrock of Judah's national identity and spirit, aggravated Jehoram's difficulties. While still heir to the throne, he had married Athaliah, daughter of Israel's King Ahab. It had been a diplomatic marriage, arranged by their fathers to seal a long-elusive alliance between the two Jewish kingdoms.

But strong-willed Athaliah had not submitted to the campaign against heathen worship in Judah that her father-in-law, Jehoshaphat, had inaugurated. After her arrival in Jerusalem as royal princess and wife of Crown Prince Jehoram, she had continued with pagan religious observances of the kind so passionately promoted by her mother, Queen Jezebel, in Israel. Her entourage, brought with her from the northern kingdom, did the same.

When Jehoshaphat died and Jehoram became king, Athaliah, now queen of Judah, championed the spread of paganism throughout her husband's realm, arousing the fury of priests and prophets and the loathing of the people. Many of the misfortunes that overtook Judah during Jehoram's reign were attributed to her transgression against the laws of Yahweh and his tolerance of them. When the king was smitten with agonizing stomach pain, possibly the result of cancer of the bowel, and died soon after, the prophet Elijah called it punishment for his sins.

During Jehoram's reign, the achievements of his father were reversed. Judah was reduced in wealth, power, and influence. Few of his subjects mourned his passing.

AHAZIAH

841–840 BCE

The manner of Ahaziah's death is of greater historical interest than his life. Of the sons of King Jehoram, only he, the youngest, survived when Philistine marauders pillaged Jerusalem while his father was away from the capital. When Jehoram subsequently died, Ahaziah, then twenty-two years old, inherited the throne of Judah.

At the time, Judah and Israel enjoyed congenial relations, underpinned by an earlier diplomatic marriage between offspring of the rulers of the two kingdoms. As a mark of friendship between the two Jewish nations that had so often suffered an adversarial relationship, young Ahaziah sent troops from Judah to the aid of his cousin, King Jehoram of Israel, who bore the same name as his late father. The Judaean troops were to fight alongside the Israelites in their war with Damascus.

When Jehoram was wounded in battle, Ahaziah went to visit him at Jezreel, the Israelite winter capital, to which Jehoram had gone to recover.

While he was at Jezreel, Israel's military commander, Jehu, staged a coup, killed the recuperating Jehoram and fatally wounded the visiting Ahaziah. Having spent little time in Judah as its ruler, he'd had little to do with administering it and had made no impression on its affairs or the ways of its people.

During most of the one year Ahaziah had been king, his mother, Athaliah, had ruled the land in his name. When word reached Jerusalem of his death, she installed herself as queen of Judah.

ATHALIAH

840–835 BCE

Like all major religions, Judaism has always been male dominated and male focused. Its annals list comparatively few females of the heroic stature of Miriam, who saved the baby Moses from Egyptian slaughter; Deborah the Judge; Judith, who killed the drunken commander of an invading Babylonian army; and Esther, who, as consort to the king of Persia, saved the lives of her people.

Though it is through matrilineal rather than patrilineal descent that Jewish identity is now considered to be passed on to a child, females are generally described as having played only contingent roles in history; important, but peripheral—like the wives of the Patriarchs: Sarah, Rebecca, Leah, and Rachel.

Only two of the fifty-two regnant Jewish monarchs were women. One was Queen Alexandra Salome of the post-biblical Hasmonean dynasty. The other was Athaliah who sat on the throne of Judah eight centuries earlier.

Daughter of King Ahab and Queen Jezebel of Israel, Athaliah had been married to Jehoram when he was heir to the throne of Judah. The marriage served the purpose of cementing an alliance between the Jewish kingdoms. When Jehoram became king of Judah upon the death of his father, Jehoshaphat, Athaliah became his queen consort.

When Jehoram died, their son Ahaziah became king but he was absent from Jerusalem through most of his brief reign. After he was slain when caught up in an army coup while visiting in Israel, Athaliah, having ruled in his name during his absence and having control of the instruments of state, took the throne for herself.

Not being descended from King David as her predecessors had been, and as required by divine mandate, she was not considered rightful ruler of Judah by its people. Her first act as queen in her own name was to confront that problem. She ordered the slaughter of David's surviving male descendants so that no one could claim greater legitimacy as ruler of Judah than herself. But she wanted more than legitimacy. In destroying the house of David with whom God had made a covenant, Athaliah also hoped to undermine the link between the people of Judah and Yahweh.

From the time of her arrival in Judah from Israel as a royal princess, she had practiced and fostered the worship of pagan deities in defiance of Mosaic law, as her mother, Jezebel, had been doing in the northern kingdom. After she made herself sovereign queen of Judah, worship of the pagan deity Baal came under the patronage of the throne in Jerusalem, and it remained so during her reign.

Temple priests were outraged, as were most of Athaliah's subjects who believed they were unique among all peoples of the world only because of their special relationship with Yahweh. As an imperious foreigner brought in from Israel, Athaliah had never been held in high esteem in Judah. To her peril, her growing band of enemies included the Temple guards who scorned her foreign ways. They also felt humiliated not to have prevented her slaughter of David's descendants.

As distaste for Athaliah grew, her subjects rallied to her grandson, Joash, the young son of the slain King Ahaziah and King David's sole surviving male descendant. He had been rescued by his aunt Jehoshaba, the wife of High Priest Jehoiada, from the queen's murderous ambition and had been kept hidden under Jehoiada's protection. Having the appropriate lineage, Joash was considered by the priests a far more suitable and desirable occupant of David's throne than his despised, paganizing grandmother.

When the boy was seven years old, the high priest and other influential figures in Jerusalem succeeded in a plot to overthrow Athaliah. In a Temple ceremony, the boy was anointed king to rule over Judah in her place.

Hearing the blast of trumpets in the coronation ceremony, and the cheers of the people as word spread of what was happening, Athaliah rushed to the Temple and attempted to disrupt the celebration. The Temple guards, who had been prepared for her arrival, blocked her way. Removing her from the Temple compound so as not to desecrate holy ground, they unceremoniously cut her down.

Her death sparked a popular backlash against the pagan practices she had promoted. Crowds smashed the temple of Baal which the queen had built in the Temple precinct and slew its officiating priest.

Through the ages, Athaliah has been stigmatized as an unmitigated villain. Suggestions that she herself might have handed the infant Joash over to the high priest for safekeeping are contradicted by the needlessness of such a gesture when she was queen, as well as by her slaughter of David's other male descendants and her effort to prevent the boy's enthronement. But accounts of her wickedness, and that of Queen Jezebel of Israel, have been seen by some as exaggerated and symptomatic of an underlying misogyny in Jewish attitudes.

The Death of Athaliah

JOASH

835–796 BCE

No king of the Jews had ever ascended the throne the way Joash did, and none ever would. As a baby he had been saved by his aunt, Jehoshaba, and her husband, High Priest Jehoiada, from death at the hands of his grandmother, Queen Athaliah, and he was anointed monarch at the age of seven in a coup consummated in the Temple in Jerusalem, during which Athaliah was killed by the Temple guards.

Dedicated to the spread of pagan worship in Judah, she had consigned Jehoiada and other priests of Yahweh to a subsidiary role in the kingdom. But for the first time in Jewish history, in successfully plotting against her, the priesthood had demonstrated overriding political power. It had been instrumental in deposing one ruler and installing another.

The high priest then effectively ruled the kingdom as regent for Joash until he was a young man. During that period, the Temple area was cleansed of pagan rites and influences.

Even after Joash was old enough to dispense with a regent, Jehoiada and the priesthood sought to dominate affairs of state and managed to do so for a time. But the king eventually extracted himself from their controlling influence.

He seized upon their failure to make essential repairs to the Temple with funds that had been provided for the work and decreed they were to receive no further funding for that purpose. Instead he supervised a campaign to raise voluntary contributions from the populace so that renovation of the Temple structure could be properly undertaken. His personal involvement was highly symbolic, closely identifying him with the spiritual commitments of his people.

But Joash owed Jehoiada his life as well as his royal elevation and not until the high priest died did the clash between the king and the priesthood reach a climax. When Jehoiada's son, the priest Zechariah, attempted to perpetuate enhanced priestly privileges and openly criticized the king for neglecting his religious duties, Joash had him executed.

He was not able to deal as effectively with other of his problems. Recent misrule had cost Judah its earlier wealth, including that accruing from control of the trade routes through previously subservient neighboring states. Denied the resources to sustain a strong army, Joash was unable to maintain his kingdom's security. The Philistines and Edomites renewed long-suspended plundering raids and the Aramaeans of Damascus made deep inroads, even advancing on Jerusalem. Joash virtually emptied his treasury to buy them off and save the capital.

His reign had been promising in the early years, after he had grown old enough to exercise authority. But his impotence in the face of invaders and marauders increasingly provoked disquiet among his subjects. Their discontent was nurtured by priests embittered by his curtailment of their authority and by leading families in Jerusalem displeased with the nation's reduced circumstances.

Officials of the royal palace were also drawn into intriguing against Joash. Two among them became his assassins.

AMAZIAH

796–767 BCE

Amaziah could not help feeling anxious when he ascended the throne of Judah. He was the son of a king who had been murdered in a plot hatched by pillars of the society he was to rule. The coup against his father, Joash, had involved important people whose support—or at least sufferance—was essential if he were to cling to his crown.

Wisely, he began his reign in a cautious, low-keyed manner. He did not at first feel secure enough even to order the death of the men who assassinated his father. When that period of his uncertainty had passed and he finally had them executed, he refrained from invoking the common practice of the period of punishing their offspring as well. His restraint was probably prompted by recognition that eminent figures in Jerusalem had endorsed the actions of his father's assassins.

Only gradually did Amaziah gain the confidence that ultimately turned him recklessly ambitious and almost destroyed Judah's independence. Having been bequeathed an army that had proved impotent against territorial encroachers and marauders during his father's reign, Amaziah proceeded to rebuild it and reform its command structure. A census was taken of all Judaean males over twenty years of age to serve as a basis for conscripting a military force capable of restoring Judah's earlier strength and influence.

Once his army was restructured, trained, and properly equipped, Amaziah sent it into combat against the Edomites who had broken free of Judaean rule decades earlier. When their resistance was crushed, Judah regained control of lucrative southern trade routes and the wealth-producing mining regions east of the Dead Sea.

His most notable victory, signifying Judah's renewed mastery in the area, was the conquest of the fortified Edomite town of Sela, later known as Petra. But to the fury of Temple priests, he had stone idols of Edomite gods carried back to Jerusalem where he took to worshipping them.

Meantime, a dispute had broken out with Israel to the north. Mercenaries had earlier been recruited from among the Israelites to join the Judaeans in the war with Edom. But they were dismissed before they could join the battle and share the spoils. Embittered, they looted and plundered Judaean towns on their way home.

Amaziah had earlier established friendly relations with Israel's King Jehoash but had come to believe his army was mighty enough to conquer the larger northern kingdom. Made rash by its success in Edom, he used the affair of the spurned mercenaries to embark on a war with Israel.

Jehoash urged him not to turn the incident into a *casus belli* between Jews. "Stay at home," he told him, "lest, provoking disaster, you fall, dragging Judah down with you."[41] But having grown determined to unite the divided land of the Jewish people under his rule, Amaziah ignored the warning.

He had, however, badly miscalculated the balance of strength between his army and Israel's. His forces were quickly and decisively trounced and he himself was taken prisoner.

The Israelites capped their victory in the field by marching on Jerusalem, plundering the treasures of the Temple, and taking senior Jerusalem figures hostage to guarantee they would suffer no further trouble from Judah. They also demolished part of Jerusalem's city wall, making Judah's capital vulnerable to reconquest by them if they deemed it necessary.

The Israelites could have retained possession of the southern kingdom at the time, achieving Amaziah's objective of reestablishing a single Jewish nation, but under their rule rather than his. The difficulties that might have been entailed and the prospect of resulting friction with neighboring states may have deterred them from such an undertaking. Having won, they were content to withdraw from Judah, though it was obliged to remain submissive to Israel, probably paying tribute.

The captured Amaziah was freed and left to preside in ravaged Jerusalem over the results of his recklessness. He was faced with the same dilemma that had plagued the closing years of his father's reign: he was surrounded by bitter and frustrated priests and officials and estranged from the leading families of the land. Conspiracy against him was inevitable, and he fled Jerusalem for his safety. But assassins pursued him to the city of Lachish, near the border with the Philistines, and killed him there.

UZZIAH

767–739 BCE

The assassination of King Amaziah, like the earlier dispatch of his father, Joash, had remarkably little immediate impact on the land they had ruled. The conspiracies that led to their elimination were not directed against the dynasty of David. Perpetuation of the Davidic royal line remained sacrosanct and continued to provide the southern kingdom with a strong measure of stability, as well as a new king. The priests, gentry, and palace officials responsible for the plot against Amaziah raised no objection when his son Uzziah succeeded his father on the throne.

Indeed, they would soon have good reason to be pleased because Uzziah's reign would be a period of notable achievement for Judah. During his time on the throne it enjoyed a stunning recovery from its recent troubles. Much of that revival can be attributed to the character of the king who was as gifted and well-intentioned a ruler as any in the history of the Jews.

The dates handed down for his reign may be mistaken, possibly including some of the first years of the reign of Jotham, his son and successor. But Uzziah (also known as Azariah) was certainly one of the longest-serving kings in Jewish history, having donned the crown at the age of sixteen, when his father was murdered. Despite a conflict with the Temple priests, he was also among the few Jewish kings to emerge with his reputation for providing for the well-being of his people virtually untarnished.

A visionary, Uzziah took steps to restructure the agricultural economy of his primarily agrarian kingdom which was often plagued by drought. The Bible says, "he loved the soil."[42] He had irrigation systems dug to improve the fertility of the land. Farmers were settled in semi-arid districts to cultivate neglected land and boost the husbanding of livestock. Parts of the uninhabited Negev Desert were made fruitful.

Dismayed by how vulnerable to foreign incursion Judah had always been, Uzziah was also obsessed with defensive preparations. To repel enemies along the kingdom's borders, he rebuilt and improved fortifications which had been demolished by marauders. Atop the strengthened walls of Jerusalem he introduced technological innovations, "clever devices ... set on the towers and corners for shooting arrows and large stones"[43] to thwart potential attackers.

He created a new class of professional officers for his army and the troops, who had often been poorly equipped, were well supplied with spears, swords, bows and arrows, slings, helmets, and metal breastplates. Brought to fighting trim, they had little difficulty in vanquishing the hostile Ammonites east of the River Jordan from whom Uzziah proceeded to exact tribute. He also captured the major Philistine centers of Gath, Jabneh, and Ashdod, putting an end to Philistine marauding raids that had long troubled both Jewish kingdoms.

Completing a process begun by his father, he regained mastery over the desert kingdom of Edom which had seized on Judah's earlier difficulties to regain its independence. Recapturing the port of Ezion Geber on the Gulf of Aqaba, he rebuilt the harbor, reopened a metal smelting center in the area, and dotted the route from Jerusalem with military outposts to safeguard access to the region. Such outposts were also planted along the trade routes within his expanded realm.

During Uzziah's reign in Judah, neighboring Israel also profited from being ruled by a dynamic and farsighted king, Jeroboam II. He and Uzziah repaired the spasmodically poor relations between their kingdoms. Allied diplomatically, militarily, and commercially, the two Jewish nations between them extended their domains over an area as extensive as the empire that had existed at the time of Solomon two hundred years earlier.

The resulting growth of commercial enterprise generated renewed prosperity in Judah. For some, it resulted in a life of luxury which lured them away from religious observances and piety, provoking the prophet Isaiah into harsh condemnation. He warned that Judah had become a "sinful nation," its people a "brood of evildoers![44]"

Despite such criticism, so highly regarded was the kingdom during Uzziah's reign that other nations in the region came to look upon him as leader of a makeshift alliance formed to resist the ever-growing menace of the Assyrian empire whose armies were on the march from the east. After Israel's King Jeroboam II died and Assyria turned the northern kingdom of the Jews into a virtual subject state of theirs (soon to be obliterated, its people dispersed), Uzziah's Judah became a regional center for defiance of the expanding superpower.

During the closing years of his reign, Uzziah was stricken with leprosy. The Bible says he was afflicted with the ailment while usurping the role of the priests. He tried to burn incense at the Temple altar, a duty and privilege the priests considered exclusively their own.

According to the historian Josephus, "A great earthquake shook the ground and a rent was made in the Temple, and the bright rays of the sun shone through it and fell upon the king's face, insomuch that leprosy seized upon him immediately."[45]

Historical evidence confirms that an earthquake did take place in the region at about the time Uzziah wore the crown of Judah. But the story may have been an embroidered account of the rift that had developed between the king and the Temple priesthood whose authority he attempted to downgrade in order to become spiritual as well as temporal leader of his people, as his ancestor David had been.

Whatever the cause of his disfiguring disease, Uzziah subsequently confined himself to his quarters in "a separate house" and was "excluded from the house of the Lord,"[46] though he continued to reign over Judah in conjunction with his son and regent, Jotham, until he died.

Ancient Jerusalem

JOTHAM

739–734 BCE

Over time, the gaps between social classes had become wide and unrelenting in the northern kingdom of Israel where the rich enjoyed benefits and privileges far beyond those available to most of the people. But Judah appears to have enjoyed a more equitable society, even when great wealth was being generated within its borders, as happened during the reign of Jotham's acclaimed father Uzziah. Recent excavations of houses of the period suggest narrower differences in social scale among its people than in the northern kingdom, a greater filtering down of wealth.

Judah was fortunate in other ways as well. Not since Ahab succeeded Omri as ruler of Israel had the Jews experienced a king's handover to a son as promising as when Jotham succeeded to the throne.

Uzziah having been stricken with leprosy and having become a quarantined recluse, Jotham was required to function as his regent until he died. He did so in a modest, unassuming fashion, making no bid to seize the crown prematurely or to initiate policies of his own.

When he became king in his own right, he expanded on the programs Uzziah had introduced to ensure Judah's security and stability. He increased the number of fortified outposts along Judah's frontiers and extended the area of Judaean dominance east of the Jordan. He tightened control of trade routes through the eastern desert territory which was vulnerable to marauders, as well as along the coastal plain. Like his father, he maintained a well-trained, well-equipped army. Unlike his father, Jotham came to terms with the Temple priests whose authority Uzziah had sought to downgrade. He also made notable structural improvements to the Temple. He was said to be "religious towards God and righteous towards men and careful of the good of [Jerusalem]."[47]

Through Jotham's dedication and perseverance, Judah sustained the confidence and stability Uzziah had brought to it. But his reign drew to a close on a note of anxiety. The increasingly territorial aspirations of Assyria had become a matter for urgent consideration. Questions of Judah's survival as an independent nation had to be addressed. At that pivotal moment, Jotham died, leaving his son, Ahaz, to shoulder the burden.

AHAZ

734–728 BCE

The Assyrians, with whom interaction had become an important factor in the Jewish experience, were founders of a sophisticated civilization whose origins dated back at least to the exodus of the Jewish tribes from Egypt. Their empire expanded and contracted over time but, at its peak, it covered territory stretching from well into present-day Turkey to the Persian Gulf and from the Caspian Sea to Egypt.

In contrast to Jerusalem, Nineveh, its capital (near present-day Mosul in Iraq) was an ultramodern city with well-laid out streets, splendorous palaces, and massive, stunning gates for its great city walls. The Hanging Gardens of Babylon, a wonder of the ancient world, may have been located there instead.

The Assyrians were the first to develop the concepts of longitude and latitude, divide the circle into 360 degrees, establish the seven-day week, and create networks of paved roads. Some of their innovations, the leather jackboot for example, served military purposes, which may have been why they were conjured up. When the actions of Assyria became a consideration for the Jewish kingdoms, it was in an expansionist phase, had already occupied much of western Asia and was bent on further conquest.

That was the grim reality Ahaz had to confront when he became king of what had been a largely untroubled Judah during the fruitful reigns of his father Jotham and his grandfather Uzziah. Facing that same Assyrian threat, other nations in the region formed a defensive alliance.

Israel and Damascus, the most exposed among them, called on Judah to join as well but Ahaz turned them down. He believed, with good reason, that the Assyrian army was far superior to any alliance that might challenge it and that attaching himself to such a grouping would serve only as a provocation.

King Pekah of Israel and King Rezin of Damascus condemned his attitude as unacceptable. They feared the presence of a neutral and possibly hostile Judah at their rear would make their plight more difficult when the expected Assyrian assault materialized.

Reacting to Ahaz's rebuff, they launched a joint invasion of the southern kingdom. Neither intended to carry the burden of actually occupying Judah at a time when they were being menaced themselves. They only wanted to force Ahaz to enroll in their anti-Assyrian alliance or make way for a replacement king in Judah who was willing to do so.

Their invading forces made rapid headway, defeating Ahaz's army and taking up positions from which they could lay siege to Jerusalem. With his capital imperiled, Ahaz contemplated calling on the Assyrians for help. The prophet Isaiah strongly advised against it. As much a realist as a religious figure, Isaiah was sensitive to the dangers involved. He pleaded with Ahaz to remain neutral and trust in God. He predicted that Israel and Damascus would be forced by Assyrian pressure on their own lands to withdraw their armies from Judah.

But unwilling to risk the fall of Jerusalem to the invaders, Ahaz spurned the prophet's advice and threw himself on the mercy of the Assyrian king, Tiglath-pileser III: "I am your servant and your son. Come and deliver me from the hands of the king of Aram [Damascus] and from the hands of the king of Israel."[48] As inducement, he sent the Assyrian ruler lavish gifts from the Temple treasury and royal palace.

The conquest of Damascus and Israel already on his agenda, Tiglathpileser was pleased to oblige, and his army easily overwhelmed theirs. The immediate threat to Judah was removed. But having pleaded for and received Assyrian assistance, Ahaz now was obliged to pledge Judah's submission to his benefactor and pay tribute.

Subservience to Assyria had religious as well as political implications. Required to journey to the newly established Assyrian base in Damascus to grovel before Tiglathpileser, Ahaz felt it prudent to pay homage as well to Assyrian deities there. He had a facsimile made of one of their altars and installed it in the Temple upon his return to Jerusalem. There could be no greater symbol of Judah's servility.

The consequences of the developments were far-reaching. The Philistines seized on Judah's troubles to reclaim mastery of the southern coastal strip and adjoining Judaean territory while Edom, liberating itself from Judah's domination, retook Ezion Geber. The port facilities there, through which Judah had traded with distant lands, were destroyed.

Ahaz was criticized in the Bible for succumbing to pagan ritual and not trusting Yahweh with Judah's fate. His submission to the Assyrians was a searing humiliation for the Jewish nation, though his infamy was partly offset by his being both son and father of men deemed to have been worthier kings—Jotham and Hezekiah.

HEZEKIAH

728–698 BCE

The fate of Judah was perilously uncertain when Ahaz died and Hezekiah inherited his throne. The expansionist Assyrians were growing ever more threatening. Soon after Hezekiah became king, they overran Israel to the north, brutally expelling great numbers of its people to places unknown, and also conquered and occupied the kingdom of Damascus to the northeast.

Judah had itself already become one of Assyria's vassal states. Its treasury was depleted through payment of tribute and loss of control of trade routes. It was further reduced in influence and power through territorial losses to the Edomites and Philistines who drew advantage from its plight. The people of Judah became profoundly demoralized as they saw their circumstances exposed to further decline, and perhaps to total disaster.

But Hezekiah refused to succumb to the widespread despair into which his people had sunk. Instead he embarked on a program of recovery from the destabilizing spiritual setbacks suffered during his father's reign. Idolatrous practices, promoted by Assyrian dominance, had undermined the distinctiveness of the Judaeans as a people, as well as their cohesiveness and solidarity. To salvage and revitalize national spirit and unity, he launched a campaign of religious revival in which traditional Jewish observances were officially promoted. Defiantly, he outlawed the worship of Assyrian idols, graven images, and gods throughout Judah.

Hezekiah also took steps to end disarray in Jewish worship. Some Jewish cult shrines had survived or sprung up anew despite the banning efforts of some of his predecessors on Judah's throne. Those places were now closed down so that the Temple, cleansed and reconsecrated, would again be the sole focus of religious worship in the land. Great numbers of people from all over the kingdom again began converging on Jerusalem for festivals and religious celebrations.

To establish Judaean identity for all Jews, Hezekiah invited those who remained in what had been Israel (now the newly established Assyrian province of Samaria) to come to Jerusalem and worship at the Temple. So energetic were his efforts to energize and purify Jewish religious identity that he is one of the most highly praised figures in the Bible: "There were none like him among all the kings of Judah after him, nor among those before him."[49] Legend has it that God pondered proclaiming him the Messiah and did not do so only because, righteous as he was, he was outshone by his revered ancestor, David.

While mounting his campaign of religious reform, Hezekiah strove to rebuild the kingdom's economic well-being through royal promotion of commercial activity and reorganization of Judah's system of taxation.

At all times he remained acutely aware of Assyria's undiminished menace. His father had neglected Judah's national security requirements, but Hezekiah did not. He took steps to strengthen fortifications along Judah's borders and the walls of Jerusalem which he extended and provided with additional towers. In a remarkable feat of engineering, a 1,700-foot-long conduit was dug through solid rock from a spring outside the walls to guarantee the maintenance of the capital's water supply, essential for the defense of the city if it came under siege, as it had in the past.

While all of that was happening, Hezekiah sought additional ways to save Judah from the fate that had befallen Israel. He considered participating with other small states in a regional anti-Assyrian defensive alliance of the kind his father had refused to join. The death of the Assyrian King Sargon II had sent a tremor through the empire he had ruled. Insurrections had broken out in parts of his vast domain. Sennacherib, his successor, had yet to prove himself an effective ruler.

With the situation seemingly in flux, the regional anti-Assyrian alliance gathered strength and purpose. It included Babylonians, Philistines, and others bridling under Assyria's domination, as well as Egypt which, under the Nubian Pharaoh Shabako, was seeking to recapture its ancient glory. Not only did Hezekiah lead Judah into the coalition but he achieved such prominence within it that Jerusalem became one of its centers.

However, Sennacherib proved himself as masterful, assertive, and ruthless as his predecessor and soon moved to assert his authority in the region. The early promise of the anti-Assyrian coalition of nations turned to grief. Rebellious Babylon was bloodily subdued and Philistine city-states either recanted or suffered the same fate.

As others hastened to renounce their insubordination and submit once more to Assyria, Judah was made to pay heavily for its defiance. Sennacherib boasted, "As for Hezekiah the Judahite, who did not submit to my yoke, 46 of his strong, walled cities, as well as the small towns in their area, which were without number … I besieged and took them. [Hezekiah] himself, like a caged bird, I shut up in Jerusalem, his royal city."[50]

Jerusalem was thrown into panic and Hezekiah lost heart. According to Sennacherib, "The terrifying splendor of my majesty overcame him, and the Arabs and his mercenary troops which he had brought in to strengthen Jerusalem … deserted him."

To save the capital and assuage Sennacherib's anger, Hezekiah paid a huge indemnity: "Thirty talents of gold and 800 talents of silver, gems, jewels, antimony, large carnelians, ivory inlaid couches, ivory inlaid chairs, elephant hides, elephant tusks, ebony, boxwood, all kinds of valuable treasures, garments with multi-colored trim, garments of linen, wood [dyed] red-purple and blue-purple, vessels of copper, iron, bronze and tin, chariots, slings, lances, armor, daggers for the belt, various kinds of arrows, countless trappings and implements of war, together with his daughters, his harem, his male and female musicians.…"

It was not enough to appease the Assyrian ruler. He sent an emissary to demand the unconditional surrender of Jerusalem. The envoy called out a threat in Hebrew, the language of the common people at the time, rather than Aramaic, the language of the city's elite. He warned that they could no more be helped by their God than other people whom the Assyrians had conquered had been saved by their deities.

But it was the Egyptians who came to their aid. Appearing at the rear of the threatening Assyrians, an Egyptian army went into battle against them and rescued Jerusalem from immediate assault. But the Egyptians were routed in heavy fighting and once more the fate of Jerusalem seemed sealed. The people of the city braced themselves for the final Assyrian onslaught. But for reasons never satisfactorily explained, Sennacherib's forces suddenly withdrew.

The biblical account suggests they were stricken by a plague administered by an angel of the Lord. The Greek historian Herodotus later wrote that a legion of rats rampaged through the Assyrian camp, destroying their weapons and gnawing away at everything made of leather or rope. But it may have been that developments elsewhere in the Assyrian domain required Sennacharib's priority attention and that of his army.

Despite this respite for Judah, the Assyrians remained an immediate and seemingly irresistible threat to its independent existence. Hezekiah accepted there was no longer any alternative to being a submissive Assyrian vassal state again and buying his kingdom's survival with tribute payments. So the situation remained for the remainder of his reign, and beyond.

MANASSEH

698–643 BCE

The domination of one nation by another is not without its compensations when the alternative for the weaker is total annihilation. For Judah, that was the situation when Hezekiah died and his son Manasseh succeeded him as king.

By submitting to the Assyrians, however reluctantly, Hezekiah had saved Judah from the fate of obliteration that Israel had suffered. But he passed on to his twelve-year-old son a land whose existence continued to depend on Assyrian forbearance.

Disagreeable though vassal status was, Judah flourished during Manasseh's reign which lasted more than half a century—longer than that of any previous king of Judah. Agrarian reform bolstered the rural mainstay of the kingdom's economy, boosted as well by partial integration into Assyria's thriving commercial activity in the region. That softened the impact of the discontent and divisive pressures generated by the king's groveling to a foreign power.

The Assyrians required only that Manasseh make certain Judah was submissive, remained untroubled by domestic upheaval, and paid its tribute on time. They may not have made religious demands on him, but the dominance of a people of great achievement supported the spread of their cultural influence. It became fashionable among privileged classes in Jerusalem to do as they did.

Though not specifically barred from doing so, Manasseh could not continue with his father's clampdown on the worship of pagan deities, some of whom were in the Assyrian pantheon of gods. Pro-Assyrian Judaean regents who administered Judah in his name when he was still a boy-king may have set the pattern by removing the curbs Hezekiah had imposed. But even after he came of age and assumed regal authority, pagan practices were officially condoned in the land, even at the Temple in Jerusalem where altars to pagan deities were newly erected.

The Bible censured Manasseh for his religious shortcomings. He was also said to have indulged in astrology, much favored by the Assyrians but anathema to those faithful to Yahweh. He "consulted ghosts and familiar spirits"[51] as well as fortune-tellers, which was deemed equally abhorrent.

Those true to Yahweh were appalled by the renewed respectability of pagan worship and associated practices. Prophets warned that because of the sinfulness of the Judaeans, the Lord would "wipe Jerusalem clean as one wipes a dish and turns it upside down.... I will cast off the remnant of My people and deliver them into the hands of their enemies."[52]

But the fate of Judah was already in foreign hands. That was apparent when Manasseh was obliged to join a score of minor kings in the region in providing supplies for the Nineveh palace of Assyrian King Esarhaddon. He was also required to send Judaean forces to serve with the Assyrians in their campaign to conquer Egypt.

Jerusalem had already become a hotbed of political rivalry. Now, because of the realities of the situation, a pro-Assyrian faction exercised overriding influence in Manasseh's court. It is even possible that an Assyrian overseer in Jerusalem made certain the king did not neglect tribute payments or stray from compliance in other ways.

An anti-Assyrian, pro-independence faction, that had been active in Jerusalem during the reign of the deceased Hezekiah, remained in existence. But its leaders were reduced to quiescence by the disastrous result of the late king's doomed defiance of Assyria and by its earlier obliteration of Israel.

Resentment of Assyrian dominance deepened and was reflected in public outbursts of discontent with how Judah was being humbled. But Manasseh ruthlessly suppressed them. The Bible says he killed so many people that the streets of Jerusalem flowed with blood. A biblical reference to Manasseh having been dragged in chains to Babylon and temporarily exiled there for having offended God with his sinfulness may refer to punishment inflicted by the Assyrians for a momentary lapse in his subservience.

Toward the end of his reign, when the Assyrians were caught up with problems elsewhere in their empire, Manasseh permitted himself a gesture of independence, strengthening the walls of Jerusalem. Such an act could have been deemed a challenge to their imperial hegemony, though whatever defiance Manasseh may have permitted himself as he grew old on the throne must have been distinctly low-keyed.

AMON

642–641 BCE

The reign of King Amon is barely a footnote in the history of Judah and the Jews. He came to the throne at the age of twenty-two upon the death of his long-reigning father, Manasseh, and ruled for only two years before being assassinated. Like his father, he bowed to the reality of the overwhelming might of the Assyrians, who remained capable of conquering and destroying Judah any time they believed they had reason to do so.

Tribute payments to Nineveh continued without interruption. Pagan religious practices, that had flourished in Judah alongside Jewish observances during Manasseh's time on the throne, continued unobstructed.

Amon's assassins were probably driven to regicide by a mixture of grievances. The anti-Assyrian faction in Jerusalem, though subdued, had remained dedicated to the restoration of Judaean independence throughout Manasseh's long reign. At the same time, a hard core of Judaeans refused to tolerate what they saw as the paganization of their kingdom. Those two fiery movements overlapped.

The king's assassins were themselves put to death by order of officials backed by landowners and other leading figures in Jerusalem bent on maintaining the status quo, whatever its defects. They feared the assassination would be regarded by the Assyrians as the beginning of a campaign against their mastery, as it probably was meant to be, and that Assyria's King Ashurbanipal might be provoked into extreme preemptive measures.

But the speedy execution of Amon's killers showed that the pro-Assyrian faction continued to be in charge in Jerusalem. The immediate coronation of Amon's eight-year-old son, Josiah, demonstrated that those who had served Manasseh, and had kept Assyria placated, retained prevailing influence in Judah and that Assyria's hegemony was not about to be challenged by them.

That was not how things would turn out.

JOSIAH

640–609 BCE

New, powerful forces were appearing on the horizons of the Jewish nation at this stage in its history, The Assyrians had for some time been the most redoubtable presence in the turbulent region. But Medes were pressing in from western Iran and what is now Azerbaijan. Fierce Scythians and Cimmerians were sweeping down from the north. Rebellion against Assyrian overlords was breaking out in Babylonia, and Egypt was once again resurgent.

Assyria was the primary target of all, and its army was being stretched beyond its ability to keep its empire from unraveling. A dramatic transformation in the power structure in the region was in the making.

That was of great consequence for the diminutive kingdom of Judah and for its King Josiah who, notwithstanding international developments, proved to be one of the most significant figures in the early history of the Jews. Josiah's contribution to the development of Judaism would turn out to be monumental and of enduring impact. He renewed the covenant between Yahweh and the Jewish people at a critical juncture, reawakening his people's sense of singularity and pride in their origins.

Josiah was only eight years old when he was anointed king as successor to his father, Amon, who had been assassinated in a plot likely to have been organized by an anti-Assyrian faction in Jerusalem. During the early part of his reign, responsibility for ruling Judah was assumed by senior figures of the dominant pro-Assyrian faction who had quickly dealt with the assassins.

But the power of the Assyrians, so recently unchallengeable, was irreversibly in decline. The death of their King Ashurbanipal, when Josiah was a young man, accelerated their downward spiral.

As customarily happened when the ruler of an imperial nation like Assyria passed from the scene, its vassal states seized the opportunity to seek independence. In this case, the pressures exerted by the region's other newly thrusting powers made the situation more tempestuous.

When the Assyrian collapse took place, it was rapid and momentous. The Medes and Babylonians ravaged Nineveh, its capital, famous far beyond the region for its grandeur and wealth. Those of its inhabitants who survived its destruction were driven into exile, a fate much like the one inflicted by the Assyrians on many of the peoples they had conquered, including Jews of what had been the kingdom of Israel.

Well before that happened, Judah, like other small regional states, had begun shaking off domination by the decaying instruments of Assyrian authority. Young King Josiah's chief advisers, belonging to the pro-Assyrian faction in Jerusalem, saw their influence gradually dissipate. When he came of age, Josiah fully relieved his regents of their responsibilities and began leading his nation along the path of defiant self-rule.

The Assyrian collapse had important religious as well as political and international implications for Judah. If pagan deities could not protect the Assyrians from the forces now arrayed against them, the attraction they held for many Judaeans evaporated, sparking a revival of traditional Jewish religious observances across the land. But an important discovery in Jerusalem had an even greater impact.

Josiah had ordered major renovations of the Temple to symbolize the reawakening of the nation's desire to be free of foreign domination. During that renovation process, High Priest Hilkiah came across a long-neglected and forgotten scroll in the Temple. A startling document, it recounted the story of the Jews since their exodus from Egypt. It also included the commandments and laws of Yahweh, their one true God, outlining the moral code basic to the Jewish faith.

The document may have been an early version of the Deuteronomy book of the Bible. It highlighted the covenant between God and the Jews.

> *If you obey the Lord your God, to observe faithfully all His commandments, the Lord your God will set you high above all the nations of the earth.... Blessed shall you be in the city and blessed shall you be in the country. Blessed shall be the issue of your womb, the produce of your soil, and the offspring of your cattle, the calving of your herd and the lambing of your flock. Blessed shall be your basket your kneading bowl. Blessed shall you be in your comings and blessed shall you be in your goings. The Lord will put to rout ... the enemies who attack you.*[53]

But the document also contained a warning of what would happen if God's trust was violated.

> *If you do not obey the Lord your God to observe faithfully all His commandments and laws ... cursed shall you be in the city and cursed shall you be in the country.... Cursed shall be the issue of your womb and the produce of your soil, the calving of your herd and the lambing of your flock. Cursed shall you be in your comings and cursed shall you be in your goings. The Lord will let loose against you calamity, panic and frustration in all the enterprises you undertake.... Your sons*

and daughters shall be delivered to another people. The Lord will drive you, and the king you have set over you, to a nation unknown to you or your fathers.... The stranger in your midst shall rise above you higher and higher while you sink lower and lower.... The Lord will scatter you among all the people from one end of the earth to the other.[54]

Josiah was excited by God's promises. But he was shaken by the accompanying warning into an appreciation of the extent to which religious observance in his kingdom had strayed from the Jewish faith, undermining the primary cohesive element in the land he ruled.

He summoned a great assemblage of the people of Jerusalem, of both high and low estate, and had the discovered manuscript read out to them. It was a highly emotional event, stirringly invoking the rich Jewish heritage, of much of which many in attendance had been unaware. Deeply impressed and moved, he and those assembled vowed to renew their covenant with God and keep all His laws and commandments. The religious renewal and reformation that swept across Judah during the remainder of Josiah's reign developed into a central component of the wider patriotic movement he had already begun promoting.

The Temple was purged of heathen altars and idols of pagan deities were destroyed. Religious prostitution was ordered outlawed. Seemingly irrepressible local shrines—where deviations from established Jewish ritual were common, and which had attracted devotees during the reigns of Josiah's father and grandfather—were shut down as dangerously divisive. Jerusalem was again to be the sole center of organized worship in Judah.

As the Assyrian collapse gathered momentum, Josiah extended his campaign of religious reform into the Assyrian province of Samaria, formerly the northern kingdom of Israel. He destroyed the surviving shrine there at Bethel which had been a primary Israelite center of Jewish cultic worship.

These religious reforms had consequences beyond their immediate effect. Deprived of local shrines at which to worship, people now sought other ways to express their spirituality. They turned to personal prayer and the reading of Holy Scriptures. Both would later play a fundamental role in religious observance, especially when synagogues came to be a major focus of Jewish life.

Meantime, the neglected tradition of celebrating religious festivals at the Temple was revived. Worshippers converged on Jerusalem from all over Judah during holy days. The public celebration of Passover was reintroduced as a major event in the calendar.

Josiah was fulsomely praised in the Bible for his piety and reforms. It says no earlier king had so earnestly "turned back to the Lord with all his heart and soul and might"[55] and that no king like him would later sit on the throne of the Jews.

Like the rulers of other lands who had previously bowed to the Assyrians, Josiah entertained thoughts of territorial expansion. Like kings of Judah and Israel who had preceded him, he may have hoped to reestablish a single Jewish nation incorporating all the land that had been part of Solomon's empire centuries before, including Samaria and Galilee.

He extended Judaean control to parts of Philistia along the Mediterranean coast and into the Negev Desert. He built new towns and renovated Judah's neglected border fortifications. Jerusalem's defenses were updated and the capital itself was expanded to accommodate a growing population. Greater commercial activity was stimulated by renewed control of the coastal trade route.

As far-reaching geopolitical changes transformed the region, Judah under Josiah once more became confident in its independence and Jewish identity. However, the entire region was in a state of uncertainty and change. In rebelling against their Assyrian masters, the Babylonians were seeking to replace them as the dominant power in southwestern Asia and were soon well on their way to doing so. The Egyptians, their own expansionist ambitions revived, sent an army to help the bruised and battered Assyrians meet the challenge of the Babylonians whom they considered a more dangerous adversary.

To do so, they had to traverse territory newly claimed by Judah. When Josiah refused to grant them free passage, the Egyptian pharaoh responded by demanding, "What have I to do with you, king of Judah? I do not march against you this day but against the kingdom that wars with me, and it is God's will that I hurry. Refrain then from interfering with God who is with me, that He not destroy you."[56] But Josiah refused to permit an affront to Judah's newfound pride. He also suspected that, despite their assurances, the Egyptians had designs on his kingdom.

Reinforced by Greek mercenaries, they were fielding forces mightier than his own. Nevertheless, Josiah led his army to block their way. The two armies met in combat near Megiddo where the Judaeans were decisively beaten by the seasoned troops they came up against. Josiah was mortally wounded in combat and carried by chariot back to Jerusalem where he died and was buried with honor.

Judah's revival during his reign would not long survive him. His land was about to become as subservient to Egypt as it had earlier been to Assyria. Further great power changes were looming in the region. The days of the surviving Jewish kingdom were drawing to a close.

Nevertheless, Josiah was to have lasting impact on Judaism. He "reformed [Judaism] with a scope and depth which was unprecedented ... and never repeated".[57] The religious laws, ethical precepts, and prescribed codes of conduct set out in the scroll discovered in the Temple during his reign, and treated reverently by him, have been cornerstones of Jewish belief, life and culture from that time to the present.

King Josiah Having the Newly Rediscovered Book of the Law Read Out to the People

JEHOAHAZ

609 BCE

Put on sackcloth
And strew dust on yourselves!
Mourn, as for an only child.
Wail bitterly
For suddenly the destroyer
Is coming upon us.[58]

After three centuries of existence, Judah was drifting inexorably toward extinction. Under Josiah, the southern kingdom of the Jews had freed itself from subservience to the crumbling Assyrian Empire. But even if the proud Josiah had not been mortally wounded by the Egyptians on the battlefield at Megiddo, and even if his army had not been shattered there, Judah would have been doomed. It was at the mercy of far more powerful forces competing for mastery in the region.

Ascending the throne, Josiah's son Jehoahaz knew the outcome of those rivalries would greatly impinge upon Judah's ways and attitudes and possibly determine its very existence. He was not the only one who realized that. Jerusalem had already become a political arena of feuding cabals siding with one or another of the powers competing in the wider regional struggles. Advisers aplenty urged the king to seek association with, and protection by, those they favored.

Assyria's rapid decline had cost pro-Assyrian advocates, who had formerly prevailed, much of their credibility. But when Josiah had been killed and Judah's army had been trounced by the Egyptians, those who had favored Egypt, having bowed to what they believed to be the harsh realities of the situation, fell into disgrace. They were edged out by a faction opposed to subservience to any foreign ruler, regardless of external pressures.

But this would-be independence movement soon found itself picking Babylon as the best possible option in a no-win situation. Long part of the empire of the Assyrians, the Babylonians had risen against their rule, put an army in the field, and were striving for supremacy over an alliance between their now-floundering former Assyrian masters and the Egyptians.

In Jerusalem, Jehoahaz attracted the support of what had evolved into the pro-Babylonian faction. But Judah would never again savor the luxury of choice. The presence of a victorious Egyptian army on Judaean soil left it bereft of options. Pharaoh Necho II imposed a heavy burden of taxes and expropriated outlying territories that Judah had ruled, cutting the kingdom well down in size.

Three months after having been crowned, Jehoahaz presented himself humbly before Necho for the Egyptians to confirm his newly acquired royal status. He was turned down. To demonstrate his absolute power over Judah, Necho ordered that the recently anointed king of Judah be put in chains and hauled off to Egypt where he died in captivity.

JEHOIAKIM

609–598 BCE

Having, by force of arms, replaced Assyria as arbiter of the fate of terminally weakened Judah, and having removed King Jehoahaz in a demonstration of their power, the Egyptians permitted his brother Eliakim to sit on the throne of the Jews. As a symbol of their authority, they assigned him a throne name—Jehoiakim.

Under Jehoiakim, Judah's continuing existence as a nation was a precarious balancing act. Tormented by a sense of hopelessness, the Jews felt abandoned by God. Idol worship, which the greatly missed Josiah had done much to eradicate, again spread through what remained of the land as many sought greater comfort from pagan deities than Yahweh was providing.

The Egyptian goddess Neith, called the Queen of Heaven, became a particular household favorite. Altars and statues of various other deities appeared again on Jerusalem's Temple Mount. Holy men warned in vain that if Judaeans did not turn away from such sinfulness, they were doomed. Jeremiah thundered a warning from Yahweh.

> *The people of Judah have done what displeases Me.... They have set up their abominations in the House which is called by My name, and they have defiled it.... I will silence in the towns of Judah and the streets of Jerusalem the sound of mirth and gladness.... The whole land shall fall to ruin.*[59]

Jehoiakim was hard pressed to pay the Egyptians the huge tribute payments they demanded. His palace and the Temple having by then been stripped of their treasures, he expropriated the required sums from the wealthy of the land. It alienated those who craved the security they thought his obeisance to Egypt could provide, and who would therefore have been his most loyal partisans.

Judah's fate and Jehoiakim's were to be decided by the result of the contest between the Babylonians—who were in the process of replacing their former Assyrian masters as the major power to the east—and Egypt to the southwest whose army was already planted on Judaean soil. Since regaining independence seemed beyond hope, bowing to the Egyptians was seen to be preferable as well as unavoidable. The Babylonians, who were ethnically much like the Assyrians who had wiped out the kingdom of Israel, were thought likely to be more oppressive.

But Jeremiah, held in popular awe, had divine intimations of an imminent decline for the Egyptians which would leave Judah exposed if it chose to be associated with them rather than the Babylonians. The prophet maintained that Nebuchadnezzar, Babylonia's crown prince and army commander, was the instrument of God's anger with the Jews for their sinfulness. He said Judah would be destroyed if it resisted Babylon and that its people would be driven into exile. Having angered Jehoiakim with his forebodings, the prophet thought it wise to go into hiding.

Spurning his warnings, the king at first conducted himself as an Egyptian puppet. But that stance proved questionable four years into his reign when, as Jeremiah had foretold, the Babylonians decisively triumphed over the Egyptians at the battle at Carchemish on the banks of the Euphrates. Positioned between the adversaries, Judah probably would then have been occupied by the victors if the Babylonian king Nabopolassar had not suddenly died.

Nebuchadnezzar rushed back to Babylon from his forward command to secure his royal succession, granting Judah respite. But the Babylonians were soon on the move again. They conquered the defiant Philistine city-state of Ashkelon on the Mediterranean coast, leveled it, and drove great numbers of its inhabitants into exile.

Trembling in expectation of similar treatment for Judah, Jehoiakim was blown about by changing circumstances. He quickly transferred his allegiance from Egypt to Nebuchadnezzar. Then, when the Babylonians once more pulled back to deal with other problems associated with the change of ruler, he again sought the protection of the Egyptians. But shaken by their defeat at Carchemish and suffering other difficulties, they were unable to provide it.

Once Nebuchadnezzar's more pressing concerns had been dealt with, he regrouped his forces, invaded Judah and laid siege to Jerusalem. At that fateful moment in the history of the Jews, Jehoiakim died a mysterious, violent death. His body was thrown from the walls of the city to show the invaders that he was dead and as a sign of Judah's submission.

In rabbinic legend, Jehoiakim is considered a figure of contempt and dishonor because of his persecution of Jeremiah and other prophets and his neglect of Mosaic laws and Jewish traditions. He is said to have committed all sorts of other crimes as well, including rape and incest, and to have been so wicked that even the earth refused to bear his remains, casting up his corpse when attempts were made to bury it.

JEHOIACHIN

598–597 BCE

No king of the Jews ever mounted the throne under circumstances as desperate as those with which Jehoiachin had to contend when he became king of Judah upon the death of his similarly named father Jehoiakim. Just eighteen years old, he was in trouble and danger from the instant he donned the crown. Having overrun his kingdom, the Babylonians were laying siege to Jerusalem.

After three anxious months, during which the people of the capital succumbed to an orgy of dread, Jehoiachin recognized that the Egyptians, his only hope of rescue, were not capable of taking on their Babylonian nemesis and extricating Judah from its predicament. To save Jerusalem and the Temple from devastation, he ordered an end to resistance. Surrendering to the Babylonians, he was led off to captivity in Babylon together with his harem and his court. In two stages, thousands of other "notables of the land" were also forcibly exiled to Babylonia.

Nebuchadnezzar confiscated what remained of the Temple treasures, but he spared Jerusalem and chose Zedekiah, Jehoiachin's uncle, to be new king of Judah. Years later, when a new ruler, Evil-Merodach, ascended the throne of Babylon, Jehoiachin was freed from what had been a comparatively agreeable captivity and was accorded the respect and treatment appropriate to his former station. But he was not permitted to return to Judah and died instead in exile some time later.

During Jehoachin's reign of less than a year in Jerusalem, the Babylonian siege of the city had isolated it from the rest of Judah which was plundered and ravaged by the invaders. Its administration had broken down. Its economy was crippled. Its priests were preoccupied with the sinfulness of the growing numbers of Judaeans who sought comfort in the worship of pagan deities. The days of the Jewish nation appeared numbered.

ZEDEKIAH

597–587 BCE

Zedekiah, the twentieth and last to wear the crown of the kingdom of Judah, was also the last of all the kings of the Jews in biblical times, the northern kingdom of Israel having been obliterated by the Assyrians more than a century earlier. During Zedekiah's reign, it became Judah's turn to suffer final catastrophe.

Zedekiah's prospects as king were slight from the beginning. Two of his brothers had preceded him on the throne: Jehoahaz, who had been led away to captivity in Egypt, and Jehoiakim, who had died young. His immediate predecessor, his nephew Jehoiachin, was imprisoned in Babylon. The Babylonians, masters of conquered Judah, had installed this twenty-one-year-old in his place.

Even a more experienced ruler would have found reigning over a shattered, subjugated land a formidable undertaking. Barely out of his teens, and torn between submission and defiance, Zedekiah was badgered with conflicting counsel from his advisers during his ten-year reign. He was urged both to seek an alliance with Egypt as a counterweight to his Babylonian masters and warned of the great dangers that could attend such a course of action.

Revered holy men similarly disputed what should be done. The prophet Hananiah, bridling at Babylonian dominance, called for rebellion against it, while Jeremiah pressed for the Babylonians to be considered an instrument of Yahweh, administering divine but temporary punishment to the sinful Judaeans. Zedekiah also had to contend with the conviction of many of his subjects that he was a false king and that Jehoiachin remained their true monarch and would return from Babylonian captivity to reclaim his throne.

At a time when adroit diplomatic maneuvering was essential if Judah were to survive, Zedekiah had neither strongly held views nor the ability to abide by decisions that had to be made. Easily swayed by articulate argument, he initially conducted himself as a compliant puppet of the Babylonians. But when the Babylonian rulers focused on consolidating their rule at home, he was persuaded to convene a secret gathering of envoys of subject kingdoms in the region—including Ammon, Edom, Moab, Sidon, and Tyre—to plot rebellion against them. When the Egyptians launched a new military campaign against Babylon and made notable progress, Zedekiah decided the time had come for Judah to join in action against its latest masters as well.

But as Jeremiah had forecast, it was a disastrous mistake. The Babylonians bounced back, severely punishing the Egyptians. The small kingdoms that had rallied to them were made to pay for their impertinence.

Once more Nebuchadnezzar's army targeted Judah, and once more Jerusalem was besieged. An Egyptian phalanx was dispatched to tangle with the Babylonians, but it was no match for them and was forced to withdraw before it could relieve pressure on the holy city. Nevertheless, Zedekiah held out there for more than two years. Not until the Babylonians brought up attack machines and blasted breaches in Jerusalem's walls did they overcome its starving and plague-ridden defenders.

The Babylonian conquest was ruthless and thorough. All Judaean resistance was crushed. The Temple, the heart of Jewish worship, was looted and demolished. Judaism's most precious relic, the Ark of the Covenant, housed in the Temple's Holy of Holies, was lost. No one knew what happened to it, or ever would again.

Jerusalem was leveled and left largely abandoned. "Lonely sits the city once great with people," mourned the writer of the Book of Lamentations. "She that was great among nations is become like a widow."[60]

Judah's other major cities were also pillaged and razed. The deportation of the Judaean elite to Babylonia, begun a decade earlier, was extended so that virtually none was left in the remains of what had been the southern kingdom of the Jews. Nobles, courtiers, officials, priests, scribes, merchants, teachers, artisans, and almost all other leading and active figures of the community who had not fled to Egypt for sanctuary were led away. Only the poorest in the land, mostly farmers, vine growers, and herdsmen, were permitted to remain. Judah was left without leadership or direction, exposed to lawlessness, and subject to encroachment by the small states on its borders.

Zedekiah and some of his court had escaped from the city before it fell but were pursued and captured. He was brought before Nebuchadnezzar. For having dared to break his oath of allegiance to the Babylonians, he was made to watch as his children were killed. Then his eyes were put out and he was led off in chains to Babylon where he died. With his death, the dynasty founded by King David more than four hundred years earlier was brought to an end.

*   *   *

In contrast to the Assyrians, who had repopulated the kingdom of Israel with people from other parts of their empire when they conquered it and dispersed its inhabitants, the Babylonians did not import strangers to settle in devastated Judah. Nevertheless, the land was strategically important in their ongoing conflict with Egypt. A measure of continuity was required there.

To replace Zedekiah and administer what was now their province of Judaea, the Babylonians appointed Gedaliah, a figure previously prominent in the Jerusalem faction that had opposed defiance of Babylon. Based in Mizpah, not far from the ruins of the holy city, Gedaliah sought to begin the process of rebuilding the land. But before he could achieve much, a member of Zedekiah's family assassinated him for presuming to replace the king and for collaborating with the Babylonians.

Fearing draconian retribution from Babylon, many of the few ranking figures still remaining in the land joined others who had earlier fled for safety to Egypt where a Jewish community was established that would survive into the twentieth century.

The murder of Gedaliah terminated the last remnant of Jewish self-rule. Partly depopulated by deportations, migration, and death, Judaea was a stricken, forsaken place. Some who had been forced to leave or who had left on their own accord drifted back in the following years. Others made pilgrimages to the ruins of the Temple to mourn and pray. But a major chapter in the history of the Jews had come to an end. For the time being, the Jewish nation had ceased to exist.

EXILE AND RETURN

The People of Judah Being Driven Into Exile by the Babylonians

BABYLONIAN EXILE

Being ejected from Judah and driven into exile in Babylonia was a shattering experience for the Jews. They had lost their homeland, their Jerusalem, their Temple and their homes, and been required to start new lives in a strange land. They had been abandoned by the God who they had believed had chosen them as His own from all peoples of the world. "The Lord has acted like a foe," they grieved. "He has laid waste Israel."[61] The roots of their religious and national identity seemed severed.

Though adrift in a foreign environment, the exiles were not widely dispersed as the "lost tribes" of the Children of Israel had been by Assyrian conquerors more than a century earlier. Instead, they were deposited by the Babylonians in a small region of southern Mesopotamia, in the town of Tel Abib and elsewhere along the Chebar River, not far from the capital of Babylon.

Once the Jews had gone through the trauma of transplantation and settling in, the Babylonians did not subject them to extreme hardship. Jeremiah proclaimed that God inclined the king of Babylon "to be merciful to you."[62] Few restrictions or obstacles were imposed on them as they went about building communities and following their chosen ways of life.

They followed God's urging, as transmitted by Jeremiah, to "Build houses and live in them, plant gardens and eat their fruit.... Seek the welfare of the city to which I have exiled you."[63] Largely spared oppression and persecution, with the passage of time some flourished in their new home. Many turned or returned to farming in a region more fertile than the one they had left. Others took up their old trades as artisans and merchants.

The wonders of Babylon—its majestic palaces, its "Tower of Babel" dedicated to the deity Marduk, its city walls wide enough for a four-horse chariot to run atop, and other trappings of a highly accomplished, sophisticated culture—must have tempted many to forsake their own heritage and adapt to new ways of thinking and living. It would have been easy or convenient to accept that the pagan gods of their conquerors had proved superior to their own Yahweh, and to worship them instead.

But for Jews who remained true to their faith, and for Judaism generally, the Babylonian exile turned into a crucial time of rejuvenation. Having been denied the Temple in Jerusalem, the nerve center and keystone of Jewish worship, and the tangible focus of their faith since the days of Solomon, they turned elsewhere to fill the great gap its destruction had left. They replaced it with the sacred texts they had brought with them from Judah. They established community meeting places in which they regularly gathered to recite from those texts, to pray and to worship.

Some such places had existed earlier in Judah and in Israel. But the phenomenon of the synagogue as the site of community religious observance and interaction for Jews was formalized and systemized in the Babylonian exile. It was to remain a permanent, central feature of Jewish life from then on and would later be the model for Christian churches and Moslem mosques.

Prayer and observance of the Sabbath and other holy days also became heightened symbols of mutual belonging, obligation, and religious distinctiveness. They provided the comforts of spiritual sustenance while the prophet Ezekiel conveyed God's promise of their eventual return to Judah. Ezekiel forecast that the breath of the Lord would revive the "dry bones" to which the exiles had been reduced.

> *I will take you from among the nations and gather you from all the countries and I will bring you back to your own land.... I will give you a new heart and put a new spirit into you.... I will cause you to follow My laws and faithfully to observe My rules ... You shall be My people and I will be your God.*[64]

However tolerable or benign life in Babylonia may have been for the deportees, nostalgia for the homeland which most of their offspring would never have seen became deeply rooted.

> *By the rivers of Babylon, we sat and wept as we thought of Zion.... How can we sing a song of the Lord on alien soil. If I forget you, O Jerusalem, let my right hand wither; let my tongue stick to my palate if I cease to think of you, if I do not keep Jerusalem in memory even at my happiest hour.*[65]

Days of mourning were designated during which people fasted in sorrow for lost Jerusalem and Zion. Thus did the Babylonian exile create the enduring phenomenon of Zionism.

The exile was a critical testing time for the Jews and might have proved disastrous for them as a distinct people. But despite their expulsion from Judah, the destruction of Jerusalem, and the considerable attractions of an exotic culture, Judaism showed itself capable of perpetuating itself away from the Promised Land.

Their faith strengthened by the circumstances of their foreign existence, Jews would never again be tempted to worship other deities as well as Yahweh, as they had at times before the exile, though a religious avowal to that effect would remain the most important single statement of their faith. Even to this day, Jews recite the *Shema* declaration of faith in their daily prayers: "Hear O Israel! The Lord is our God. The Lord is one."

The experiences in Babylonia shaped much of the pattern of subsequent Jewish life. Isadore Epstein, editor of an English translation of the Babylonian Talmud, said the people of Judah shared the fate of "captivity" suffered by the ten tribes of the long-vanished northern kingdom of Israel. But, "whilst the other tribes vanished and merged with their conquerors, Judah alone survived.... Out of the crucible of exile and affliction, Judah emerged, purged and purified, into a new people—the Jews. Spreading quickly throughout the earth, the Jews carried wherever they settled a new message—Judaism."[66]

Historian and scholar Yehezkel Kaufmann said, "The religion of Israel emerged [during the Babylonian captivity] from its national matrix and began to function as a universal historical force.... The Torah book was compiled and Israel became the people of the book."[67]

∗   ∗   ∗

For all its significance, the Babylonian experience was a comparatively brief episode, lasting between fifty and seventy years. Momentous geopolitical developments in the region determined what would follow from it. By the time the exile began, mighty Babylonia was in decline and about to be challenged by a rising new power. In a corner of its empire, Cyrus, a local chieftain of part-Persian origin, had launched a campaign of conquest that vanquished the Babylonians with remarkable rapidity and made their dominion part of his own.

Though he ultimately built a Persian empire reaching from India to Egypt, Cyrus dedicated himself to a struggle against evil, as ordained by his Zoroastrian religion which stressed tolerance of other peoples' beliefs and ways. In addition to following the precepts of his religion, Cyrus believed people who did not feel oppressed were easier to rule. The Greek historian Herodotus wrote, "Of all men, the Persians most welcome foreign customs."[68]

Cyrus issued what has since been regarded as the first-ever charter of human rights. It decreed, among other things, that the religions and customs of the various peoples of the Persian Empire were to be respected. Those who had been transplanted from their homes by the Babylonians were to be permitted to return to them in safety. The exile of the Jews, a seminal experience in their history, was coming to an end.

Cyrus issued an extra decree for them. In addition to being permitted to return to Judah, they were instructed to rebuild their Temple in Jerusalem. What was more, Cyrus directed that those among the Jews who chose not to return to Judah should assist in that task.

> *The Lord God of Heaven … has charged me with building Him a house in Jerusalem, which is in Judah. Anyone of you of all His people—may his God be with him, and let him go up to Jerusalem that is in Judah and build the House of the Lord God of Israel, the God that is in Jerusalem, and [let] all who stay behind … assist him with silver, gold, goods and livestock, besides the freewill offering to the House of God that is in Jerusalem.*[69]

Though Cyrus may have been influenced by his wish to plant a loyal, reliable, and highly motivated people where they would defend what was then Persia's border with Egypt, he seemed a divine instrument to the Jews in Babylonia. The prophet Isaiah said God considered him His anointed and His shepherd. The return to Judah he authorized and promoted opened a new chapter in the annals of the Jewish people. It is anyone's guess what course their history might have taken if Cyrus had not permitted the Judaean exiles to reclaim their ancestral homeland.

**Cyrus Liberating the Jews From their Babylonian Exile
And Restoring Treasures Looted From Their Jerusalem Temple**

RETURN TO ZION

Like their return from Egypt almost eight centuries earlier, the return of the Jews from Babylonia was in waves, beginning in 538 BCE. This new exodus also involved a hazardous trek of hundreds of miles. Sheshbazzar (who may have been a son of exiled King Jehoiachin, though never king himself) led the first contingent of returnees. The first governor of Judah under the Persians was Sheshbazzar's nephew, Zerubbabel. He and Jeshua, a descendant of Zadok, high priest during Solomon's time, provided the initial leadership for the returnees. (Sheshbazzar and Zerubbabel may have been different names of the same person.)

Not long after the first exiles returned to Jerusalem, work on rebuilding the Temple began. A new foundation was laid in the ruins of the old and an altar for the worship of Yahweh was erected. However, expectations of an immediate glorious renaissance were to be disappointed.

The number of returnees was at first too small to make much impact on the land, and shortages of construction materials had to be overcome. Jerusalem and the other cities of Judah remained largely in ruins. What had been the southern kingdom of the Jews had become a part of the Persian province of Samaria and was called Yehud.

The Jewish homeland had dwindled in size from what it had previously been. During its time of troubles, its neighbors—the Philistines, Edomites, Ammonites and Moabites—had annexed some of its territory. For a long time, it was effectively limited to an area extending no further than thirty-five miles from Jerusalem.

Difficulties arose too between the returnees and the offspring of those Judaeans who had not been driven into exile decades earlier. They had adjusted to their own situation over time. They had not experienced the spiritual renewal of the exiles and had not adapted to the important changes the practice of Judaism had undergone in exile. They were offended by the attitudes of the returnees who considered themselves the sole inheritors of the covenant with God. Nor did neighboring lands take well to the Persian-sponsored return of the exiles. They did what they could to obstruct the Temple's reconstruction.

Those problems soon forced suspension of the project. Almost thirty years passed following the return from Babylonia before the Temple was rebuilt, and then it was only after Persian King Darius I, apprised of the neglected wishes of his predecessor, Cyrus, interceded to order all concerned to "Allow the work of this House of God to go on."[70]

The construction of the second Temple was seen as a renewal of the covenant between Yahweh and the Jews. At the joyful dedication celebration, twelve goats were among the animals sacrificed, one for each of the original tribes of the Jews.

Whatever gratification and comfort the rebuilt Temple engendered, times were hard in the land. Crops failed. Ever-greater numbers fell into debt. Community spirit broke down. The divorce rate, not previously significant among Jews, soared.

The prophet Malachi railed against sinfulness in the land. He censured those "who practice sorcery, who commit adultery, who swear falsely, who cheat laborers of their hire."[71] He condemned those who took advantage of widows, orphans, and foreigners. Crime was rife. The religious laws of Judaism were more often breached than observed and its rituals were commonly neglected.

The forecasts of the prophets notwithstanding, Judah had not again become a great land. It remained a small, impoverished, sparsely populated corner of a Persian province, under the administration of the Persian governor in Samaria.

In due course, more Jews in exile were drawn to the call of Zion. But it was little more than a drifting in of small groups, families, and individuals as Jewish communities established themselves in what had become the Diaspora in various cities of the Persian Empire and Egypt. No great numbers were anxious to migrate to a land none of them remembered from personal experience. They retained their Jewish identity and remained religiously observant, but they believed life in the Diaspora, where some were to achieve high rank and position, to be more congenial, secure, and stable than living in Jerusalem would be.

However, their reluctance to take up their lives in the reestablished Jewish homeland did not dampen their identity with it or their concern for what was happening there. Nehemiah, who rose to the rank of cup bearer and favorite of Persian King Artaxerxes, was distressed by what he heard of the collapse of standards and social cohesion in Jerusalem and how vulnerable it had become to marauders. He begged Artaxerxes for permission to rejuvenate the city and rebuild its shattered walls.

Artaxerxes was dismayed by the possibility of unrest in Persia's strategically positioned Yehud. Not only did he grant Nehemiah's request for permission to put things right, but he provided him with materials to rebuild Jerusalem's defenses and with an armed escort. He also decreed that Yehud should become a separate province, no longer subject to the governor of Samaria. Nehemiah was to be its governor.

Arriving in Jerusalem in 445 BCE, Nehemiah immediately began establishing a sense of order. Military measures were introduced to provide security for the populace, especially during the rebuilding of the walls. To repel marauders, construction workers kept weapons within easy reach, and armed sentries were posted on the walls during the night as the work proceeded. Everyone was instructed to rally for battle if an alarm trumpet were sounded.

Once the walls were rebuilt, families from other towns in Judah were recruited to live in the still thinly populated capital. Under Nehemiah's spirited leadership, Jerusalem developed a renewed sense of tenacity and purpose. Under his direction and that of the priest-scribe Ezra, strict religious observance and high standards of personal behavior were enforced, including observance of the Sabbath. To obstruct commercial activity on the prescribed day of rest, the gates of Jerusalem were kept closed from Friday afternoon until after nightfall on Saturday. The cost of maintaining the Temple was divided among the city's families.

More than ever before, the Torah, with its account of Jewish origins and destiny, became part, not only of the religion of the people, but of their living history as well. Corrupt practices by priests were exposed and prohibited. Marriage with non-Jews, which had been practiced even by the exalted King David, was banned.

This new Judah remained a Persian protectorate but the return of the Jews from exile gave the land a renewed historical and religious underpinning. Greater numbers continued to live in the ever-more-widespread Diaspora, but over time, new waves of "returnees" were drawn to Jerusalem by the national-religious revival. The Jewish people were again one nation under Yahweh. Wherever they lived, and whatever other allegiances they had, they considered Zion their spiritual home.

The era of the kingdoms of the Jews, and of the kings who ruled over them, had been relegated to history. Governors responsible to the kings of Persia administered their Jewish province but hereditary high priests, some more pious, conscientious, and principled than others, retained secular as well as spiritual authority over the people. They led the nation in worship and maintained the sanctity and official sanction of religious law.

It was a period of low international profile for once-turbulent Judah. It was for the most part isolated even from Samaria and the people of the former northern kingdom of the Jews.

With protracted peace and security, the population of Jerusalem, and of the entire province, gradually increased substantially. Ever-greater contact was established and maintained with Jewish settlements in Mesopotamia and elsewhere in the Diaspora.

Rebuilding the Temple

THE GREEK CHALLENGE

After the walls of Jerusalem had been rebuilt, the people of Judah lived in peace according to their own laws and culture for more than a century. For the most part, they were neither oppressed by the Persians who ruled their land, nor pressured to adapt to non-Jewish ways.

But their situation changed after Alexander the Great, having conquered the Persian Empire, returned from his triumphs in Asia. Judaea, as it came to be known by its Hellenized name, fell to him without a struggle in 332 BCE.

According to legend, a delegation of Judaean elders, led by High Priest Simon the Righteous, met with Alexander to assure him of the loyalty of the Jews and plead that they be permitted to continue to govern themselves. Little concerned about a place as small as Judaea, and not inclined to interfere with the domestic customs and traditions of the many lands he conquered, Alexander is said to have assured the Judaeans they could retain a large measure of independence and offered them animals to be sacrificed on his behalf at the Temple. Though the entire region would come under the influence of the Hellenic culture and Greek language which Alexander and his heirs brought with them, the high priests and officials of Judaea were permitted to administer the land with little external interference.

After Alexander died, his senior commanders contested among themselves for control of his empire. Judaea became a part of the battleground between them. Its people often suffered grievously as rival armies crisscrossed their territory, living off the land.

The struggle for mastery in Judaea ultimately was between the descendants of Ptolemy and Seleucus, two of Alexander's senior officers. Ptolemy had established the capital of his domain at the newly founded Egyptian city of Alexandria, the Jewish population of which was to grow larger than that of any other city in the ancient world. Seleucus, meantime, became king of a region that including Syria and stretched deep into Asia. His capital was at Antioch in northern Syria.

Ptolemy and his successors were the first of the Hellenic potentates to establish long-term dominion over Judaea. They were content to leave the administration of the province to its hereditary high priest. As senior figure in the land, he had political as well as religious responsibilities in consultation with a Judaean council of elders which would evolve into the Sanhedrin religious court. Also wielding authority were a group of Judaean families who effectively formed an aristocracy in Jerusalem, gaining eminence and wealth through royal favor, family links, priestly connections, tax farming privileges, and commerce.

After more than a century, in 198 BCE, the army of Antiochus III, the Seleucid ruler of Syria, overthrew Ptolemaic Egyptian rule in Judaea. Like the Ptolemaic kings, he permitted Judaeans to govern themselves. But throughout the long period of Hellenic dominance—whether by the Ptolemies of Egypt or the Seleucids of Syria—the influence of Greek culture had a powerful impact on Jewish existence.

Large numbers of Hellenized gentiles settled in Judaea and the surrounding region. The Hellenes were great city builders. Greek cities and settlements were founded and flourished in Judaea and the area around it, including Ptolemais (Acco) on the Mediterranean coast, Philoteria on the shore of the Sea of Galilee, and Philadelphia (Amman) across the Jordan River. Temples to Zeus, Jupiter, Apollo, and other Greek deities were erected in those cities, though not in Jerusalem.

Pagan ideas and values spread across the land. They had little influence in rural areas of Judaea where devotion to traditional ways remained largely unchallenged. But in major centers, many Jews were attracted to Greek customs and practices.

Greek increasingly became the language of educated people who forsook what had become the Aramaic vernacular of the common folk. Greek ways were *de rigueur* for members of the social and intellectual elite and those who aspired to join them. Many in Jerusalem knew the Bible only through Greek translation. As a matter of course, many newborn children were given Greek names. Many took to equating Yahweh with Zeus, the senior deity in the Greek pantheon.

A chasm opened between Jews who clung to the more austere ways of their forebears and those who sought to adjust to changing conditions. Many families were bitterly divided over whether Hellenization undermined Jewish identity or was the invigorating wave of the future for Jews. Members of the elite of society—landowners, merchants, officials—were the most readily Hellenized.

Youths were particularly attracted to Hellenized ways. For young Judaean men, the height of fashion was the standard attire of youths wherever Hellenization had sunk roots or was doing so—in Alexandria as in Antioch, in Athens as in Sparta. They might, for example, strut about Jerusalem in high-laced boots, chlamys (a short toga-like garment broached at the shoulder), and broad-brimmed hats. Even priests were to be found among the Hellenizers. Young priests were known to abandon services at the Temple to rush off to watch and even participate in Greek athletic contests.

Three major strands of belief and practice developed. Ultra-pious Hasidim insisted on strict observance of religious law and ritual, and total rejection of foreign ways. Hasidic practices sometimes carried piety beyond the prescriptions of Mosaic ordinances. For example, some refrained from sexual intercourse on all days except Wednesdays because of calculations that resulting births might otherwise occur on and disturb the Sabbath.

In diametric contrast to the Hasidim, extreme Hellenizers favored unqualified acceptance of Greek influences and abandonment of old customs. Moderates shunning both extremes believed a *modus vivendi* was possible between the old and the new, remaining generally true to Jewish law and practices while adopting many Hellenized ways.

However, Jewish and Greek ideals were fundamentally irreconcilable. The Jewish tradition held that the highest good was a belief in the one God with whom the Patriarchs had made a covenant, plus the observance of religiously established standards of justice, virtue, and propriety. In contrast, Greek culture considered humans to be the measure of all things, esteeming most highly such attributes as physical beauty, artistic inspiration, and logically generated truth.

According to Jewish standards, the Greek search for beauty and art was as often as not an excuse for immodest and obscene displays of the human figure, and the Greek search for truth was attempted justification of impious sophistry, an insult to the concept of the incomparable wisdom of Yahweh.

An open clash between the two cultures erupted in Judaea after arch-Hellenizer Antiochus IV Epiphanes ascended the Seleucid throne of Syria in 176 BCE. Antiochus's primary objective was to conquer Egypt, as the illustrious Alexander had, and overthrow his Ptolemaic rival there. Cementing his control of Judaea on the land bridge between Syria and Egypt became an important strategic consideration for him.

When High Priest Onias, who favored the less oppressively Hellenizing Ptolemaic Egyptians, displayed his pro-Egyptian stance in Jerusalem, Antiochus replaced him with Joshua, Onias's brother, more commonly known by his Greek name of Jason. Jason not only paid well for the appointment but also pledged to transform Jerusalem into a totally Hellenic city.

Among the steps he took to achieve that goal was building a gymnasium in Jerusalem to promote Greek sports, including nude wrestling. Some wrestlers, ashamed of having been circumcised and fearing the taunts of the spectators, underwent remedial surgery to disguise that fact.

Jason was soon replaced as high priest by Menelaus—who paid the hard-pressed Antiochus a bigger bribe than his predecessor and offered to be even more energetic in promoting the Hellenization of Jerusalem, consistent with Antiochus's requirement that all his subjects "should be one people ... each abandoning his particular customs."[72] Like Jason, Menelaus used his exalted status to authorize sacrifices in the temple of Zeus. The resulting outrage extended beyond the puritanical Hasidim to more moderate elements in Jerusalem and to elsewhere in the land.

By then, a third power with interest in the situation had become involved in the geopolitics of the region, with major consequences for Judaea. When a Syrian army defeated the Egyptians in battle, Antiochus might have succeeded in adding Egypt to his Syrian empire if it had not been for Rome.

The Romans had established themselves as masters of the eastern Mediterranean, and much else. The Syrian Greeks grudgingly accepted that Rome was unlikely to tolerate the expansion of a presumptuous and potentially challenging lesser power.

To make that point, an emissary was sent from Rome to order Antiochus to withdraw from Egypt and warn of serious repercussions if he proved defiant. When Antiochus asked for time to consider, the Roman envoy drew a circle on the ground around where he sat and commanded him to give his reply before he dared to step out of it. Antiochus had no option but to yield.

In his frustration, Antiochus grew even more determined to maintain control of Judaea against possible Egyptian efforts to pry the province from his grasp. When a rumor that he had died sparked a wave of violence between pro-Syrian and pro-Egyptian factions in Jerusalem, he believed an uprising against him was in the making. Continuing discord between Jewish Hellenizers and those clinging to traditional Jewish ways seemed to confirm his suspicions.

He had long considered Jewish resistance to Hellenization a barbaric irritant and, more importantly, a challenge to his rule. Furious over his Egypt fiasco, Antiochus vowed to stamp out such insubordination forever. According to the Roman historian Tacitus, he intended to "abolish Jewish superstition"[73] and firmly spread "Greek civilization" across Judaea.

In the year 167 BCE, a contingent of his troops was dispatched to Jerusalem with orders that it act firmly to restore absolute Syrian authority there. Mass slaughter and destruction was the result.

Much of the city was set ablaze and the Temple was desecrated. A towering structure, called the Akra, was built on a hill overlooking the Temple and turned into a garrisoned citadel. Its presence was to guarantee obedience to Syrian decrees. The holy city, the center of Jewish life, was now dominated by a fortified enclave in which was quartered a threatening force of foreign pagans, assisted by collaborators among Hellenized Jews. Resistance to Syrian rule was to be ruthlessly suppressed.

Nevertheless, the Jewish rebellion Antiochus had feared was in the making.

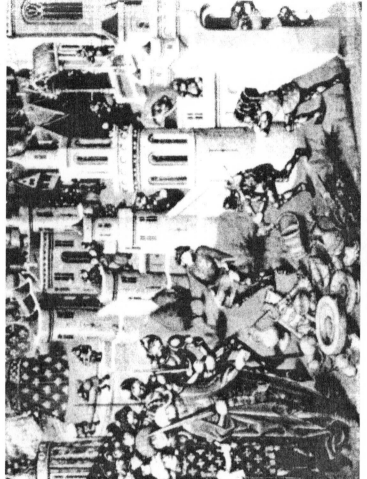

Antiochus Pillaging Jerusalem

THE HASMONEANS

THE MACCABEE REVOLT

The attempt by Syrian King Antiochus IV to forcibly Hellenize Judaea was the greatest threat Judaism had faced since the Babylonian exile four centuries earlier. All Jewish practices were to be outlawed and uprooted. All measures thought necessary to achieve that objective were to be rigorously implemented.

The Temple in Jerusalem was to be rededicated to Zeus and rituals of sacrifice to pagan gods were to be made obligatory. Jewish festivals and observance of the Sabbath were abolished by law. Circumcision was outlawed on pain of death. The Temple was stripped of its treasures. These were sent off to replenish Antiochus's depleted treasury.

Many Jews found not to be complying with the new order were crucified. Many Jerusalemites fled the city for the towns of the countryside where it might be more possible to live and worship as they wished. But troops were sent throughout the land to force submission to Antiochus's decrees.

In the village of Modein, not far from Jerusalem, a Syrian officer instructed Mattathiah, the elderly local priest, to show the way to the villagers by offering a sacrifice to a pagan god. Mattathiah refused, saying he would not abandon "the covenant of our fathers."[74] What was more, he struck down a Hellenized Jew who stepped forward to make the required gesture in his place. He then also killed the Syrian officer and, with his five sons, attacked and killed the officer's troop escort.

Mattathiah knew the Syrians would react harshly to this challenge to their authority. He called upon all who wished to remain true to the laws of Judaism to flee with him and his sons—John, Simon, Judah, Eleazar, and Jonathan—to the nearby hills, not far from present-day Ramallah, where they would continue their defiance of Antiochus.

It was a small group but Mattathiah and his followers had a thorough knowledge of the hiding places and escape routes of the countryside while those who would be sent to destroy them did not. They used their advantage to evade their Syrian pursuers and punish Jews who succumbed to Hellenizing pressures. They swept down on outlying towns and villages to destroy pagan altars, circumcise Jewish boys whose parents had neglected that religious requirement and "saved the law from the hands of the gentiles."[75]

The elderly Mattathiah did not live long after the incident at Modein. Before he died, he chose his third son, Judah, called Maccabeus (The Hammer), who had obvious leadership skills, to take command of his band of insurgents. With the aid of his brothers, Judah Maccabee would transform the spontaneous act of a handful of insubordinate villagers into a national liberation movement.

The Maccabees, as they came to be known, formed the first organized Jewish military force in four centuries of foreign rule. They ambushed troops dispatched to crush them and terrorized Hellenized Jews. As word of their exploits spread, others came to join their ranks, raising concern in Antioch, the Syrian capital from which Judaea was being administered.

Apollonius, the governor of the region, was led to believe he was dealing with no more than a bothersome band of fanatics. He was confirmed in that belief when the troops he sent to wipe them out scattered them in their first encounter. But the Maccabees regrouped and followed their setback with a well-executed ambush during which they massacred those sent to track them down—Apollonius among them.

His defeat and death jolted the Syrians and a larger contingent was dispatched to annihilate the expanding band of Jewish insurgents. But the Maccabees, now numerous enough to engage in set-piece battle as well as ambush, again were victorious.

Despite his limited combat experience, Judah Maccabee became skilled in surviving the worst his much-more-powerful adversaries were able to inflict. Having learned that rebellious ultra-pious Hasidim had been slaughtered for refusing to defend themselves against the Syrians on the Sabbath, he ruled that the Maccabees would not refrain from fighting on the religiously prescribed day of rest when circumstances required.

At the time, King Antiochus was committed to leading a campaign of conquest in Iran, far to the east. He empowered Lysias, his most senior official, a member of his royal family, to act as his regent during his absence from Antioch, with instructions that he blot out all memory of the Jews in Judaea. To make certain Syria would never be troubled by them again, he was to settle "strangers in all their territory"[76] in their place.

A far stronger force than before was organized to finish off the Maccabees. Slave-trading merchants were encouraged to tag along with this army so that they would be able to buy, shackle, and cart off captured Jewish fighters when victory was achieved.

But the earlier confrontations had taught Judah Maccabee important lessons in defensive tactics. He lured his adversaries into futile and draining battlefield maneuvers before trouncing them convincingly. When still another Syrian army was sent to make good that defeat, he prevailed again.

The setbacks the Syrians suffered had gone beyond mere humiliation. Lysias realized the stability of their entire empire, also under pressure in some of its remote regions, could be shaken. He sought a compromise to calm the situation and offered the Maccabees a general amnesty. He said that he would urge Antiochus to withdraw the edicts banning Jewish worship and practices. Furthermore, the Maccabees would not be blocked from entering Jerusalem.

Only three years after Mattathiah had touched off the insurrection with an act of defiance against a lowly Syrian officer in a countryside village, the guerrilla army led by his sons trooped into the holy city in triumph. They were not pleased that the Akra, the Syrian garrisoned citadel there, remained intact, but tolerated its presence for the time being.

Once in place in Jerusalem, Judah began rooting out the most conspicuous manifestations of Greek influence. Altars and idols of Zeus and other pagan deities were torn down. The Temple was cleansed and rededicated in a festival of thanksgiving and prayer that lasted eight days. People from other parts of Judaea converged on the capital to take part. Torchlight processions dramatized the occasion.

Thus did the holiday *Chanukah* come into existence, to be celebrated for a week and a day every year from that time on. According to legend, only a small quantity of the special oil needed during the ceremony for the Temple's rededicated candelabra could be found, but it remarkably lasted a full eight days.

The Maccabees had scored such striking success against so formidable an enemy that even many of Jerusalem's Hellenized elite rallied to them. Riding a wave of glory, Judah now embarked on a bid to transform what had been a religious uprising into a national movement that would overthrow foreign domination and reclaim other areas that had been part of the Jewish nation in earlier times.

He sent armed probes into Gilead, beyond the Jordan, and into Galilee. Where the forces at his disposal were not strong enough to overcome the resistance of majority gentile populations, Jews subject to persecution among them were brought under escort back into Judaea proper and resettled there. He also launched sorties to the south against Idumaea (the Greek name for the land previously known as Edom) and against the Philistines along the coast.

It was far more than Lysias believed he would have to allow when he sought a compromise with Judah. Such challenges to Syrian control of the region could not be endured. He revived plans to end the Maccabee insurrection and led an army into Judaea, the most powerful yet assembled against the rebellion, to finally do the job.

As well as a strong cavalry contingent and light and heavy infantry units, Lysias's army included fearsome battle elephants on which were mounted turrets from which archers could launch showers of arrows. The Syrian garrison holding out in its Jerusalem Akra citadel broke out to assist the attacking army. This time the final destruction of the Maccabees and their rebellion seemed inevitable.

However, external developments saved them. King Antiochus succumbed to illness and died while on the military campaign that had taken him far from Antioch. A struggle for power erupted among rival candidates to succeed him on the throne. For Lysias (leading an invading army about to overwhelm the Jewish rebellion), Antioch, rather than Judaea, was the place to be at that moment.

In recognition of the situation and the seeming futility of endlessly tangling with the Maccabees, he again offered a peace treaty in which Jews would be free "to live according to their own laws as formerly."[77] Antiochus's edicts abolishing Jewish worship, which had initially provoked the insurrection, would definitely be withdrawn. Syria would retain sovereign power over Judaea and would continue to appoint its high priest as chief religious and (effectively) secular authority but would otherwise no longer interfere in Judaea's internal affairs.

It was not enough for Judah and his Maccabees. They still insisted on independence for Judaea and feared their leadership of the freedom movement would be undermined. But the people of Jerusalem welcomed with relief the Syrian promise that prohibitions against Jewish observances would be cancelled and that peace would be restored to the land. Not even the Hasidim, who had earlier given the Maccabees strong support, withheld their approval. Their religious freedom was their overriding concern. They did not even question Syria's appointment of the Jerusalem priest Alcimus as high priest, though he had Hellenistic leanings and had the support of Hellenized Jews. Descended from the tribe of Levi, he was accepted as genealogically qualified for the post.

Judah was obliged to defer to the popular craving for peace. But, guarding his options, he cautiously withdrew his Maccabee fighters from Jerusalem.

His suspicion of Syrian intentions soon proved justified. Once new High Priest Alcimus had arrived in Jerusalem with a strong Syrian troop escort, it became apparent that his task was to ensure that Syrian rule would never again be challenged and that the Hellenization of Judaea would not again be obstructed.

Once more the Maccabees entered the fray. The Syrian force propping up Alcimus in Jerusalem was not permitted to return to Syria unchallenged when its mission was thought to have been fulfilled. It was attacked and harassed by Maccabees on its way home and harried by people in towns and villages along its line of withdrawal.

His position threatened and his life in danger, Alcimus fled to Antioch to save himself. Popular outrage at Syrian duplicity, and belated admiration for Judah's refusal to submit, made him a hero throughout the land: a famous warrior, an acclaimed leader of his people in their renewed longing for independence, an historic figure in his own time.

But he realized that the odds would ultimately be against his triumph over Syrian might, which remained massive compared to his own, and he sought external support. Suspicious of Syrian aspirations, the Romans, to whom he dispatched envoys, responded favorably. They offered a mutual defense alliance with Judah and asked the Syrians, "Why have you made your yoke heavy on our friends and allies the Jews? If they complain about you again, we will do them justice and make war on you by land and sea."[78]

It was a diplomatic success for the Maccabees, but the Syrians knew it had no immediate military bearing on the situation. Though generally respected, the Romans had by then developed a reputation for making pronouncements they were not always prepared to act upon when coping with more pressing commitments elsewhere, as they were at that moment. Choosing to risk Roman displeasure in this situation, the Syrians resumed offensive operations in Judaea, their army slaughtering all in its path regardless of complicity in the renewed rebellion.

It was a brutal onslaught, demoralizing all but the most dedicated and fearless of the Maccabee fighters. Grown war weary, many gave up hope and drifted back to their towns, villages, and farms until only eight hundred were left. Judah led them in rearguard action against the Syrians, but his time of glory was nearing its end. In 160 BCE, he fell in battle at the head of his shrunken band of warriors. The survivors scattered.

The Maccabees appeared finally to have been crushed. Eleazar, one of Judah's brothers, had been killed earlier. Believing mistakenly that a richly ornamented battle elephant was carrying the successor to King Antiochus, he ferociously battled his way through the troops around it, thrust his spear into the elephant's underbelly, and was crushed when it toppled over on him. John, the oldest of Mattathiah's sons, by nature more peaceful than his brothers, was killed by hostile desert tribesmen while guarding Maccabee supplies and baggage. Mattathiah's youngest son, Jonathan, now succeeded to leadership of what little remained of the uprising.

The Syrians had meantime become increasingly preoccupied with unrest in other parts of their dominion and the struggle for succession to the throne in Antioch. It left them less disposed to expend military resources on the now much diminished, though seemingly endless, Maccabee provocations.

Facing a less determined adversary and driven both by religious fervor and nationalist spirit, Jonathan relaunched the guerrilla campaign for Judaean independence. Though he was denied Jerusalem by the Syrians and the Jewish Hellenizers, within a few years he had gained mastery over much of the rest of Judaea, a matter of renewed anxiety in Antioch.

It soon became obvious to rival contenders for the Syrian crown that if Jonathan could relieve them of the burden of strife in their Jewish province, he would make a better ally than adversary. Competing for his friendship, they engaged in a courting process that resulted in his appointment as high priest of Judaea, effectively its ruler. Mattathiah, who had launched no more than a local uprising, would not have imagined such a thing possible for one of his sons.

Though nominally still subject to Syrian authority, Jonathan proceeded to manipulate rival factions in Antioch, taking liberties far beyond his authorized high priestly powers. He strengthened Jerusalem's defenses and fortifications elsewhere in the province, and began building a professional army. At one stage, he sent a contingent of Jewish troops to Antioch to restore order on behalf of one of the claimants to the Syrian throne. He gained such respect there, and his military forces grew to be so formidable, that he was able to extend his authority to neighboring territory that was also still nominally under Syrian jurisdiction.

Shrewd and pragmatic, Jonathan also went some way toward healing divisions within the Jewish nation. The Hasidim objected to him as high priest. Neither a blood descendant of King David's high priest, Zadok, nor even of the priestly tribe of Levi, he was considered by them unqualified for that revered role. But others were pleased with the measure of self-rule he had won for Judaea. Hellenized Jews, once the nemeses of the Maccabees, came to look upon Jonathan as a tolerant leader and effective ruler, capable of securing the conditions that permitted them to follow their chosen ways in peace.

Despite his achievements, he did not become as adept at intrigue as some whom he tried to manipulate. Seeking to extract further advantage for Judaea from the power struggle in Antioch, he was lured into captivity by one of the claimants to the Syrian throne and murdered by him.

During the time Jonathan had been master of the fate of the people of Judaea (160–143 BCE), he transformed what had been an unstable province, riven by strife and subject to foreign oppression, into a seminational, self-ruled entity respected by other states in the region.

*   *   *

The murder of Jonathan stirred demands throughout Judaea that his brother Simon, the last of the original Maccabees, succeed him. Without troubling to seek approval from any of the figures contending for power in Syria, Simon assumed the role Jonathan had played as de facto ruler of Judaea.

With him, "The yoke of the Gentiles was removed from Israel"[79] says the Book of Maccabees. It was the beginning of a new period in which the Jewish people would again be free, in name as well as fact, to rule themselves.

At a great assembly in Jerusalem of "priests, people, rulers of the nation, and elders of the country,"[80] Simon was formally declared "high priest, governor general and ethnarch of the Jewish people and priests … to exercise supreme authority over all." He had served Jonathan as chief adviser and general and was not unfamiliar with the difficulties and opportunities that now were his to deal with.

Like Jonathan, Simon seized upon the ongoing leadership rivalries in Syria to seek advantage for Judaea. Political paralysis in Antioch permitted him to starve out the Syrian garrison at Jerusalem's Akra citadel which had been an important symbol of Syrian rule. He then sent his fighters to take first Gezer in the Judaean hills, which dominated the road to the coast, and then the port of Jaffa—providing Judaea with access to the sea.

To demands for their return to Syrian control, Simon replied, "We have neither taken other men's lands nor have we taken possession of that which belongs to another but only of the inheritance of our fathers."[81] When a Syrian army was sent to punish such impudence, it was beaten back.

For the first time since the death of King Zedekiah and the destruction of the first Temple more than four centuries earlier, the Jewish nation was again master of its own fate. Under Simon, "leader of the Jews,"[82] it grew stronger and self-assured and developed a thriving economy. Bitter differences between Hellenizers and those adhering to Jewish traditional practices were for the moment muted.

> *The people cultivated their land in peace; the land yielded its produce and the trees of the field their fruit. Old men sat in the squares, all talking about the good times, while the young men wore the glorious apparel of war. [Simon] supplied the cities with food and equipped them with the means of defense, till his glorious name reached the ends of the earth. He brought peace to the land, and Israel was filled with happiness. Every man sat under his vine and his fig tree, with no one to disturb him.… He strengthened all the lowly among his people and was zealous for the law; he suppressed all the lawless and the wicked.[83]*

Judaea's improved circumstances gained it international respect. Rome recognized its sovereignty by renewing the treaty of friendship it had less meaningfully agreed to earlier with Judah Maccabee.

Emulating the habits of neighboring potentates and harking back to the grandeur of Solomon, Simon established an opulent court in Jerusalem. After spending most of his adult life as a fighting man on the run, he took to living in what his austere father Mattathiah would have considered degenerate splendor, though he would have approved of Simon's continued strict personal observance of Jewish religious law and practices.

Simon ruled Judaea for nine years without serious reversal. But like his brothers, he died violently. He was assassinated by his son-in-law, Ptolemy, whom he had appointed governor of Jericho and who hoped to seize power in Judaea with Syrian support. After killing Simon, Ptolemy took two of his sons prisoner.

Simon's third son John Hyrcanus (Hyrcanus I), a commander of the Judaean army, was also supposed to have been eliminated in the coup. But Hyrcanus was tipped off at his field command post and dealt with those coming to kill him. He then rushed to Jerusalem to organize its defense against an expected Syrian-backed assault. He was immediately proclaimed high priest and ruler of Judaea as successor to his murdered father.

His coup having failed, Ptolemy barricaded himself in a fortress town near Jericho, taking his mother-in-law—Hyrcanus's mother and Simon's newly widowed wife—as an additional hostage. When Hyrcanus arrived to lay siege to the town, Ptolemy led her and Hyrcanus's two captured brothers out onto its wall and threatened to hurl them to their deaths unless the siege was lifted. His mother cried out to her son, urging him to ignore the threat. But Hyrcanus withdrew to save her and his brothers. Ptolemy killed them anyway, escaped from the town, and fled across the Jordan River. His subsequent fate is unknown.

*   *   *

John Hyrcanus was an audacious figure, cut from the same mold as his Maccabee forebears. But barely had he assumed leadership of Judaea when the Syrians, never reconciled to the independence it had achieved and encouraged by the turmoil following Simon's assassination, dispatched an army to oust him and claim mastery of the land once more. Jerusalem came under a siege so threatening that those too old or infirm to help defend the city were put outside its walls to save food for those who could.

If the Syrians had not had to divert forces to cope with difficulties elsewhere, they might have retaken the holy city at the time. Nevertheless, they maintained a strong enough presence in Judaea to force Hyrcanus to bow to Antioch, pay tribute, and even to send fighters to serve under them in a war against the Parthians, the rising power in the east.

It was a losing war for the Syrians whose empire had already begun to fragment in the face of the challenge of the Parthians, who were of Iranian origin. Their forces were overstretched and their imperial authority was undermined by dynastic rivalries. Under those circumstances, Hyrcanus was able to relaunch the campaign for the full Judaean independence sought by his father and his Maccabee uncles. Not only did he succeed but, strengthening the already sizable army he had inherited, he ventured beyond the territory to which Judaea had been confined as a Syrian province to seek sovereignty over all the land where Jews had held sway at the peak of their power centuries earlier.

Samaria, Galilee, and large parts of Transjordan were reclaimed. Idumaea was absorbed into Judaea. To preempt the development of potentially divisive elements there, the Idumaeans were forcibly converted to Judaism. It was one of the two episodes in the history of the Jews during which they imposed religious conversion on others[8]. The Idumaeans were Arabs, considered to be descendants of Esau, the twin brother of the Patriarch Jacob. Some soon came to occupy important positions in Judaea. It was from converted Idumaean stock that King Herod the Great would later spring.

The Romans, their empire expanding, had been closely monitoring developments in the region. For them, anything that hastened the collapse of Judaea's Syrian overlords, whom they would replace in due course, was worth pursuing. The Roman Senate offered Hyrcanus expressions of friendly regard as a warning to the Syrians against trying to reassert their authority over him. Hyrcanus also established amicable contact with Egypt where the large Jewish community in the city of Alexandria was on excellent terms with Queen Cleopatra III.

Peace returned to the land of the Jews during Hyrcanus's time as their leader and ruler. The clash of armies no longer disrupted the harvest. Trading ships sailed from busy Mediterranean port cities that had been absorbed into Judaea. Main caravan routes were once more part of its domain. Gifts of great value poured in from Jewish communities in Egypt, Mesopotamia, and elsewhere in the widening Diaspora.

Within Judaea, independence and security achieved, rival religious political and philosophical movements flourished, most notably those of the Sadducees

---

8.   Not long afterward, Hyrcanus's son Aristobulus would conquer Ituraea, north of Galilee, and also forcibly convert its people to Judaism.

and Pharisees who contended for political as well as religious supremacy in the land.

The Sadducees, named after Zadok, the first high priest under King Solomon, were conservative by attitude and religion. They believed Jews should be bound only by what was contained in the five books of the Torah and rejected what came to be known as rabbinic elaborations affecting the more personal and spiritual nature of an individual's relationship with God. The Sadducees included the elite figures and sections of society: the Temple hierarchy, senior administrative officials, landowners, high-ranking military officers, and merchants. Their privileged positions in the community dictated their views on public policy. They distrusted populist movements that might disrupt the status quo and did not find nonreligious Hellenizing influences necessarily objectionable.

The Pharisees—their name means the separated ones, a title that may originally have been given them by their critics—were the spiritual successors of the Hasidim. They believed that Judaism was a personal, emotional experience rather than merely the formal adherence to ancient practices that it was to the Sadducees. They held that the laws of the Torah were subject to interpretation to provide a guide for everyday life, and that patterns of Jewish worship and moral behavior prescribed by religious luminaries were also to be revered.

The Pharisees denied that the Jerusalem Temple hierarchy, which had at times been an instrument of foreign domination, enjoyed exclusive right to pass judgment on standards of behavior. They wanted Judaea to be ruled by the descendants of David, as ordained by God, rather than by a man like Hyrcanus who was increasingly remote from the aspirations and beliefs of the ordinary people.

Though less well placed in government and society than Sadducees, the Pharisees had a much larger popular following which included the lesser priesthood, scribes, artisans, and small landowners. They had a particularly wide following in the towns and villages of Judaea where the comforts of deeply personal religious feeling and observance were much cherished. Josephus said they had "so great a power over the multitude that when they say anything against ... the high priest, they are ... believed."[84]

Concentrating on spiritual and ethical values, the Pharisees believed political policies should be determined by religious needs and moral standards. In contrast, the Sadducees saw divine worship and matters of national policy as separate and unrelated.

Those differences had practical consequences because the national and religious survival of the Jews had long been linked. The principles of the Pharisees more readily inspired Judaean liberation sentiments like those held by the Macca-bees. They contained a greater dynamic than the Sadducees could provide.

Hyrcanus was at first close to the Pharisees, but he soon tired of their criticism of his Hellenistic leanings, and they were dismissed from councils of state and other positions of influence in Jerusalem. In their place, the Sadducees came to be the dominant political force in the land.

A third grouping during this period was the Essenes, deeply devout figures for whom the worship of God and the study of the Torah were the only purpose of existence. They withdrew from society to form semi-monastic communities from which women were excluded. They lived communal lives based exclusively on study and diligent observance of religious law. They were relatively few in num-ber and had little effect on the politics or fate of Judaea, though they played an important role in the evolution of Jewish mystical thought. Some scholars have suggested that Jesus was an Essene.

*   *   *

During the years in which Simon ruled Judaea (143–134 BCE) and those in which John Hyrcanus did so (134–104 BCE), Judaea became a strong, confident nation. Almost seventy years had passed since Mattathiah had sparked a religious uprising against tyranny. When his grandson, Hyrcanus, died, kings were about to sit on the throne of the Jews once more.

THE HASMONEAN
MONARCHS

ARISTOBULUS I

(104–103 BCE)

Judah Aristobulus, oldest son of John Hyrcanus and grandson of Simon Maccabee, believed it natural and proper for him to succeed his father as ruler of Judaea.
His father thought otherwise.

According to the testament Hyrcanus left when he died, Aristobulus was to
succeed him as high priest of the Jews but not as their leader. Instead, Aristobulus's mother, Hyrcanus's widow, whose name has been lost in history, was to be
"mistress of the realm."[85]

However, the sense of filial devotion, which had led the five Maccabee sons of
Mattathiah to rally around their father in defying Syrian tyranny, was lost on
Mattathiah's great-grandson. The circumstances were greatly changed; Judaea
had become a very different place, and Aristobulus was not about to be thwarted
by parental decree.

His mother may have been named mistress of the nation but he was well
placed to organize a coup against her. Having been a commander of the Judaean
forces in combat in Samaria and Galilee, he had little difficulty persuading the
army that the right to rule Judaea was his rather than hers, regardless of his late
father's wishes. Her overthrow was easily executed. He simply had her imprisoned and declared himself monarch. Thus was the Hasmonean dynasty founded,
the name possibly derived from that of a Maccabee ancestor. Through no choice
of their own, the Jewish people had a king once more.

There was little in Aristobulus's personal behavior in which his subjects could
take pride. In addition to having his mother thrown into a dungeon, where she
was left to starve, Aristobulus imprisoned three of his brothers to prevent them
from challenging his authority.

His fourth brother, Antigonus,[9] was spared a similar fate because they were
friends and had fought alongside each other against the enemies of Judaea.
Together they had led their father's campaign of conquest in the north.

Aristobulus's act in proclaiming himself king of the Jews provoked much discontent among the Pharisees because he was not a lineal descendent of King

---

9.   Though never a king, he is identified as Antigonus I to distinguish him from Antigonus II who was.

David. They were also dismayed by the increasing Hellenization of the leadership of the land. Judaea had become an independent state with a powerful army, but that army was swollen with non-Jewish mercenaries. Syria's attempt to force Jews to abandon Judaism and adopt Hellenistic ways had provoked the Maccabee uprising but, while Jewish worship continued to prevail, those ways were becoming increasingly fashionable in Jerusalem.

Aristobulus had deviated so far from the resolve of his Maccabee forebears to root out Hellenic influences that, upon claiming the throne, he adopted the title *Philhellen*—one who hold things Greek in high regard. But he and his father had done so much to strengthen and enlarge the independent Judaean state that disquiet was confined to conspiratorial grumbling. He relentlessly snuffed out dissent where it surfaced.

Nevertheless, Aristobulus's reign was doomed to brevity. Within a year of declaring himself king, he was stricken with severe abdominal pains and had to confine himself to his palace. It coincided with the festival of *Sukkoth*. His cherished brother, Antigonus, returned to the capital and went to the Temple to celebrate the holiday, as was expected of a member of Judaea's leading family, and to pray for the king's recovery. Unfamiliar with Temple niceties, Antigonus arrived at the Temple attired in battle dress and escorted, as usual, by armed soldiers.

Malcontents and conspirators at court spread rumors that his martial dress on such an occasion indicated he was preparing to seize power in the land. Aristobulus's wife, Queen Alexandra Salome, was among those who cast aspersions on the intentions of the king's brother. Her sick husband was showing no sign of recovery and the queen feared that Antigonus would soon succeed him on the throne. If that happened, he might consider her a threat and treat her as brutally as her husband had treated his deposed and imprisoned mother.

When the rumors of conspiracy involving his brother reached the king, he summoned Antigonus to his palace, sending him word that he was to come unarmed. It was to be a test. The king's bodyguard was instructed to lie in wait for him. They were to let him pass if he was unarmed and unescorted, but to kill him if he was not.

However, Queen Alexandra bribed the messenger carrying the king's summons to Antigonus, and the message he carried was altered. As revised, the message led Antigonus to believe his brother wished to see the new armored battle dress he'd had made for himself in Galilee. When he approached the royal palace attired as if for combat, the king's bodyguard cut him down.

Though he had, in effect, ordered his brother to be killed, Aristobulus was overcome with grief. His physical condition deteriorated and he soon died. He had been king for just one year. Upon his death, the three of his brothers he had imprisoned were freed and Alexander Jannai, the eldest of them, ascended the reestablished throne of the Jews.

ALEXANDER JANNAI

(103–76 BCE)

Alexander Jannai, the second Hasmonean monarch, took an unusual path to the throne of the Jews. He was a prisoner one day, king of Judaea and high priest the next. When his brother Aristobulus, who had imprisoned him as a possible threat to his position, died after only one year on the throne, twenty-two-year-old Jannai was freed from captivity and anointed his successor. He then married Salome Alexandra, widow of the late king, despite a biblical injunction banning high priests from marrying widows.

Under Jannai (Jonathan), the Jewish nation grew bigger and stronger than at any time since the days of Solomon. He secured most of Palestine's Mediterranean coastline and expanded his domain north and south and east of the Jordan River. But his reign was marked by virtually ceaseless foreign wars and domestic turmoil, consequences of his territorial aspirations and his manner of ruling his subjects.

Jannai was a harsh ruler. Great numbers of his subjects were slaughtered for daring to object to his conduct of the affairs of state. His truculent nature might be attributable to his experiences during his early years. Josephus writes that he was "hated by his father as soon as he was born."[86] He was forbidden to come into his presence and was banished as a boy to Galilee. His outlook on life would not have been softened by his having been confined to a dungeon by his brother.

His earliest attempts at territorial enlargement for Judaea were thwarted by Ptolemy Lathyrus, a son of Egypt's Queen Cleopatra. Having failed in his effort to depose her, Ptolemy had fled in fear of his life to Cyprus from where he was subsequently summoned by the people of the free city of Ptolemais in the bay of what is now Haifa. Besieged by Jannai's army, they begged him to save them. Gathering an army of mercenaries, Ptolemy invaded Judaea.

He drove the Judaean forces back as far as the Jordan River and proceeded to roam across the land, slaughtering and looting. So wide-ranging and thorough was Ptolemy's rampage that if Cleopatra had not intervened, the Hasmonean dynasty might have been terminated by him so soon after it had been founded.

Fearing her son's wider aspirations, the Egyptian queen sent strong detachments under two of her generals, the Jewish brothers Helkias and Ananias, to come to the aid of the embattled Jannai and foil Ptolemy's attempt to establish himself as ruler of Judaea. Their success led Cleopatra to contemplate turning the Hasmonean Jewish kingdom into an Egyptian province. But she was persuaded that the Judaeans made better friends than subjects and she restored Jannai to his throne.

His brush with disaster did not deter him from reviving his expansionist program. He rebuilt his shattered army and led it into Transjordan. After conquering parts of Nabataea, in what is now southern Jordan, he crossed the land to take Gaza and other coastal areas.

By then, many Judaeans, and particularly the Pharisees who resented his Hellenic leanings, had become exasperated with their king. Aside from his costly and destructive military adventures, he neglected his duties as high priest, a position that he apparently considered unworthy of his attentions and for which he was anyway not deemed to have proper genealogical qualifications.

When he appeared publicly in Jerusalem, he excited little enthusiasm among his disgruntled subjects. At a *Sukkoth* celebration at the Temple, he was jeered by the crowd and pelted with citrons which worshippers had brought along for use in the holiday rituals. Enraged, Jannai ordered his mercenaries to deal firmly with the situation. Thousands were massacred.

Once order had been bloodily restored, he set off again on his mission of conquest, returning to Transjordan to complete his victory over the Nabataeans. This time, however, his forces were routed and he barely escaped with his life. He fled back to Jerusalem where the exasperation of the Pharisees flared again in public demonstrations of discontent by their followers. It exploded finally into open rebellion and six years of civil war across Judaea.

Ultimately recognizing he could not crush dissent, Jannai stepped back from confrontation with the Pharisees and sought reconciliation with them. But having suffered grievously at his hands, they rejected his overtures and turned to the Syrians for help in relieving them of this tyrant. The Syrians readily responded; the Pharisee call for help was an opportunity for them to reclaim the Judaea they had lost to the Maccabees. The army Demetrius III dispatched to destroy Jannai was reinforced by thousands of Judaeans anxious to be rid of their king. Jannai's defenders were easily routed, leaving Jerusalem open to conquest by Demetrius.

Realizing now that the Temple and their nation were again about to be conquered by a foreign army and that Judaea might again lose its independence, the Pharisees executed a rapid turnabout. They made peace with the hated Jannai and sent their supporters rushing to swell the ranks of his decimated army. The Syrian advance on Jerusalem was halted and Demetrius withdrew from Judaea, hastened on his way by word of fresh unrest at home.

Once more saved from disaster, and secure again on the throne, Jannai responded to his rescue by the Pharisees by taking vengeance on them and their supporters for their earlier disloyalty. The mass killings he ordered included particularly grotesque acts of cruelty. In one case, eight hundred were crucified and, as they slowly died on their respective crosses, he had the throats of their wives and children cut in front of them. To escape such atrocities, thousands of Judaeans fled for sanctuary to Jewish communities in Egypt and Syria.

Others went into hiding within Judaea. Some may have joined the community of the semi-monastic Essenes, established near the Dead Sea. Jannai may have been the "wicked priest" mentioned in the Dead Sea scrolls which were discovered by archeologists almost two thousand years later.

Having decimated or cowed the Pharisee rebels, Jannai once more launched his campaign of territorial acquisition. He sent forces against Arabs in Transjordan, the Hellenic city-states in the north, and elsewhere in the region, adding extensively to Judaea's area of control or influence.

Opposition to him at home having been silenced and success in his military adventures having been achieved, Jannai underwent a striking change in character. The harshness with which he had been dealing with his subjects was eased. As a measure of calm settled over Judaea for the first time during his reign, he came to be more readily accepted by his subjects, even attaining some popularity.

He did not have long to enjoy it. Stricken with malaria, he continued to lead his army on combat missions but was increasingly incapacitated.

Before dying, he arranged for his wife, Alexandra Salome, to succeed him on the throne. During his last days, he was said to have regretted the crimes he had committed against his people and advised her to make peace with the Pharisees so that the divisions in the nation he had done so much to exacerbate could be healed.

ALEXANDRA SALOME

(76–67 BCE)

Alexandra Salome (Shelomtzion) was one of only two women ever to have ruled the Jewish nation in their own right, rather than as the wives of reigning kings. The other was Queen Athaliah who had sat on the throne of the kingdom of Judah eight centuries earlier.

Among the extensive reforms that were enacted during Alexandra's reign, one had especially historic consequences. A unique marriage contract, called a *ketubbah*, was introduced and made obligatory. One element of the *ketubbah* was designed to protect the interests of women in an unprecedented fashion: if men divorced their wives, they were required to provide resources to protect their abandoned spouses from being impoverished as a result. That support requirement would evolve in due course into the principle of alimony. The *ketubbah* also gave women special rights to their husbands' property if they were widowed, to help them sustain themselves.

Alexandra was herself twice widowed. Her first husband was King Aristobulus I who died young after ruling for only one year. She became reigning queen of Judaea, at the age of sixty-four, upon the death of her much-longer-reigning second husband, King Alexander Jannai.

It might easily have been otherwise. As Jannai lay terminally ill with malaria while with his troops in action in Transjordan, Alexandra told him she feared what might happen to her and their two sons after his death in view of the "ill will your nation bears you"[87] because of his brutal rule.

Jannai knew her fears were well grounded and advised her to keep his imminent death secret until a fortress, under siege by his soldiers, fell to the Judaeans. He said she would then be credited with that victory and, having thereby gained the backing of the army, she should return to Jerusalem and come to terms with the leaders of the Pharisees whom he had persecuted. He said they "had great authority ... both to do hurt to such as they hated and to bring advantages to those to whom they were friendly disposed."[88]

Alexandra followed that advice and benefited from it. Favoring the popular Pharisees over the previously prevailing elitist Sadducees was the route to the wide public acclaim her husband had never enjoyed. Besides, although *he* had persecuted the Pharisees, *she* had always been sympathetic to them and to their more spiritual style of worship. Now she acted quickly to free Pharisee leaders he had imprisoned and invited those who had fled his wrath to return to Jerusalem from exile. It was enough to shield her from discredit for having been the wife of a despised ruler.

Because she was a woman, the queen could not also hold the office of high priest as her husband had. She bestowed that potentially influential position on her eldest son, Hyrcanus II, a lightweight figure little concerned with either politics or priestly duties.

Openly favored by the queen, the Pharisees quickly filled the gap the new high priest left open. They ousted Sadducees from the Sanhedrin court and council of elders they had previously dominated, and replaced them with their own appointees. Leading Sadducee figures said to have been implicated in the earlier murder of Pharisees were executed.

Among the prominent Pharisees who returned from exile was Simeon ben Shetach who is believed to have been the queen's brother and who became leader of the Sanhedrin. For the first time, the Pharisees became the dominant political, as well as religious, force in Judaea. They launched a campaign to reinstate long-lapsed strict adherence to religious law and observance. Neglected religious holidays were revived and enlivened with torchlight processions, trumpet fanfares, celebratory dancing, and much ceremony. Far-reaching reforms of the religious and legal institutions of Judaea were instituted, as was a vigorous program of education, strong on religious study. Formal schooling for the young was introduced.

The administration of justice was reformed, notably to provide legal protection to people falsely accused of crimes, a practice which had grown widespread. With Alexandra's backing and supported by the instruments of the state, a sense of public responsibility for vulnerable members of society was promoted. The introduction of the *ketubbah* marriage contract to protect divorced wives was part of that process. At the time, most men possessed only the land on which they lived and/or the livestock by which they earned their livings, so the requirement that they provide for their abandoned spouses had the effect of sharply reducing the incidence of divorce.

During Alexandra's reign, Judaea was for the most part a land at peace both within its borders and in the wider region. To reinforce the link between national and religious identity, every Judaean over the age of twenty was required to contribute a half shekel a year to the upkeep of the Jerusalem Temple. It was not a great burden but it served its purpose. Collections for the Temple were also made in Jewish communities in Egypt, Syria, Mesopotamia, and elsewhere.

Though such contributions were not obligatory in distant places, huge amounts of gold, far more than was needed for the Temple's maintenance, regularly poured into Jerusalem from the Diaspora, transported by regularly scheduled, heavily guarded caravans. The Temple grew famous for its accumulating treasure, descriptions of which inevitably were exaggerated and aroused much envy in foreign courts.

Domestic tranquility having been established, Alexandra was free to devote her attention to foreign affairs—a crucial matter at a time of international upheaval. She doubled the size of her army, mostly by hiring mercenaries, and thereby gained the respect of the rulers of neighboring states, from whom she took hostages of high social standing to guarantee peaceful relations. But except for an abortive move against Damascus, she did not launch campaigns to extend the borders of her realm.

Her only serious problem was with Armenia to the north. The Armenian King Tigranes conquered Syria and threatened to invade Judaea with an army mightier than any Alexandra could field. But she bought Tigranes off with sumptuous gifts and soon the need to meet the menace of Roman legions at his rear compelled him to withdraw from the region without following through on his threat to Judaea.

Toward the end of Alexandra's largely untroubled reign, intrigue, which had earlier been an unsettling feature of the Hasmonean royal court, surfaced once more in Jerusalem. The queen's older son, High Priest Hyrcanus, was first in line to the throne, but his brother Aristobulus II had other plans.

A cunning conspirator, Aristobulus rallied to the cause of the persecuted, formerly preeminent Sadducees and pleaded their case before his mother. Extracting from her authorization for them to seek sanctuary from Pharisee vengeance in various fortified towns in the land, he proceeded to forge a power base among them there. With Sadducee backing and units of the Judaean army over which Alexandra had given him command, he intended to assert his claim to the throne when she died.

His intentions became an open secret in Jerusalem. His brother Hyrcanus, the queen's chosen heir, and Pharisee leaders pleaded with her to act against Aristobulus's threat to them and to the unity of the nation. But she refused to believe the situation was as precarious as they claimed. Seventy-three years old at a time when few people lived past the age of fifty, she may have been too weary or too ill to appreciate what was happening. She died soon afterward, leaving a situation fraught with danger to the unity of the nation.

Alexandra would turn out to have been the last independent monarch of the Jews. She had been a popular, benevolent, and effective monarch for most of her nine-year reign. But it was to be followed by civil war.

HYRCANUS II, ARISTOBULUS II, ANTIGONUS II

67–37 BCE

The closing chapter in the history of the Hasmonean kings of the Jews is a tale of family strife, civil war, and the beginnings of Roman rule in Judaea. It is the story of three kings for whom the troubled affairs of the nation were of little concern compared to questions of their personal fortunes.

When Queen Alexandra Salome died, Hyrcanus II, the older of her two sons, succeeded her on the throne as she had ordained. But unlike the dynamic grandfather after whom he had been named, Hyrcanus had little interest in matters of state and was generally lackadaisical. In sharp contrast, his brother, Aristobulus II, was spirited, ambitious, and determined to seize the crown.

As soon as word came that Alexandra had died, Aristobulus marched on Jerusalem with army units he commanded in Judaean towns where he had cultivated strong support during the last years of his mother's reign.

Newly enthroned Hyrcanus sent his army to meet his younger brother's challenge. But many of his soldiers switched allegiances and joined the forces of the more inspiring Aristobulus. Demoralized, Hyrcanus's remaining troops were decisively beaten in a clash at Jericho.

Resuming his march on Jerusalem, Aristobulus took the city, seized the Temple and would have appropriated the throne as well if his brother had not willingly handed it over. Now having even less of a wish to carry the tedious burdens of public duty, Hyrcanus was content to live an uneventful life, with the comforts accessible to a prince of the royal blood.

The amicable accord between the brothers was sealed with a public fraternal embrace and with the marriage of Aristobulus's son Alexander to his cousin, Hyrcanus's daughter Alexandra. The people of Judaea welcomed their reconciliation with relief. Even the rivalry between the Pharisees and Sadducees was toned down.

However, what had transpired was not universally welcomed. Members of the entourage of the obliging, retiring Hyrcanus had expected that he would remain king and that they would enjoy the status and benefits that would thereby flow to them. By accepting downgraded status, he was downgrading them as well. One of his courtiers was particularly outraged by the agreement between the brothers and was to play a role of considerable consequence in the history of the Jews.

Antipater was son of the governor of the Judaean-dominated Arab land of Idumaea. Its inhabitants, including Antipater's family, had been forcibly converted to Judaism when the first Hyrcanus had ruled Judaea some five decades earlier.

Shrewd and manipulative, Antipater had maneuvered himself into the position of chief adviser to the lackluster young prince, Hyrcanus. But he saw no future in being the confidant of a figure who had abandoned his claim to the throne and who disclaimed all interest in public affairs.

His own position devalued and his aspirations frustrated, Antipater resolved to change the mind of his timid superior. He persuaded Hyrcanus that his brother, anointed king in his place, had treated him cruelly by usurping the throne, and also was criminally corrupting the religious standards of the nation.

Hyrcanus did not much care and wished to be left in peace. But Antipater persisted, warning that Aristobulus would have him murdered. He insisted his brother would have no choice but to eliminate the continuing threat to the throne posed by the mere existence of his older sibling, the rightful king.

Harping relentlessly on such warnings, Antipater persuaded Hyrcanus to flee for his life across the Jordan River to Petra, capital of the Arab kingdom of Nabataea. He had already bribed the Nabataean king to give him sanctuary. He also arranged for the elders of a dozen Judaean-ruled Arab towns in Transjordan to supply an army to take Jerusalem and retrieve the lost crown for weak-willed Hyrcanus.

With a force of fifty thousand Arabs, the freshly emboldened Hyrcanus marched on the holy city where he received the important backing of the leaders of the Pharisees. Just as thousands of Judaeans had switched to the side of hard-driving Aristobulus when he had snatched the crown from his older brother, now thousands deserted the usurper king to support the sidelined, more legitimately regal Hyrcanus.

Much weakened, Aristobulus's defending army was routed in battle. He and the forces remaining faithful to him were driven back by the Nabataeans through Jerusalem to the Temple Mount where they held out until, as recurred so often in the early history of the Jews, an external element intervened in the situation.

The Roman general, Pompey, already celebrated for his exploits in the eastern Mediterranean and elsewhere, was in the process of expanding Rome's dominance across the region. He had already turned Syria into a Roman province and now had his eyes on Judaea. Aristobulus and Hyrcanus both knew he had the military might to decide which of them would be its king.

For promising a hefty bribe, Aristobulus, beleaguered in his Jerusalem stronghold, received the support of a lesser Roman official who had established a forward command post in Damascus. The official ordered the attacking Nabataeans supporting Hyrcanus to end their siege of the Temple Mount and withdraw from Judaea, which they did.

But Pompey himself was never in the business of simply settling foreign disputes. His aim was to bring Judaea under his command and enhance his reputation with the Senate back in Rome. He would determine which of the rival brothers seemed more likely to serve his purposes. Regardless of what had previously been decided, they felt obliged to send envoys to Damascus to seek Pompey's favor when he arrived there.

Hyrcanus maintained that, as Alexandra Salome's oldest son, he was born to be king of Judaea and was therefore its legitimate ruler. He also insinuated that Aristobulus had once allied himself with the enemies of Rome, something he himself would never do. In response, Aristobulus, shakily clinging to the crown, said that had been long ago and insisted his personal qualities made him better qualified to rule. He said his older brother was simply unfit to be king of a Roman protectorate state.

Weighing their arguments, Pompey concluded that the weak-willed Hyrcanus, propped up by his shrewd adviser, Antipater, would be easier to control. He was, however, reluctant to drive Aristobulus into a defiant military response. Having to attack and take his fortified position in Jerusalem would delay his triumphant return to Rome from his march of conquest across the region.

He instructed the brothers to work out a compromise of their own. Aristobulus saw that as a Roman trick, a prelude to his removal as king. But realizing that the forces at his command would be unable to hold out long against a battering by Roman legions, he told Pompey that if he were permitted to remain monarch, he would obligingly hand all his fortified positions in Judaea over to him; Jerusalem would be Rome's for the asking.

It was a tempting offer but one which the desperate Aristobulus could not fulfill. Most people in the holy city were willing to surrender its independence to spare its destruction and their lives, but a hard core of his men refused to follow his lead and end their resistance to Roman rule. When Pompey responded by marching on Jerusalem, he found them still entrenched on the Temple Mount.

So well positioned and fortified was the Mount that when vigorously defended, it could only be seized by means of a strong attack from the north, and only if the ravine in front of the city wall there was filled in to provide the attackers with suitable assault positions. After completing that arduous task, the

Romans constructed battle towers on the landfill to overlook the defenders and they brought up attack engines.

Despite the intensity of their assault, resistance was sustained in Jerusalem for three months. But the Romans were ultimately able to break through the wall, rampage across the Temple Mount, and take the Temple. The Roman historian Cassius Dio said if the Jews "had continued defending it on all days alike," instead of being unwilling to fight on the Sabbath, Pompey "could not have got possession of it."[89]

Some twelve thousand were slaughtered in the Roman assault and the aftermath, including Temple priests who, as if oblivious to what was happening around them, were cut down as they proceeded with their usual rituals at the altar. When one was killed, another stepped forward to take his place.

After all resistance was crushed, Pompey entered the Temple with an armed escort and made his way to its Holy of Holies. He did no damage, wanting only to see that mysterious chamber which, according to religious law, only the high priest was permitted to enter. His act of sacrilege aroused no significant popular protest in cowed Jerusalem and symbolized the final end, in 63 BCE, of independence for the Jewish nation in ancient times.

Infuriated by the casualties sustained by his legionnaires, the time and effort required to conquer Jerusalem, and the poor impression it must have made in Rome, Pompey stripped Judaea of much of the territory the earlier Hasmonean kings had acquired, including Samaria, the coastal region, and Jordan valley. Having once been a province of Seleucid Syria, it was now made part of Roman Syria whose governor was to administer the land from Damascus. The Jewish monarchy, reestablished by the offspring of the Maccabee guerrilla fighters a century earlier, was abolished.

As for the feuding royal brothers, the submissive Hyrcanus was permitted to remain in Jerusalem as high priest and titular ethnarch of Judaea (leader of the people) while the Romans took to governing the land.

Headstrong, ambitious Aristobulus was less fortunate. Upon Pompey's triumphal return to Rome, he was required to trudge in procession in front of his ornately decorated chariot, along with other conquered kings and princes.

But that was not the end of him. He soon escaped Roman captivity, returned to Judaea, gathered an army, and tried to reclaim the throne. But he was defeated, recaptured, and sent back to Rome.

Nor was that yet the end of Aristobulus. Soon after he had been imprisoned again, Julius Caesar and Pompey took to contesting supreme leadership of the Roman republic. Their rivalry turned into a wide-ranging civil war that spilled over into Judaean affairs. Caesar, supreme in Rome, saw imprisoned Aristobulus as an instrument he could use against Pompey's preeminence in the now-Roman-dominated Middle East. He arranged for him to return to his homeland once more, this time with an escort of two legions.

This sometime king of the Jews was to seize Judaea on Caesar's behalf and eliminate his brother Hyrcanus who owed his continuing position as ethnarch and high priest to Pompey. But while preparing for his campaign, Aristobulus was poisoned by Pompey's acolytes and finally, permanently, removed from the scene.

Meantime back in Jerusalem, the Machiavellian Antipater increasingly overshadowed Hyrcanus, the other onetime king, whose tireless, supremely efficient adviser was busily furthering his own interests. Antipater had established his own lines of contact with the Romans and had made a timely switch of allegiance from Pompey to Caesar, arranging for Judaean troops to back Caesar's campaign against those in Egypt who sided with Pompey. Hyrcanus also did what he could to win Caesar's favor. He used the reverence in which his high priestly rank was held to urge the influential Jewish community in Egypt to back Caesar's cause there.

Caesar was duly appreciative. He confirmed Hyrcanus as hereditary high priest and ethnarch of Judaea. Antipater did even better. Despite his earlier support for Pompey, Caesar saw him as even more qualified to serve his and Rome's interests and appointed him procurator of Judaea. In that role, he outranked his former master, Hyrcanus.

Though Antipater was not popular with the people of Judaea, his diplomatic maneuverings served them well. Through him, Caesar authorized reconstruction of Jerusalem's defensive walls which had been demolished by Pompey's legionnaires. He restored Galilee to Judaea, as well as cities in the plain of Jezreel and other territories of which it had been stripped. Judaeans would no longer be required to billet Roman troops or furnish recruits for Roman legions. Taxes imposed on Judaea would be reduced. Caesar also extended his benevolence to Jewish communities in Roman-ruled cities in the Diaspora. He decreed that they be permitted to run their own affairs. The traditional Jewish customs and form of worship were not to be interfered with. Existing ordinances to the contrary were to be withdrawn. In Alexandria, one of the great cities of his empire, Caesar ordered that the Jews, who had lost equal status under the law with the city's Greek majority, should have their rights restored.

Hyrcanus was named a *friend* of Rome; no small honor. But he continued to be eclipsed in all matters of state by Antipater who was awarded elevation to

Roman citizenship. Hyrcanus was also soon overshadowed by his nephew Antigonus, the son of his younger brother and adversary, the poisoned Aristobulus. This Antigonus (Antigonus II) was to be last of the Hasmonean kings.

$$*\qquad *\qquad *$$

Like his royal father, Antigonus II had been taken prisoner when the Romans under Pompey overran Judaea. Like his father, he had trudged along with other vanquished kings and princes in the procession that was part of the celebration marking Pompey's return to Rome from his victories abroad.

Pompey was subsequently defeated by Caesar in their contest to be supreme ruler of the Roman Empire, and he was assassinated. Antigonus seized on those developments to try to persuade Caesar that changes were necessary in Judaea. He charged Procurator Antipater with being an untrustworthy servant of the Romans and urged that he, as son of Aristobulus, should succeed his poisoned father on the Jewish throne.

Caesar was not persuaded. He chose to retain the services of the efficient Antipater and for Antigonus's uncle and enemy Hyrcanus to continue as high priest and ethnarch of Judaea. It was less likely to complicate the situation in a strategic region much given to complications.

But Antigonus persisted in his quest for the crown and saw a new chance to achieve his objective in the turmoil unleashed when Caesar was assassinated. Proclaiming himself king by right of inheritance, he gathered an army, invaded Judaea and marched on Jerusalem. A Judaean army commanded by Antipater's son, Herod, repelled his attack, but events nevertheless conspired in his favor.

Caesar's death, and the subsequent poisoning of Antipater by a rival, deprived Judaea of its two most effective champions. It lost its favored status in Rome and was soon subject to extortionate tax demands. Dismayed by the turn of events, the Judaeans drew hope from a comparatively new challenge to the Romans. A powerful army, spearheaded by armored cavalry, had swept out of the northeast to establish a new dynasty in Persia and thwart the regional plans of the Romans.

The Parthians drove the Romans from Syria and Phoenicia and advanced into Judaea where, given the new Jewish disenchantment with Rome, they were welcomed as liberators. Young Antigonus, who had been sidelined by the Romans, also cheered their arrival, the Parthian invaders now championing his claim to the throne. Their leaders may have been influenced by his promise of vast treasure and, according to Josephus, "500 women."

The defense of the holy city against the Parthians was commanded by Antipater's son Phasael, who had been appointed tetrach of the city by the Romans, and by Phasael's younger brother, Herod. The attack coincided with the Feast of Pentecost (*Shevuoth*) when the unstoppable convergence of thousands of Judaeans on Jerusalem to celebrate the festival confounded their defense plans.

When the Parthians appeared before the walls of the city, Phasael offered to resolve the problem through negotiations. Against Herod's advice, he went to Parthian command headquarters to see what might be done. He was immediately taken prisoner. Fearing he might be made a hostage, Phasael committed suicide.

Assessing the situation he confronted and the resources at his disposal, Herod, now in sole command in Jerusalem, believed resistance would be futile. He slipped away under the cover of night before Antigonus, with a strong force of Parthians, stormed the city.

His uncle Hyrcanus, the ineffectual ethnarch and high priest, was taken prisoner. Reluctant to execute him because of his priestly status, Antigonus had his ears cut off (personally bit them off, according to Josephus), automatically terminating his position as high priest. Religious law held that only men without physical blemish could hold priestly office. He was sent to live in Babylon, where the well-established Jewish community treated him with respect.

Flush with success and in command in Jerusalem, the Parthians formally installed Antigonus as king of Judaea. But the setback for the Romans proved no more than a temporary embarrassment from which they soon recovered. Barely had he settled on the throne when his position came under threat.

Herod had gone to Rome where, blessed with his father, Antipater's, powers of persuasion, he won the support of Octavian (later to be renamed Augustus and to become Rome's first emperor) and Mark Antony, both members of Rome's ruling triumvirate. He assured them that if they made him its king, Judaea would again be a devoted and reliable tributary. That was good enough for them and the Roman Senate which then went through the motions of officially awarding him the crown.

The Jews now had two kings: Antigonus, shakily seated on his throne in Jerusalem, and Herod, determined to replace him with the help of the Romans. Funded by them, he began his march to power by gathering an army of mercenaries. Landing at Ptolemais, he overran Galilee and most of Judaea. But he was not strong enough to take Jerusalem until Roman legions came to his aid after they had thrown back the Parthian challenge elsewhere in the region. Even with their help, a five-month siege of the holy city ensued. Food shortages threatening mass starvation ultimately forced Antigonus to submit. His three-year reign (40–

37 BCE) had been marked by nothing but war and his struggle to survive, and he failed at both.

This last king of the Hasmonean dynasty was brought before Mark Antony who had him beheaded. As for Hyrcanus II, the banished former ethnarch and high priest who had briefly once also been king, the triumphant Herod invited him to return from his exile in Babylonia to Jerusalem where he was to live as an honored guest of the crown. But the famously paranoid Herod soon imagined this earless, ineffectual, pathetic figure, who had never wanted to occupy a position of responsibility, to be a threat. He had him executed.

Having ruled Judaea for more than a century, the Hasmoneans had now made way for one of the most extraordinary figures in the history of the Jewish monarchy.

THE IMPACT OF THE ROMANS

HEROD THE GREAT

37–4 BCE

Herod was among the most accomplished of all the kings who sat on the throne of the Jewish nation. During his reign, Judaea prospered and was secure. Under him, it was transformed from what had been reduced to a landlocked ministate into a kingdom almost as large as the Jewish nation had ever been, and was highly regarded internationally despite having become a client state of the Romans.

He beautified Jerusalem, spectacularly rebuilding the poorly maintained Temple and embellishing many of its other buildings. He also undertook lavish architectural projects elsewhere in the land, constructing splendid new cities, including Antipatris near the coast, named after his father; Cypros near Jericho, named after his mother; and Phasaelis in the Jordan Valley, named after his dead brother.

He undertook massive public works projects, building reservoirs and aqueducts to improve water supplies to urban areas. He was effective in furthering the interests of Jews widely dispersed in the Diaspora and was revered by them. He was a figure of significance throughout the region, hence his designation as *Great*.

Herod was also a brutal tyrant, often teetering on the edge of homicidal insanity, and he was loathed and feared by his subjects because of it. They scorned his subservience to Rome and held him in disdain because of his heritage. He was neither of legitimate royal descent, having been appointed king of the Jews by the Romans, nor even of Jewish ancestry. His father, Antipater, was of Idumaean origin, a descendant of pagan Arabs who had been converted to Judaism a century earlier under the Hasmoneans.[10]

Herod was twenty-five years old when he was first widely recognized as a headstrong figure, not to be ignored. Antipater had been appointed Roman procurator of Judaea by Julius Caesar and, in that capacity, named his son governor of the turbulent Galilee. Despite his youth, Herod quickly acquired a reputation for ruthlessness in crushing a rebellious Galillean religious movement and summarily executing its leader and some of his followers.

---

10. Herod's mother, a Nabataean Arab, was not a Jew. That has raised questions about whether Herod therefore was not Jewish either. But the Torah does not decree that Jewish identity is conferred only through matrilineal descent or conversion, though that was later considered the rule, as it is today, though not in Reform Jewry. There is no indication that it was an issue of religious law in Herod's time.

While killing in combat was permissible, the Sanhedrin court in Jerusalem had exclusive authority to authorize death sentences. Arousing its anxiety with his insubordinate behavior, Herod was summoned to answer for taking the law into his own hands, a transgression that could have earned him execution. In keeping with his already achieved reputation for audacity, he tried to frighten the Sanhedrin by arriving for his trial with an armed escort but fled before he could be sentenced.

Capable of great charm, Herod became popular with Roman luminaries by making it clear that he was prepared to serve their interests in troublesome Judaea and liberally sprinkling them with gifts. They responded by overlooking his youth and the criminal charges outstanding against him in Jerusalem and appointed him governor of Samaria and the Bekaa Valley in Lebanon, putting him well along on the path to power in Judaea.

His rise was interrupted when Julius Caesar was assassinated in 44 BCE, sparking turmoil in the Roman leadership. The subsequent power struggle spilled over into the wider Roman Empire, helping the Parthians, the latest power to rise in the east, to wrest mastery in much of the Middle East from Rome.

Overrunning Judaea, the Parthians sought out the figure who they believed would best represent their interests as king in Jerusalem. They settled on the man whose royal aspirations the Romans had scorned: Antigonus II, son of the deceased King Aristobulus II.

Though they had not been given a choice by the Parthians, the elevation of this last of the Hasmonean monarchs to the throne was welcomed by the Judaeans; Rome had proved an extortionate taskmaster since Julius Caesar's assassination.

But Herod remained determined to rule Judaea. He tried to gather an army of Nabataean Arabs to retake Jerusalem, but nothing came of it. He then went to Egypt to see what backing he could find there. But receiving only an offer from Queen Cleopatra of a senior position in her army, he went on to Rome to seek better prospects from leading figures there he had previously come to know. They included Julius Caesar's adopted son Octavian and the late Caesar's stalwart Mark Antony.

With the backing of such luminaries, with a record of allegiance to Rome, and despite his lack of a genealogically legitimate claim to the crown, Herod was named king of Judaea and its high priest by the Roman Senate and authorized to install himself in those positions.

With resources supplied by his backers in Rome and in the Diaspora, whom he had assiduously cultivated, Herod landed at Ptolemais, gathered a mercenary army of Jews and gentiles, and quickly swept across Judaea, obliterating all resistance. But the Roman reinforcements he needed to storm fortified Jerusalem and depose Antigonus were tied down fighting Parthians elsewhere and could not come to his aid.

For the next three years, much of Judaea was a battlefield between the forces loyal to Antigonus—or just anti-Roman—and those at Herod's disposal. Even after Roman legions were free to come to his assistance, the defenders of Jerusalem held out against him for five grueling months.

The Roman commanders were so enraged by their losses when the city finally fell that they permitted their normally disciplined legionnaires to slaughter and plunder at will. Their rampage was so unrestrained that Herod felt obliged to plead with and bribe them to stop so the city he was to rule would not be left a desert. Antigonus was captured and beheaded, terminating the royal dynasty of the Hasmoneans.

At the age of thirty-eight, Herod mounted the throne of the Jews in Jerusalem to become their king. Throughout his thirty-three-year-reign, he remained a compliant vassal of Rome, accepting that the military preponderance of the Romans meant their domination of Judaea could not be challenged and that much could be gained from submission to them, both for himself and for the Jewish nation. He was comfortable in a Roman-ruled environment, having been educated to accept Graeco-Roman values and achievement as the best that civilization had yet produced.

For their part, the Romans were pleased to have a figure in command in Jerusalem who was ruthless enough to keep the peace among—and raise the required taxes from—a notoriously volatile people, someone who was also capable of effectively confronting any of Rome's adversaries who might seek to pass through this strategically important land link between Asia and Africa.

In pursuing his personal and national aims, Herod was always careful to remain on the best of terms with whoever was in command or likely to be in command in Rome. Without compunction or hesitation, he switched his allegiance from Mark Antony to Octavian when they became rivals and it seemed advantageous to do so, both for himself and for Judaea.

As king of Judaea, Herod proved to be one of its most assiduous administrators. Ruling forcefully through an efficient bureaucracy, he restored law and order which had collapsed across the land during long periods of war and civil strife. Robber bands which had established themselves in various parts of the land were crushed and thieves in the cities found their chosen profession had become dangerous to pursue. Farmers could tend their fields without fear of marauders, and people were again safe in their homes and in the streets of their cities.

Herod transformed the face of the country by launching a series of major construction projects. He turned a sleepy port into the magnificent city of Caesaria, named in honor of his patron, Octavian, who had become the first Roman emperor and had taken the name Caesar Augustus. Its vast artificial harbor, an outstanding engineering feat, was one of the wonders of the ancient world. So spectacular was Caesaria that it was called Little Rome and later, under direct Roman rule, would replace Jerusalem as administrative capital of Judaea.

Herod also rebuilt Samaria into one of the most splendid cities in the region, renaming it Sabaste (Greek for Augustus). He constructed or adorned a string of other cities in the land, dotting them with theaters, hippodromes, aqueducts, and palaces, including a magnificent edifice at Masada to which he intended to withdraw if threatened. He built fortresses on the borders of the kingdom for national security, permitted to do so by the Romans who were confident of his allegiance.

Employing diplomatic skills, bribes, and the personal friendships he forged with Roman leaders, he was permitted to extend the territory and settlements of the Jewish nation deeper east in Transjordan, north of Galilee, and elsewhere. It once more became as extensive as it had been during the high point of the Hasmonean rulers.

Through displays of military might and the distribution of gifts, he greatly enhanced the reputation of Judaea among other nations of the region. He built the first Jewish navy and sent a fleet into the Black Sea to assist a Roman military campaign there. To the Romans, he became one of the most valued regional rulers in their empire.

Herod's fame and generosity spread far and wide. He had temples, gymnasia, baths, markets, and other public projects constructed at Judaean expense in Tyre, Damascus, Athens, Sparta, Pergamun, Rhodes, Berytus (Beirut), and other cities of the eastern Roman Empire. He had a two-mile-long main thoroughfare of Antioch paved with polished marble and flanked with colonnades. He rescued the Olympic Games from seemingly terminal financial embarrassment and was elected honorary life president of the Olympics for his magnanimity.

Under Herod, Judaea enjoyed the benefits of greatly increased foreign trade and domestic commercial activity. The irrigation projects he sponsored fertilized formerly barren land. Though a willing servant of Rome, he managed to keep the Romans from interfering in Judaea's internal affairs, not that they wished to do so as long as the taxes they imposed were paid and he kept the peace in this strategic region.

He promoted the well-being of Jewish communities elsewhere in the Roman Empire—notably in Rome, Alexandria, Antioch, and Damascus—effectively intervening on their behalf with the ruling authorities and gaining for them special administrative privileges by order of the Roman emperor. In sharp contrast to the hostility he generated at home, he was much admired and respected in the Jewish communities of the Diaspora, though he displayed little personal attachment to Jewish religious law or custom. When elected king of Judaea by the Roman Senate, he had gone with Mark Antony and Octavian to the Capitoline Hill in Rome to offer sacrifices in gratitude at the Temple of Jupiter.

But to gain the affection of his estranged subjects, he tried to avoid excessively offending their religious sensibilities. The work he had done on the Holy Temple made it even grander than Solomon's original edifice. (The exterior and external courts and galleries would not be completed until after his death.) He forbade his sister to marry an Arab prince who refused to be circumcised. Prominent Jewish scholars, notably the philosopher Hillel, were drawn to Jerusalem from the Diaspora and encouraged to flourish there. When Pharisees, most organized in their objections to his rule, and members of the semi-monastic Essene sect, refused to pledge allegiance to him, he relieved them of the obligation to do so. When times were hard for the people, he sold off treasures of his palace to help feed the needy.

Nevertheless, most of the population continued to think of Herod as an imposition, a creature of a foreign power, a Jew remote from Jewish roots, a brutal despot who slaughtered those he imagined were a threat to him. His victims included most of the members of the Sanhedrin which he emasculated. He had the harmless, earless eighty-two-year-old former king Hyrcanus II, whom he had magnanimously invited back from exile in Babylonia, put to death. His seventeen-year-old brother-in-law Aristobulus III, whom he had been persuaded to name high priest, was drowned at his instruction by fellow bathers in a swimming pool at Jericho when it appeared that the popular youth might become a favorite of the Romans and a rival for Rome's affections. Fearing palace conspiracies, he had three of his own sons executed. Wearying of his eccentric behavior, Augustus Caesar mused it would be safer to be Herod's swine than his son.

In a fit of unwarranted jealousy, and believing (probably with justification) that she was plotting against him, he executed the beautiful Miriamne, the Hasmonean princess who had been the favorite of his several wives. Theirs had been a grotesque relationship. He loved her deeply but she made no secret of hating him after her young brother had been murdered on his orders and after discovering that, when he left Jerusalem on state business, he left instruction that if he died while away, she was to be put to death. After she was killed, he had her body embalmed in honey to enjoy her physical presence a while longer.

In the New Testament Gospel of Matthew, Herod is described as ordering the massacre in Bethlehem of all boys under the age of two when informed that a new king of the Jews, Jesus Christ, had been born there.

In addition to being appalled by his brutality and grumbling about high taxes, Judaeans were offended that his senior officials and administrators were predominantly gentiles or Hellenized Jews and that his army, especially its officer corps, consisted mostly of non-Jewish mercenaries from various corners of the Roman empire. Activities at the Greek stadiums he built in Judaea, in which gladiators were matched against wild beasts, were an offense against Jewish custom and traditional behavior. So were immodest displays at the Greek theaters he built and supported.

He chose and dismissed high priests on whims, ignoring the hereditary principle that was supposed to influence such choice, and he effectively eliminated the important role in society and government they had previously played. He turned spies loose on society to uncover conspiracies and executed alleged conspirators on mere suspicion. According to Josephus, plagued by frustration about his unpopularity, he "would oftentimes himself take the habit of a private man and mix with the multitude in the nighttime and make trial of what opinion they had of his government."[90]

During Herod's declining years, the disaffection and hatred of the populace grew ever more intense, compounded by horror at his murderous rages. At times, he took to meandering through the corridors of his palace in agony from intestinal cancer and weeping over loved ones he had slaughtered. However, even shortly before his death, he was not yet too debilitated to order that young men be burnt alive for destroying a golden eagle that had been placed above the great gate of the Temple in honor of Rome.

Having always been considered an enemy and interloper by most of his people, Herod died at the age of seventy. News of his death coincided with the approach of Passover, during which Judaeans normally flocked to the Temple in Jerusalem to celebrate the holiday.

They now had something more to celebrate and also a venue for organized popular demands for post-Herodian reforms. So clamorous were their demonstrations that Herod's son Archelaus, named in his will as prime beneficiary of the kingdom, sent troops to disperse the crowd. Three thousand people were cut down in the process, a slaughter that seemed part of Herod's final testament.

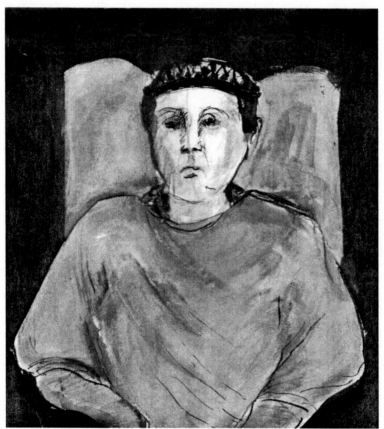

Herod the Great   Barbara Gelb

THE AGRIPPAS

AGRIPPA I
41–44

The death of Herod the Great marked the start of an interval in the history of the kings of the Jews. More than four decades would pass before another would wear their crown.

Herod had left a will naming his son Herod Archelaus as his royal successor. But Roman approval was necessary and Augustus Caesar declined to give it. The throne was to be left vacant. Emperor Augustus ruled that Archelaus would have to be satisfied with the less-than-royal rank of ethnarch of Judaea, Samaria, and Idumaea. Of two other princes named in Herod's will, Archelaus's brother, Herod Antipas, was appointed governor of Galilee and of Peraea, east of the Jordan River; his half brother, Herod Philip, was made governor of Ituraea in present-day Lebanon.

The transition was not as orderly as Augustus hoped. Disdain for Herod's family and resentment of Roman dominance was rife in Judaea and sparked riots. Archelaus tried to put them down ruthlessly, provoking even greater unrest.

The situation spiraled so dangerously out of control that the Roman governor of Syria had to dispatch three legions to restore order. Thousands were crucified. In the New Testament Gospel of Matthew, it is said Joseph took his wife Mary and child Jesus to Nazareth in Galilee rather than stay in Judaea because life under Archelaus had become precarious.

Augustus soon had enough of his appointee. Responding to appeals from Judaea and Samaria, he banished Archelaus to Gaul. The land was turned into a district of the Roman province of Syria, to be administered by a succession of procurators. There were to be fourteen of them over the next sixty-four years, each answerable to the governor of Syria. Their main tasks were to maintain order and make certain taxes were collected.

Their capital was Caesarea, the modern port city Herod had built, rather than Jerusalem, which was downgraded in Roman perceptions. The Sanhedrin lost what little authority it had managed to retain as a judicial, administrative, and religious council during Herod's reign and the procurators regularly took it upon themselves to appoint and dismiss high priests.

The collapse of even the pretense of Judaean autonomy promoted the growth of Jewish extremist sects, notably the Zealots, religious militants who dedicated themselves to the emancipation of Judaea from foreign tyranny by revolutionary means.

Among those militants were the so-called *Sicarii*, political assassins who often operated singly, murdering prominent Judaeans they considered collaborators with the Romans. They would trail their victims on crowded streets of Jerusalem or close in on them at public gatherings, stab them with the *sicas* (daggers) they concealed under their cloaks and then melt into the crowd, sometimes joining in cries of outrage when others realized what had transpired.

Not all procurators found the activities of the Sicarii objectionable. Procurator Antonius Felix is believed to have conspired with them to eliminate High Priest Jonathan because of complaints he made about how badly Judaea was being administered. Described by Tacitus as "wielding the power of a king with all the instincts of a slave,"[91] Felix is said to have arranged Jonathan's murder by the Jewish extremists because he knew his superiors in Syria and Rome would not have authorized his official execution.

Other radical sects shunned violence, some of their members preferring to live lives of celibacy, poverty, and devout worship in semi-monastic communes isolated from the outside world. Scornful of the Jerusalem priests whom they considered servants of Rome, they preached the imminent arrival of a Messiah to liberate Jews from oppression and herald the establishment of the kingdom of heaven.

John, son of the priest Zacharias, later to be called the Baptist, urged Jews to cleanse themselves spiritually through baptismal submersion in the River Jordan. They were to repent their sins and make ready to welcome the Messiah and savior whom John recognized in the person of his cousin, Jesus.

Only a small minority of Judaeans was directly affiliated with the radical sects or bands. For the most part, members of the Judaean elite were content to live under Roman rule. Sadducees tended to believe *Pax Romana* offered social and economic stability and that, if treated with deference and respect, the Romans would refrain from interfering in their lives or obstructing their religious observances.

In contrast, the Pharisees, who reflected the feelings of most Judaeans, harbored nationalistic and religious resentment of foreign domination, and particularly of the abuses of procurators. But most also disapproved of Zealot extremism, opposed violent resistance to Rome and believed it could lead only to bloodshed and destruction.

Growing up during this period of turbulence, Herod's grandson Herod Agrippa (Agrippa I) lived in Rome, remote from all of that. His father was

Herod's son, Aristobulus, who, with two of his brothers, had been slain by Herod to preempt any possible conspiracies by his offspring. Agrippa's grandmother Miriamne, who had been Herod's favorite wife and whom he had also murdered, had been a Hasmonean princess. Agrippa could therefore claim royal legitimacy through both the Herodian and Hasmonean lines.

As a consequence of his royal antecedents and his grandfather's high-ranking Roman connections, Agrippa had associated and been educated with the sons of other luminaries and aristocrats. Emperor Tiberius's son, Drusus, was a close friend, and the emperor himself was fond of him.

But being part of such an illustrious social grouping had its problems. Unlike some of Agrippa's playmates with whom he gambled, debauched, and got drunk, his resources were limited. While still a young man, he found himself greatly in debt and obliged to leave Rome.

His uncle Herod Antipas,[11] tetrarch of Galilee and Peraea, found him a sinecure in the new town of Tiberias (named after Emperor Tiberius), on the Sea of Galilee. But Agrippa had become addicted to a much more cosmopolitan setting and restlessly shifted from one place to another seeking to recapture a life of youthful abandon.

After accumulating further debts, he fled back to Rome where he was welcomed by his old cronies and his family contacts. He became a particular friend of Caligula, the emperor's chosen heir. When Tiberius died and Caligula succeeded him, he appointed Agrippa king of Ituraea in the north. It was an act of friendship rather than policy—the Romans remained in charge—and was quickly followed by the extension of Agrippa's domain to include Galilee and Peraea, though not Judaea proper.

Despite his royal rank, Agrippa chose to stay on in Rome. His circle of influential friends continued to expand, but life at the nerve center of the Roman Empire, even for the well connected, was hazardous.

Questions had long been raised about the balance of Caligula's mind and now the emperor was growing increasingly deranged. He was subject to sudden extreme mood changes which could prove fatal to anyone who aroused his ire, often for no reason whatever, even if they were otherwise favored.

Declaring himself divine, Caligula commanded that monumental statues of him be erected and that they be worshipped. At great risk, Agrippa persuaded the

---

11. Herod Antipas was the Herod described in the New Testament Gospel of Luke as contributing to the Roman decision to crucify Jesus Christ. He had also ordered the execution of John the Baptist after John accused him of adultery.

demented emperor-god to rescind an order that such a statue be erected in the Temple in Jerusalem, an act of sacrilege that might have triggered a rebellion against Rome across Judaea.

A wave of relief swept through Rome and the empire when members of his Praetorian guard assassinated Caligula. By now widely respected and admired in Rome, Agrippa played an important role in resolving the dangerous confusion that followed. Acting as intermediary between the Praetorian Guard and the Senate, he helped negotiate the choice of Claudius, a childhood friend, to be Caligula's successor as emperor.

Claudius gratefully rewarded Agrippa by adding Judaea, Samaria, and Idumaea to the smaller kingdom Caligula had previously awarded him. Judaea again had a king and the Jews once more had a nation of their own.

Roman dominance over Judaea remained intact, but it was a benevolent dominance now. Gone (for the moment) were the procurators, occupying legions, and foreign tax collectors. Though deferring to Rome when infrequently pressed to do so, the Jewish nation was able to rule itself again.

The character of Agrippa, who was now thirty-one years old, had completely altered. The young wastrel had become a responsible, constructive ruler, as faithful to his Jewish origins as to Rome. He managed to resolve that potential conflict of national allegiances to the satisfaction of his subjects in a way that his grandfather Herod the Great had not.

He chose to live in Jerusalem rather than Caesarea so that the holy city was restored to its role as administrative as well as religious capital of the kingdom. So scrupulously did he observe religious law that he became a favorite of the Pharisees despite his Roman connections while, because of those connections, the Sadducees also held him in high regard, especially when he persuaded Rome to reduce the taxes imposed on the people of Judaea.

Unlike Herod, Agrippa was a popular king but, like Herod, he interceded effectively with the Romans on behalf of Jewish communities in the Diaspora. He did much to revive the Jewish nation's spirit and regain for it the respect in the region that had fallen away while the Romans directly governed it.

But Agrippa's reign was cut short. In the year 44, while opening Olympic Games in Caesarea in honor of Claudius, he was stricken with severe stomach pains and died. Intrigue and conspiracy were relentless features of the Roman world and enemies of the emperor may have poisoned him.

Agrippa had occupied the throne of the Jews for just three years and was only thirty-four years old when he died. In view of what he had achieved as a ruler and international figure, and of what followed, his early death was a disaster for the Jewish nation.

AGRIPPA II

53–100?

The last king of the Jews never was their actual monarch. Upon the death of Agrippa I, Emperor Claudius considered naming his son Julius Marcus Agrippa (Agrippa II) to succeed him. But Claudius was persuaded that the youth, still only seventeen years old, was too young to carry the responsibility of maintaining order in a land that had so often been subject to upheaval

Instead, Judaea was absorbed into the Roman province of Syria, as it had been after Herod the Great died. Procurators, subordinate to the governor of Syria, were once more appointed to administer it from the port city of Caesarea.

But as a tribute to his friendship with young Agrippa's father, and because his family retained important connections in Rome, Claudius found a royal position for him when he came of age. He was to be king of Chalcis in the Bekaa Valley. Galilee, south of it, and other northern segments of the land were later nominally added to his domain.

To calm the anger of the people of Judaea now that they had again fallen under direct foreign rule, the Romans also made Agrippa guardian of the Temple in Jerusalem. He was authorized to name the high priest and maintain a royal palace in the holy city. But that was the extent of his exalted status. The Jewish nation was to remain under direct Roman rule and administration.

The best of the procurators they appointed to govern Judaea were experienced officials who wanted to fulfill their duties with as little bother as possible so as to advance their careers, while—as was considered standard behavior by a Roman imperial official serving abroad—pocketing enough loot to help keep them reasonably comfortable in their old age. But some of the procurators were little more than oppressive plunderers who saw Judaea only as a place to build great personal fortunes. Whatever their quality and abilities, none of them sympathized overly with such Jewish peculiarities as refusing to worship more than one god, circumcising their male offspring, and nurturing independence movements.

Even Procurator Tiberius Julius Alexander, who had been born into a leading Egyptian Jewish family and was a nephew of the celebrated Jewish philosopher, Philo, had difficulty coping with an alienated population dotted with religious and political extremists, except through heavy-handed policing that aggravated popular resentment. Conditions grew ripe for the spread of religious and nationalist movements which were troubling to both the Romans and the official Jewish leadership. A small group of devout Jews anxiously awaited the establishment of the kingdom of God on Earth to be heralded by the return of Jesus, who had been called king of the Jews by Procurator Pontius Pilate when sanctioning his crucifixion.

Aspiring messiahs wandered about urging the people to cease their sinful ways. One of them, Theudas by name, said he would divide the waters of the Jordan River and lead his people into the desert to escape heathen subjugation. He aroused enough unrest for the Romans to have him beheaded. Another was an Egyptian Jew who gathered a crowd of followers and led them to the walls of Jerusalem which he said would fall at his command, permitting them *en masse* entry to overwhelm the Roman garrison in the holy city. He too was summarily dealt with.

Other radical movements presented a serious immediate challenge by promoting armed rebellion. Even Judaeans who preferred to refrain from open opposition to the Romans sometimes found themselves caught up in heated or violent protest demonstrations. Some were spontaneous reactions to the harshness of the standard Roman response to unrest: restoring control as quickly as possible regardless of how much blood was shed in the process. Incidents of civic turbulence became frequent, as when a soldier publicly tore a Torah to pieces in Jerusalem and when another made obscene gestures to a group of Jewish worshippers.

Agrippa was anxious about the growing turmoil, but his area of authority in the holy city was confined to administration of the Temple and was circumscribed even there. Nor did Judaeans generally hold him in high regard. Many were offended that he was custodian of the Temple only by courtesy of his imperial masters. There was also much gossip that Agrippa had a criminally incestuous relationship with his sister Berenice who lived under her brother's roof for a time. (She later became the mistress of Emperor Titus.)

Their Roman rulers considered the Judaeans narrow-minded primitives incapable of appreciating the wonders and grandeur of the well-ordered civilization that was being bestowed on them. The politician and orator Cicero said, "The practice of their sacred rites was at variance with the glory of our empire, the dignity of our name, the customs of our ancestors."[92] Roman historian Cassius Dio said Jews "are distinguished from the rest of mankind in practically every detail of life and especially by the fact that they do not honor any of the usual gods but show extreme reverence for one particular divinity."[93] Jewish outrage over misrule and abuse mounted in tandem with Roman exasperation. Even heavy-handed Roman policing could not contain the situation. With no authority capable of exercising control, Judaea staggered toward a breakdown of social order.

Murder became so common that the Temple priests suspended the practice of sacrificing an animal as a sin offering each time innocent blood was shed because of the great number of animals they would have had to slaughter. When by chance a Sicarii assassin was apprehended, his colleagues kidnapped a prominent figure to exchange for his release.

Robber gangs terrorized the countryside and class antagonisms deepened. The rich were increasingly singled out for assault and theft. Nor were the normally law-abiding elements of society always at peace in those turbulent times. When Agrippa appointed Joshua ben Gamaliel to replace Joshua ben Damnai as high priest, the latter refused to bow out and their rival advocates clashed bloodily in the streets of Jerusalem.

The appointment of Gessius Florus to be procurator of Judaea in the year 64 dragged the situation toward a violent climax. Aside from being of brutal disposition, Florus saw his posting exclusively as an opportunity to become rich. He plundered the Judaean cities he was supposed to administer and even tapped the Temple treasury.

Angered by the protests of the Jews and by public mocking of his venality, Florus turned his troops loose to loot and murder. The Jews reacted with a fury that leading figures of their moderate majority attempted, with growing futility, to channel into appeals to Rome for justice. The situation cascaded toward crisis.

Fearing the worst, Agrippa, in his role as guardian of the Temple, tried to persuade the people that the abuses to which they were being subjected were aberrations and that Rome could be relied upon to see that justice ultimately prevailed. Addressing a huge gathering, he urged patience and warned that rebellion would be futile against the forces of an empire that had vanquished kingdoms in Asia, Gaul, Spain, Germany, and even Britain behind its sea moat that should have provided its people far more protection than the walls of Jerusalem. He told the people, "Other nations by the thousand, bursting with greater determination to assert their liberty, no longer resist. Will you alone refuse to serve the masters of the whole world?"

> Where are the [fighting] men, where are the weapons you count on? Where is the fleet that is to sweep the Roman seas? Where are the funds to pay for your expeditions? What gives you the confidence to defy the power of Rome?[94]

Agrippa warned that rebellion not only would be crushed but would also have calamitous consequences for Jews throughout the Roman Empire. "There is not a region in the world without its Jewish colony. All these, if you go to war, will be massacred by your opponents"

Saying what most people in Jerusalem accepted as true, Agrippa was heard in respectful silence. But when he urged submission to hated Procurator Florus until Rome sent a replacement for him, it was more than the people were willing to grant. Popular outrage had taken on a momentum of its own and many in the crowd refused to be restrained.

He was shouted down and some hurled stones at him. Forced to recognize that his effort to calm the situation had failed, he hastily withdrew from Jerusalem

Passions grew even more heated. Articulate, forceful leaders emerged from the ranks of the militants to promote, organize, and lead open defiance. The possibility of averting an outright clash with Rome was rapidly eroded.

Mortified and disheartened, Agrippa sided with the Romans in the hope of saving Judaea from destruction, even sending detachments to try to support their continued rule. But he could play only a peripheral role in what was about to transpire.

WAR WITH ROME

66–70

By the summer of 66, war in Judaea appeared inevitable. Opinion among the Jews was sharply divided. Most of them probably favored fighting for independence from Rome if it could be achieved without great bloodshed. But religiously motivated Zealots insisted on freedom from foreign rule and oppression no matter how it was achieved and whatever the price. Other fervent nationalists demanded the same. Jews who believed continuing Roman rule was the best possible option under the circumstances had been politically emasculated by developments.

Bitterness had been deepening in intensity for years, fueled by the brutal and corrupt actions of the most recent Roman procurators. Now the Zealot and nationalist revolutionaries were driving the pace of events. Pharisee leaders, the religious figures most influential among the people, sympathized with the Zealots, but were averse to violence. In their resulting confusion, they lost the influence they might have wielded.

If there was a single act that sparked the war, it was committed by Eleazar, captain of the Temple guard in Jerusalem. A fiery young man of privileged status, Eleazar was the son of former High Priest Ananias to whom he probably owed his position. With the support of others enraged by the cruelty and venality of Procurator Gessius Florus, he brushed aside the disapproval of the senior priesthood and cancelled the usual daily Temple sacrifices on behalf of Emperor Nero.

That was more than a snub to the Romans. It was a public disclaimer of subservience to them and virtually invited reprisal.

A band of Zealots, led by Menahem, son of Judas, had already overwhelmed the Roman garrison at the Masada fortress overlooking the Dead Sea to the south. The Romans would have considered the Masada event an isolated episode by a band of fanatics who would soon be dealt with without great difficulty. But Eleazar's impudence at the Temple could not be so lightly dismissed. Nor could the support it received at a public assembly of the people of Jerusalem who had gathered afterward to assess the situation. Their prevailing mood was furious defiance of Roman tyranny.

Fearing further turbulence would lead to catastrophe, leading Jerusalem moderates rushed messages to Procurator Florus in Caesaria, the Roman administrative capital, and to King Agrippa, the official guardian of the Temple. They urged them to take action before Jerusalem tumbled into a whirlwind of unrest and disorder.

Hoping the situation would deteriorate still more to justify his harsh, blundering administration, Florus did nothing. But fearing the worst, Agrippa sent a troop of two thousand cavalrymen, who quickly secured much of the holy city.

However, the Zealots, led by Eleazar ben Simon (a man also of distinguished priestly family), were not easily intimidated. They seized the Temple and its adjoining district. Bolstered by an influx of armed Zealot recruits, Eleazar's followers then forced the withdrawal of Agrippa's horsemen, along with a contingent of Roman troops, to Herod's fortified palace on the fringe of the city. In little more than a week, most of Jerusalem had come under the control of the Zealots, who proceeded to take drastic action to consolidate their authority.

They set fire to the municipal archives which contained records of debts, mostly owed by the poor to the rich. They also torched King Agrippa's Jerusalem palace and the home of former High Priest Ananias, father of the rebellious captain of the Temple guard. He was accused of having used his office to enrich himself at the expense of lesser priests. Together with other prominent figures, he went into hiding to escape the wrath of the extremists.

Eleazar ben Simon now turned his attention to Jerusalem's Antonia fortress. Situated next to the Temple, the fortress had been built by Herod and named in honor of his friend and patron Mark Antony. Long garrisoned by Roman soldiers, it had been the most distinctive symbol of Rome's supremacy in Jerusalem. Its capture was the greatest challenge yet to Judaea's imperial rulers. There was more to come.

As people in the holy city grew increasingly anxious about the possible consequences of the extraordinary events through which they were living, the insurgents there received additional reinforcements. Menahem and his Zealot followers arrived from the Masada fortress they had captured.

Claiming leadership of the rebellion, Menahem launched a reign of terror. He had Ananias dragged from his hiding place and executed. Others who suffered at his command included prominent Jerusalemites who had protested to Rome about the conduct of the procurators, but who also had little sympathy for the insurgents. He permitted Agrippa's horsemen to leave Herod's palace and Jerusalem in safety, but not the Roman soldiers who remained surrounded there.

Having made his presence felt, Menahem went to the Temple attired in elaborate robes, as if revealing himself to be king of the Jews. Already offended by his presumption and the challenge to his leadership of the uprising, Eleazar ben Simon declared only God would thenceforth rule the Jewish people. Aspiring king Menahem was driven from the Temple and killed, together with many of his followers. Others escaped and returned to their stronghold at Masada where they would dominate the nearby Dead Sea area and hold out against the Romans for years.

The Roman soldiers still holding out in Herod's Palace in Jerusalem, now facing starvation, agreed to surrender to the Zealots if their lives would be spared. They were promised safe conduct but were cut down after emerging and laying down their arms.

Writing later, Josephus, present in Jerusalem at the time and no fan of the Zealots, said that to most Jews, "it seemed the prelude to their destruction. They saw no way to undo the provocation they had given for war and the City was stained by such guilt that they must expect a visitation from heaven if not the vengeance of Rome. There was universal lamentation and the streets were full of long faces, every decent citizen being terrified at the prospect of paying for the misdeeds of the insurgents."[95]

With the holy city in ferment, trouble also flared in Caesarea. As word of what had transpired in Jerusalem spread, gentiles loyal to Rome massacred great numbers of Jews there. In revenge, Jews attacked gentiles in towns and villages elsewhere in Judaea. Throughout the land, people who had lived in peace were at each other's throats. The land was succumbing to murderous anarchy.

Among those for whom the situation had turned personally alarming was Cestius Gallus, the Roman governor of Syria. He was responsible for maintaining peace and control in the region and would be held accountable in Rome if he failed to do so. In the autumn of 66, two months after the first incidents of open Jewish defiance of Rome, he patched together a force consisting of the battle-trained Twelfth Roman Legion, contingents from other legions, additional cohorts of infantry and cavalry, and detachments sent by the leaders of regional lands submissive to Rome, including King Agrippa.

Ravaging towns and villages and engaging in wanton slaughter, this army made its way to Gibeon, six miles from Jerusalem, where it made camp before laying siege to the capital.

Rather than await an assault by this formidable force, the insurgents in the city burst out for a ferocious surprise assault on Cestius's bivouacked forces. They killed many before racing back to within Jerusalem's walls. It was a bold foray but Cestius's army was still formidable, and he was left still determined to take Jerusalem.

On the scene and convinced that most of his fellow Jews opposed and dreaded war with Rome, Agrippa sent two envoys to the city to negotiate the peaceful restoration of Roman authority. But Zealot leaders were unwilling to consider concessions of any kind. Knowing that others would welcome a peace agreement, they intercepted Agrippa's envoys outside the city walls, killed one and wounded the other, sending him fleeing.

Seeing no reason for further delay, Cestius's army now advanced on Jerusalem, taking positions on Mount Scopus overlooking the city, and then entering it in force. The insurgents were made to pull back to the more easily defended Temple area. Some among them now urged their leaders to sue for peace to avoid futile slaughter. But the most militant of the Zealots were in control. Those suggesting negotiations were executed as cowards and traitors.

But the stubborn Zealot refusal to give way soon seemed to have been justified. Just as Cestius's troops appeared about to storm the fortified Temple Mount, he called off the attack and ordered his army to withdraw from Jerusalem.

It may have been that in recognizing the to-the-death doggedness of the Zealots, and examining the strength of their Temple Mount defenses, he decided that with the autumn rain season about to begin, it would be best to pull back and resume his attack at a more favorable time.

Josephus later contended that if Cestius "had chosen at that very hour to force his way inside the [Temple] walls, the City would have been his immediately and the war brought to an end.... Thus it came about that the war lasted so long and the Jews were overwhelmed by irretrievable disasters."[96]

Whatever Cestius's reason for abandoning the attack, he was not permitted to withdraw unchallenged from Judaea. Zealot fighters poured out of Jerusalem to harass his troops as they pulled back. At Beth Horon, ten miles from the city, where Judah Maccabee had vanquished a Syrian army two hundred years earlier, the Roman army sent to make short work of the Judaean upstarts was ambushed and decimated. What remained of Cestius's legion was forced to abandon large stores of arms and supplies to the insurgents. It also lost its treasured Eagle standard, a grave humiliation.

It was the most devastating military defeat the Romans had sustained since their legions had been mauled in the forests of Germany six decades earlier. No longer dismissible as a minor tussle in a far-off place, it was a disaster Rome could not fail to avenge. Peace advocates in Jerusalem could no longer hope war could be averted.

The victory at Beth Horon was, however, an enormous morale stimulant for Judaeans, even for many moderate figures who had been convinced the Zealots were leading the Jews to catastrophe. They now came to believe that independence from Rome, or at least greater self-rule, was a possible outcome of what had been happening.

They had been warning against provoking Rome's retribution but realized that to have any influence on the course of events they would have to become part of the armed liberation movement. Indeed, they would have to take command of it from the hotheaded Zealots, and they proceeded to do so. Their way was paved by divisions that had sprouted in insurgent ranks and by popular recoil in Jerusalem against Zealot extremism.

In the winter of 66–67, Ananus, another former high priest, backed by other senior figures hoping for peace with Rome, gained leadership of what effectively became the provisional government of a new Jewish republic. The Romans gone and Zealot assertiveness curbed, some measure of normality returned to Jerusalem. Order was restored in the city. Pilgrims again streamed in. Daily rituals at the Temple continued as before. The Sanhedrin functioned as a sort of national assembly. The walls of the city were strengthened. Coins were minted.

But the reality of the rebellion and what probably lay ahead could not be ignored. Plans had to be made by those who assumed command of Judaea to organize resistance to the expected Roman punitive onslaught.

The land was divided into military districts. Among those assigned to organize local resistance, Eleazar ben Ananias, the captain of the Temple guards who had terminated Temple sacrifices for the Roman emperor, was dispatched to command in Idumaea in the south and twenty-nine-year-old Joseph ben Mattathiah, later to be known as the historian Josephus, was sent to organize the defense against the Romans in Galilee in the north. (Josephus would soon bow to the inevitability of Roman victory, surrender, change sides, and become an aide to the Roman war commanders.)

Around this time, the group of Jews who believed the crucified Jesus was the Messiah slipped out of Jerusalem. Willing to "render onto Caesar the things which are Caesar's,"[97] they opposed the looming war. They made for the Jordan and crossed the river to find sanctuary in the city of Pella.

Until then, they had constituted the heart and central authority of their faith. But like others hoping for peace, they were enfeebled and shocked by the turmoil, and now by their self-imposed exile from the holy city. However, through the efforts of St. Paul (who had once been a Pharisee) and other evangelists, Christianity was already taking root in a scattering of predominantly gentile cities elsewhere in the Roman Empire, from which it would spread and, over time, become firmly established.

*   *   *

As the Jews prepared for war, the Romans did the same. Emperor Nero had been stunned by the mortifying rout of Cestius's legion at Beth Horon. He realized the Judaean uprising could have repercussions throughout the empire and had to be dealt with immediately. But crushing it had clearly become too great a task to be left to the governor of Syria.

Nero summoned general and former senator Titus Flavius Vespasian out of retirement and instructed him to restore Roman rule to vexatious Judaea with utmost haste. Vespasian had won battle honors in Britain vanquishing fierce resistance to the Roman occupation there and had served as Roman proconsul in Africa. By early 67, nine months after the start of the Jewish insurrection, he had gathered the necessary resources and was ready to begin crushing it.

At his disposal were three legions and additional contingents—some sixty thousand men in all. Having made his way to Syria, he began his campaign by launching assaults on the rebels in Galilee. The rocky terrain of much of that northern region provided the insurgents with excellent defensive positions and, in some places, they held out to the last man. But resistance to overwhelming Roman might was futile. By early autumn of 67, Vespasian had conquered all of Galilee. By the end of the year, much of the rest of the land had been similarly "pacified."

The relentlessness and rapidity of Vespasian's advance left the leaders of the provisional government in Jerusalem in despair. If Galilee had fallen so quickly, what hope was there for the rest of the land? They were forced to recognize that independence from Rome stood little chance of emerging from the struggle. The best they could hope for was a negotiated peace in which the Romans would spare Judaea further destruction and possibly appoint a less oppressive procurator to rule them.

But such a timorous conclusion to the uprising was out of the question to those who had launched it. Eleazar ben Simon and his Zealot followers had no doubt that God was on their side and refused to consider any agreement with Rome short of full independence.

To underscore their refusal to sanction any other alternative to war, they made the Temple their stronghold and defiantly chose, by lots, a high priest of their own. They ransacked private homes for food and supplies and killed prominent figures they deemed treacherous representatives of the old order, including resident members of Agrippa's royal family.

Their presence and actions were a threat and an embarrassment to the provisional government which was clinging to the hope that a settlement short of total capitulation could be negotiated with the Romans. In desperation, Ananus, as provisional government leader, called on the people of Jerusalem to force the Zealots out. "They have seized the strongest place in the city," he cried out to them in anger. "From now on the Temple must be spoken of as a citadel and a fort. Tyranny is strongly entrenched [there]. Will you really wait for the Romans to recover our holy places? Why don't you rise, you spiritless creatures ... and ... kick out your tormentors?"[98]

In characteristically assertive fashion, Eleazar's Zealots did not merely stand their ground when faced with such a challenge. Not waiting to be attacked, they swarmed out of their Temple bastion to try to seize all of Jerusalem and demonstrate their staying power.

Aroused by Ananus's harangue, a force of Jerusalemites had quickly assembled and met their foray. Many were killed on both sides before the Zealots were driven back onto the Temple Mount and then into the Temple's inner forecourt where they barred the gates to protect themselves from annihilation. Ananus was unable to penetrate their defenses, or was reluctant to further desecrate sacred ground with bloodshed. But he posted a strong guard to confine them.

*   *   *

By then, many rebels who had survived the Roman onslaught in other parts of Judaea had converged on Jerusalem to continue their resistance. Some had joined the Zealots but most had gathered around another figure, John ben Levi, of Gischala, who had put up robust but unavailing resistance to the enemy in Galilee before escaping to the capital. John and his followers had been welcomed as valiant fighters by the people of Jerusalem and lent badly needed support to their moderate leadership.

But within months, by the winter of 67–68, John had grown disenchanted with the provisional government. He had not given up the fight against the Romans but had come to believe its leader, Ananus, was prepared to do so—that he was willing to surrender the holy city rather than defend it against Vespasian's legions. Sent to negotiate with Eleazar on behalf of the provisional government, John instead told the Zealots that Ananus was bent on destroying them and betraying Jerusalem to the enemy.

The Zealots did not intend to let either happen. Though Eleazar and his men were still confined to the Temple inner forecourt, he managed to sneak runners out to seek help. The messengers went to Idumaea to tell the virulently anti-Roman Idumaeans that Ananus had to be stopped. Converted to Judaism less than a century earlier and retaining the zeal of converts, twenty thousand rallied to the call and marched on the holy city to save it from Ananus's supposed treachery. Learning of the imminent arrival of the enraged Idumaeans and fearing what might happen if they linked up with Eleazar, Ananus had the city gates locked and guarded, forcing the Idumaeans to camp outside the walls after their long trek. But under the cover of a thunderstorm, Zealots slipped out of their Temple confinement and, the alertness of the gate guards having been blunted by the ferocity of the storm, they let the Idumaeans into the city.

Furious at how they had been treated, and convinced Ananus was a traitor, they then joined the Zealots in a destructive rampage. The short-lived provisional government of Judaea was destroyed in a surge of terror. Ananus was slain, as were his most prominent supporters. Slaughter was widespread, as the Zealots and their newly arrived allies took command throughout Jerusalem.

As the situation stabilized, the Idumaeans discovered that, contrary to what they had been told, there had been no plot to deliver the city to the Romans. Bitter at having been duped, most trudged home, leaving Eleazar and his Zealots in a position to exercise sole mastery in the capital.

However, the situation had by then grown more complicated. The ranks of John of Gischala's insurgent followers had grown much larger than those of the Zealots. They had been swollen by some of the Idumaeans who had stayed on in the city, as well as by insurgents who had continued to converge on the capital from elsewhere in the land while fleeing the Roman march of conquest.

At first, John's men and Eleazar's Zealots avoided clashes. Acting as head of a new provisional government, John concentrated on preparing for the inevitable assault on Jerusalem by Vespasian's legions. He strengthened the city's fortifications and had food and water stored against a siege. He also sent word to members of the large Jewish community in Babylon, urging them to press their rulers, the Parthian adversaries of the Romans, to hurry to the aid of Judaea.

Meantime, another figure had emerged as a leader in the war for Judaean independence. Simon bar Giora was more a social revolutionary than a Zealot. Simon, whose patronymic suggested he was the son of a convert, had distinguished himself in the destruction of Cestius's legion at the start of the war. Subsequently ransacking the homes of the rich, and promising rewards to the poor, he had gathered a formidable guerrilla army and had taken control of much of the south of the land not yet overrun by the Romans.

Simon's successes, strength, and the proximity of his base of operations to Jerusalem, worried Eleazar who considered him a threat to the leading Zealot role in the insurrection. He sent a troop of fighters to destroy the challenge he presented. But Simon's men easily fought them off.

Meantime, John of Gischala had become exasperated by Eleazar's leadership pretensions in the city when his partisans there were much more numerous. His men went on the attack and drove the Zealots back to within the Temple precinct again while he assumed command of the rest of Jerusalem.

As the people of the city struggled to survive lawlessness, food shortages, chaos, and confusion, the leadership of the resistance continued to fragment. Conflict had already begun brewing in the ranks of John's followers. Some objected to his dictatorial behavior, others to the conduct of some of his men. According to Josephus, they donned female attire, applied makeup to their faces, and, approaching "with mincing steps, then in a flash" drew swords "from under their dyed cloaks [and] ran every passer-by through."[99]

In the spring of 69, malcontents among John's men, joined by surviving moderate notables, called on Simon bar Giora to march his corps of guerrilla insurgents into Jerusalem and facilitated their entry through its walls. They wanted him to free the city from the tyranny of their increasingly autocratic leader, John, the delinquency of some of his followers, and the threat of a Zealot resurgence. Most of all, they wanted him to address their primary concern—the imminent Roman assault.

Confronted by Simon's more powerful force, John and his remaining corps of disciples were driven back to the high ground of the Temple Mount, forcing the smaller group of Zealots back to their old confinement within the Temple's inner forecourt.

But hopes that Simon would free Jerusalem from strife among the insurgents, so the threat of Roman conquest could properly be met, were soon seen to have been in vain. Instead of unitary command, the city now had three contending rebel leaders. Simon ruled most of the city, John and his men commanded the Temple Mount, and Eleazar and his smaller band of Zealots remained locked and defiant in the Temple's inner forecourt.

While awaiting the Roman onslaught, the three factions kept up running battles among themselves: "There were three generals, three armies," Tacitus observed. "[B]etween these three there was constant fighting, treachery and arson."[100] They clashed with swords, javelins, and spears. Simon erected towers from which his fighters set up catapults, earlier seized from the Romans, to fling heavy missiles at John's men in the Temple's outer areas while they, caught in the middle, exchanged lesser missile attacks with Eleazar's confined Zealots.

*   *   *

While the contest between the insurgent groups had been developing, Vespasian's legions had got on with their task of overrunning Judaea. After capturing all of the north and securing the coastal strip, the Romans had extended their control to much of the rest of the land. At Vespasian's newly established headquarters in Caesaria, his senior officers urged an immediate assault on Jerusalem to finally snuff out the insurrection.

But Vespasian wanted no repeat of the disaster that had befallen Cestius's legion. Such an occurrence would not sit well in Rome. From refugees and defectors, he was well informed about the factional turmoil in the city and preferred to let the insurgents exhaust themselves in their internecine struggles before he struck. But when he finally decided to mount his assault on the city, word of a momentous development in Rome made him change his plans.

Emperor Nero had committed suicide. Faced with mutiny in his army, threatened by sedition among his imperial bodyguard, declared an outlaw by the Roman Senate, mentally unhinged and increasingly weird in behavior, Nero had been persuaded that taking his own life was the way to solve his problems.

A power struggle for Rome's imperial throne ensued. The year 69, in which the fate of the Jewish nation hung in balance, came to be called the Year of the Four Emperors. Three former senior imperial figures—Galba, Otho, and Vitellius—succeeded each other in rapid succession. But none had sufficient backing from the army or the Senate, and each was violently deposed within months.

Kept informed, Vespasian thought it best to await instructions about how to proceed in Judaea from whoever finally remained emperor. There was his future to consider. In view of Rome's hothouse political climate, such a consideration could be important for his future, and even his life.

With the upheaval in Rome leaving the contest for the imperial succession unresolved, Vespasian also examined whether he himself had sufficient backing to become emperor. As a result of his earlier achievements and rank, he certainly would have support in important circles.

That support was quickly forthcoming. Urged by Tiberius Alexander, former procurator of Judaea and now Roman Prefect of Egypt, the two legions under his authority there declared for Vespasian in what was probably a carefully orchestrated plot. Vespasian's own legions in Judaea rapidly followed suit. So did legions in other parts of the empire and the Roman navy on the Black Sea. Such strong backing from the military was all he needed.

Departing Judaea for Rome in the closing days of 69 to don the imperial purple, Vespasian left the winding up of the war in Judaea to his twenty-nine-year-old son, Titus, an experienced battle commander who had personally led troops in combat in Galilee. The insurgents in Jerusalem could expect no further respite from him. Nevertheless, there was no pause in the three-way Simon-John-Eleazar struggle in the city. It was as if whatever the Romans were up to was of secondary significance to them.

*   *   *

In the spring of the year 70, thousands of pilgrims, lulled by the suspension of Roman military operations, converged on Jerusalem to celebrate the Passover holiday there. In accordance with tradition, the Zealots permitted worshipers to enter their Temple inner forecourt stronghold for holiday rituals. With weapons concealed under their cloaks, some of John's fighters infiltrated as well, attacked the Zealots in their stronghold, and quickly decimated them. Those who survived were absorbed into John's ranks, while his men continued to trade missiles with Simon's fighters beyond the Temple precinct.

Meantime, Titus's three legions, reinforced by a fourth, began taking up positions to lay siege to Jerusalem. Once they were in place, attack towers were erected and siege ramps, battering rams, and catapult engines were brought up.

Only when it became apparent that missiles from those engines would soon come crashing into the city did Simon and John stop fighting each other and begin joint defensive operations against their common enemy. Sorties, some verging on the suicidal, were launched through the city walls to destroy or damage the enemy's heavy equipment. "The bolder spirits," Josephus wrote, "sprang forward in tight groups, tore to pieces the screens over the engines, and falling on the crews overpowered them, not so much by skill as by reckless courage."[101]

Daring as those raids were, they could have only limited success against the great numbers of legionnaires at Titus's disposal. But when the actual assault on the city began, he was confronted by a series of shrewdly devised, meticulously executed counterattacks. The ingenuity of some of those forays, taking the Romans completely off-guard, contrasted sharply with the folly of the earlier self-destructive divisions among the insurgents.

But Roman might in manpower and equipment could not be long withstood. Sustaining massive casualties—while inflicting the same on the Jews—Titus soon took two of the city's three defensive walls.

At that stage of the battle, he halted his attack, regrouped his forces, and held a massive parade of his troops in full view of the remaining wall but beyond harm's reach. The display of its long, disciplined ranks was meant to convince the insurgents that their choice was surrender or death. No request for talks having come from the insurgents in response, Titus assumed they preferred the latter and resumed his assault preparations.

The situation was now desperate for the people of Jerusalem and the pilgrims who had flocked there. Much of the grain that had been prudently stored for the expected siege had been destroyed during fighting between the insurgents, and Titus blocked all further food shipments into the city.

Starvation stalked its streets and homes, overwhelming decency and propriety, even within families. "Wives robbed their husbands, children their fathers, and mothers their babies, snatching food out of their very mouths."[102] Searching for food, insurgents and bandits broke into homes where locked doors suggested a meal was being eaten within. The besieged city was stricken with a hunger-driven wave of mayhem, murder, and theft.

To intensify the food crisis, Titus allowed people to enter Jerusalem through his lines but threw an almost impenetrable blockade around the city, letting no one out. He contemplated simply maintaining the blockade and letting hunger bring the insurgents to their knees. But he was in a hurry to add an important, possibly essential military victory to his family's reputation so soon after his father's still precarious elevation to the office of emperor, as well as to gain battle honors for himself. (Nine years later, he would succeed his father as ruler of the Roman Empire.)

The assault was resumed. After heavy fighting, in which the Romans were repulsed for a time, Jerusalem's third wall fell to them. Now they had to take the Temple, to which all the remaining active insurgents had withdrawn.

Here "arrows and spears were of no use to either side." Romans and Jews "drew their swords and closed; in the milling mass it was impossible to distinguish one side from the other.... The carnage on both sides was terrible.... There was room for neither flight nor pursuit.... Those in front [had to] either kill or be killed" with those behind pressing forward "leaving no space between the opposing lines."[103]

Once more, the tenacity of the insurgents halted the Roman advance. Roman historian Cassius Dio wrote that it was as if the Jews "had discovered a piece of rare good fortune in being able to fight near the Temple and fall in its defense."[104] But to conquer it and win the war, Titus was also willing for his men to take heavy casualties, and they did. As Tacitus pointed out, the Temple "was like a citadel" with its own walls, and "the porticoes around it constituted excellent defensive positions."[105]

Titus passed word along that he would spare the precious Temple if the insurgents came out to fight in the open. Their response was to set fire to the structure's colonnades to block Roman access. Some legionnaires added to the flames by hurling firebrands into the Temple. The blaze was soon out of control.

As the flames rose to the sky that summer's day of the year 70, the anniversary of which is still considered a day of mourning by observant Jews, the people of Jerusalem "sent up a cry that matched the calamity."[106] Legend has it that as fire engulfed the Temple, priests rushed to the roofs, "flung the keys up to the heavens and cried out, 'Master of the universe, here are the keys with which you entrusted us. We have not proven trustworthy custodians.'"[107]

The deteriorating discipline of the legionnaires had now completely broken down. Infuriated by their huge losses and the refusal of the remaining insurgents to recognize the futility of their continuing resistance, they ran wild, putting to the sword everyone they came across. "There was no pity for age, no regard for rank; little children and old men, laymen and priests alike were butchered."[108]

Insurgents broke out of the blazing Temple into the city, where they fought on until cut down. Others tried to escape through Roman lines or hide in tunnels and sewers. But most were forced to surrender, including Simon bar Giora who appeared from a subterranean passage bizarrely wearing a white shroud under a purple cloak

It had taken the Romans five months to take Jerusalem. Final victory was achieved in early autumn of the year 70. Countless pilgrims were among the great number of Jews who were killed during the battle for the city, which Titus then reduced to rubble. The Temple, consumed by flames and its remains plundered, was destroyed, never to rise again.

Captured insurgents not executed on the spot were led off into captivity. Some would later be made to fight each other in gladiatorial contests in the stadium at Caesarea. John and Simon was among seven hundred Jewish captives, "picked for their exceptional stature and physique"[109] taken to Rome to be displayed before crowds in Titus's triumphal procession, along with scrolls of the law, a golden menorah, and other precious items saved from the Temple. John was then imprisoned for life while Simon, seen by the Romans as the chief outlaw, was executed.

The war had lasted four years but was not yet completely over. The clifftop fortress of Masada near the Dead Sea, seized by Zealots when the war began, was still in their hands. It did not fall until the year 73 when, doomed to be overrun, its besieged defenders killed their own wives and children and committed suicide rather than be taken prisoner. Two women and five children survived to confirm what had been done.

The war with the Romans had lasted four years and ended with their total victory. Resulting death and devastation was extensive across Judaea. Jerusalem was left in ruins. The destruction of the Temple over which Agrippa had been custodian effectively terminated whatever remained of his limited official connection with the former kingdom of the Jews. He remained titular king of the northern territories the Romans had awarded him, but they had become appendages of the Roman province of Syria in all but name, and even that miniature kingdom was gradually reduced in size by Roman decree.

Agrippa spent most of his remaining years in Rome, serving no significant political or religious function. Well before his death around the year 100, the Jewish monarchy had ceased to exist. There would be no more kings of the Jews.

Jewish Prisoners and Temple Treasures Paraded in Titus's Triumphal Procession in Rome

AFTERMATH

The slaughter, destruction, and consequences of the war with Rome were the greatest calamities the Jewish nation had suffered. So many Jews had died in the conflict, and Jerusalem and other Judaean population centers had been so devastated, that continuing the struggle for independence was out of the question. Shattered Jerusalem was now little more than a base for the Roman Tenth Legion. Rome's rule was draconically reimposed on the land and steep new taxes were levied.

But this was still a province of Rome in a region of strategic importance. When the dust settled, survivors were permitted to pick up their previous lives as much as the changed circumstances allowed. Synagogues had already become places of worship and cultural life in many places. The Temple destroyed and the senior priesthood having been a victim of the war, they became the channels of national-religious continuity.

With the return of peace and calm, the Romans permitted the revival, with reduced authority, of the dissolved Sanhedrin as a religious council at the coastal town of Jabneh, south of present-day Tel Aviv. Soon the new center of Jewish cultural and religious life, Jabneh was where rabbinic Judaism first flourished. Scholars and spiritual leaders lived and worked there. They set about inspiring new vigor and spirit in Judaism after the catastrophe of the war. They ruled on questions of religious law, did much to systematize the Torah, and revised the content and order of formal prayer. They composed the Hagadah for Passover service and redesigned the Jewish calendar. Pilgrims from cities of the Diaspora converged on Jabneh during holiday times.

Judaea gradually recovered from the bitterness and much of the destruction of the war. The rubble was cleared from ruined cities (including Jerusalem) which again became active centers of urban life. After Hadrian became emperor in 117, pronouncements attributed to him left the impression that he would rebuild Jerusalem, which was still largely leveled, and permit it to become the sparkling center of the Jewish world again, with the Temple gloriously reconstructed.

That was not his intention. It was true that Hadrian planned to rebuild Jerusalem, but as a Roman pagan city to be named Aelia Capitolina. (Aelia was his family name and the Capitoline hill in Rome was the site of the empire's main temple, dedicated to its primary deities.) Where the Jerusalem Temple had stood, on a site still sacred to Jews, a temple to Jupiter, rather than to the God of the Jews, would be erected.

Hopes and elation over an expected revival of their holy city collapsed among the Jews as word of Hadrian's actual plans circulated. Cassius Dio said, "Soon the whole of Judaea had been stirred up and the Jews everywhere were showing signs of disturbance, were gathering together, and giving evidence of great hostility to the Romans."[110]

Another of Hadrian's rulings provoked even greater bitterness. Appalled by the practice of castration in some parts of his empire, he outlawed mutilation of the flesh; this was deemed to include circumcision, which Jews considered a biblically ordained sacred rite. The first signs of organized resistance brought further proscriptions. Jewish religious services were banned, as was observance of the Sabbath and religious holidays.

In the year 132, the Jews of Judaea again rose in rebellion against Rome. They were led by Simon bar Kosiba, a charismatic figure who was called Bar Kochba (Son of the Star) by the most eminent Jewish spiritual figure at the time, Akiva ben Joseph, who claimed Simon was the king Messiah.

The guerrilla campaign he commanded initially confounded the legions Hadrian sent to destroy it. Unlike the fighters in the earlier war with Rome, Bar Kochba's followers drew strength from being united under his sole, absolute command, from his meticulous operational planning, and from wide popular support.

The war raged for three and a half years, during which Bar Kochba established mastery over most of Judaea. But Roman might again decided the outcome. "As to those who perished by hunger, pestilence or fire," said Cassius Dio, "no man could number them. Thus almost the whole of Judaea was laid waste."[111]

Cities were leveled once more. Much of the land was reduced to wilderness and Jews were expelled from Jerusalem. Bans were imposed on Jewish religious observance, Torah study, synagogue gatherings, and circumcision. So many Jews were sold into slavery that the slave market was saturated. Judaea, like Jerusalem, was divested of its historic name. It was now to be part of a region called Syria Palestina, from which the name Palestine would evolve.

Antoninus Pius, Hadrian's successor as Roman emperor, relaxed the restrictions imposed on Jews and Jewish worship. But as a geographic entity, the Jewish nation had been obliterated.

Jewish identity, based on religious and cultural heritage and birthright, had, however, by then already been firmly implanted across the Diaspora—in Rome, ironically, where there had been a Jewish community for at least a century, in Syria, Alexandria and other Egyptian cities, cities of North Africa, and the islands of the Eastern Mediterranean. The largest and most significant Jewish community was in Mesopotamia, modern-day Iraq, which became the primary center of Jewish scholarship and the source of the Babylonian Talmud, the most authoritative rabbinic commentary on Jewish law, ethics, and customs. The office of exilarch (leader of the Diaspora) had already been established there, its holder reputedly a lineal descendent of King David.

Over the centuries, centers of Jewish worship and culture would develop—in Spain and various other parts of Western Europe, the cities of the Ottoman empire, Poland, Russia, Ukraine, later America, and ultimately, the modern nation of Israel. Scholars, spiritual figures, and other leaders of the Jewish people would arise. Many religious Jews prayed for the coming of the Messiah to bring God's splendor to the world, and still do. But never again would there be a king of the Jews.

ENDNOTES

[1]. "King David and King Solomon," Naylor, James Ball, "David and Solomon"

[2]. "I will make of you," Genesis 12:2

[3]. "In those days," Judges 17:6

[4]. "Saul has slain," 1 Samuel 18:7

[5]. "Tomorrow you and your sons," Ibid., 28:19

[6]. "Your glory, O Israel," 2 Samuel 1:19

[7]. "In distress," 1 Samuel 22:2

[8]. "I will give you," 1 Chronicles 17:8

[9]. "The sword shall never," 2 Samuel 12:10

[10]. "won away the hearts," Ibid., 15:6

[11]. "as numerous as the sands," Ibid., 17:11

[12]. "My son Absalom," Ibid., 19:1

[13]. "love for those who hate," Ibid., 19:7

[14]. "King Adonijah," 1 Kings 1:25

[15]. "I will establish his line," Psalms 89:30

[16]. "Be strong," 1 Kings 2:2

[17]. "Thus," says the Bible, Ibid., 2:46

[18]. "to test him," 2 Chronicles 9:1

[19]. "what was displeasing," 1 Kings 11:6

[20]. "an ancient tribal," Heaton, 11

[21]. "Your house and your kingship," 2 Samuel 7:16

[22]. "the heavy yoke," 2 Chronicles 10

[23]. "still go up," I Kings 12:27

[24]. "worse than all," Ibid., 16:25

[25]. "ivory palaces," Amos 3:15

[26]. "they shall go wandering," Hosea 9:17

[27]. "They have sold," Amos 2:6

[28]. "but not with My sanction," Hosea 8:4

[29]. "I will turn Samaria," Micah 1:6

[30]. "There is no honesty," Hosea 4:1

[31]. "As for Menahem," Pritchard 194

[32]. "I will gather you." Ezekiel 11:17

[33]. "Almighty God," James, M.R. "The Lost Apocrypha of the Old Testament," 104

[34]. "Do not ask," Sholem, Gershom, "Sabbatai Sevi," 338

[35]. "The Egyptian Jews," Ibid., 343

[36]. "There are quite," Ausubel 217

[37]. "Your father made," 2 Chronicles 10:4

[38]. "My father made," Ibid., 10:11

[39]. "We have no portion," Ibid., 10:16

[40]. "Should one give aid," Ibid., 19:2

[41]. "Stay at home," Ibid., 25.19

[42]. "he loved the soil," 2 Chronicles 26:10

[43]. "clever devices," Ibid., 26:15

[44]. "sinful nation," Isaiah 1:4

[45]. "A great earthquake," Josephus, "Antiquities," 9:10:225

[46]. "a separate house," 2 Chronicles 26:21

[47]. "religious towards God," Josephus, "Antiquities," 9:11:236

[48]. "I am your servant," 2 Kings 16:7

[49]. "There were none like him," Ibid., 18:5

[50]. "As for Hezekiah," the Tayor Prism at the British Museum

[51]. "consulted ghosts," 2 Kings 21:6

[52]. "wipe Jerusalem clean" Ibid., 21:13

[53]. "If you obey" Deuteronomy 28:1

[54]. "If you do not obey," Ibid., 28:15

[55]. "turned back to the Lord," 2 Kings 23:25

[56]. "What have I to do with you," 2 Chronicles 35:21

[57]. "reformed [Judaism]," Lowery, 190

[58]. "Put on Sackcloth," Jeremiah 6:26

[59]. "The people of Judah," Ibid., 7:30

[60]. Lonely sits the city," Lamentations 1:1

[61]. "The Lord has acted," Ibid., 2:5

[62]. "to be merciful," Jeremiah 42:12

[63]. "Build houses," Ibid., 29:4

[64]. "I will take you," Ezekiel 36:24

[65]. "By the rivers of Babylon," Psalms 137

[66]. "whilst the other tribes," Epstein, 54

[67]. "The religion of Israel," Kauffmann, XIII

[68]. "Of all men," Herodotus, "The Persian Wars," 1:135

[69]. "The Lord God of Heaven," Ezra 1:2

[70]. "Allow the work of this House," Ibid., 6:7

[71]. "who practice sorcery," Malachi 3:5

[72]. "should be one people," 1 Maccabees 1:41

[73].   "abolish Jewish superstition," Stern, vol. 2, 28

[74].   "The covenant of our fathers," 1 Maccabees 2:20

[75].   "saved the law," Ibid., 2:48

[76].   "strangers in all," Ibid., 3:36

[77].   "to live according to their," Ibid., 6:59

[78].   "Why have you" Ibid., 8:32

[79].   "The yoke of the Gentiles," Ibid., 13:41

[80].   "priest, people, rulers," Ibid., 14:47

[81].   "We have neither taken," Ibid, 15:33

[82].   "leader of the Jews," Ibid., 13:42

[83].   "The people cultivated their land," Ibid., 14:8

[84].   "so great a power," Josephus, "Antiquities," 13:10:288

[85].   "mistress of the realm," Ibid., 13:11:302

[86].   "hated by his father," Ibid., 13:12:321

[87].   "ill will…," Ibid., 13:15:399

[88].   "had great authority," Ibid., 13:15:402

[89].   "had continued defending," Stern, vol. 2, 350

[90].   "would oftentimes," Josephus, "Antiquities," 15:10:367

[91].   "wielding the power," Stern, vol. 2, 29

[92].   "The practice of their sacred," Ibid., vol. 1, 198

[93].   "are distinguished from the rest," Ibid., vol. 2, 351

[94].   "Other nations by the thousands," Josephus, "War," 2:360

[95].   "it seemed the prelude," Ibid., 457

[96].   "had chosen at that very hour," Ibid., 529

[97].   "render onto Caesar," Matthew 22:21

[98].   "They have seized," Josephus, "War," 4:173

[99].   "with mincing steps," Ibid., 561

[100]. "There were three generals," Tacitus, "The Histories" 5:12

[101]. "The bolder spirits," Josephus, "War," 5:280

[102]. "Wives robbed their husbands," Ibid., 430

[103]. "arrows and spears," Ibid., 6:75

[104]. "had discovered," Stern, vol. 2:375

[105]. "was like a citadel," Ibid., 30

[106]. "sent up a cry," Josephus, "War," 6:253

[107]. "Master of the universe," Finkelstein, "Jews," 148

[108]. "There was no pity," Josephus, "War," 6:271

[109]. "picked for their exceptional," Ibid., 7:118

[110]. "Soon the whole of Judaea," Stern, vol. 2, 392

[111]. "As to those who perished," Armstrong, 163

CHRONOLOGY

(Early dates are approximate)

Exodus 1280 BCE
Judges 1200–1020
Saul 1020–1000
Ishbosheth 1000–998
David 1000–961
Solomon 961–931

Divided Kingdoms

Kingdom of Israel 931–722	Kingdom of Judah 931–587
Jeroboam 931–910	Rehoboam 931–914
Nadab 910–909	Abijah 914–911
Baasha 909–886	Asa 911–871
Elah 886–885	Jehoshaphat 871–848
Zimri 885	Jehoram 848–841
Omri 885–874	Ahaziah 841–840
Ahab 873–853	Athaliah 840–835
Ahaziah 853–852	Joash 835–796
Jehoram 852–841	Amaziah 796–767
Jehu 841–813	Uzziah 767–739
Jehoahaz 813–797	Jotham 739–734
Jehoash 797–782	Ahaz 734–728
Jeroboam II 782–747	Hezekiah 728–698
Zechariah 747	Manasseh 698–643

Shallum 747	Amon 642–641
Menahem 747–742	Josiah 641–609
Pekahiah 742–740	Jehoahaz 609
Pekah 740–731	Jehoiakim 609–598
Hoshea 731–724	Jehoiachin 598–597
Assyrian Conquest 722	Zedekiah 597–587

Babylonian Exile From Judah, Including Early Deportations 597–538
Judah Under Persian Rule 538–336
Hellenic Rule of Judaea Begins 336
Maccabee Revolt 168
Judah Maccabee 166–161
Jonathan Maccabee 161–143
Simon Maccabee 143–135
John Hyrcanus
135–104
Aristobulus I
104–103
Alexander Jannai 103–76
Alexandra Salome 76–67
Hyrcanus II, Aristobulus II, Antigonus II 67–37
Roman Dominance from 63 BCE
Herod 37–4
Herod Archelaus 4 BCE–6 CE
Direct Roman rule 6–41
Agrippa I 41–44
Agrippa II 53–100 (?)
War with Rome 66–73
Fall of Jerusalem 70
Fall of Masada 73
Second War with Rome 132–135
Creation of the State of Israel 1948

LIST OF ILLUSTRATIONS

King David Bringing the Ark of the Covenant to Jerusalem, *Library of Congress*
Map: Tribal Areas, *www.bible.ca/maps*
The Prophet Samuel Blessing Saul, *Gustave Doré*
King David, *Chartres Cathedral*
David Mourning the Death of His Son Absalom, *Gustave Doré*
King Solomon, *Gustave Doré*
The Temple of Solomon, *Matthaeus Merian the Elder*
Map: Kingdom of David and Solomon, *www.bible.ca/maps*
Map: The Kingdoms of Israel and Judah
Omri's Coup Against Zimri, *Unkown Artist, XVII Century*
King Ahab Mortally Wounded in Combat with the Syrians, *Julius Schnorr von Carolsfeld*
Scholem, Gershom, *Sabbatai Sevi: The Mystical Messiah*
Syrians Abandoning Their Siege of Samaria, *Unknown Artist, V Century*
King Jehu Prostrating Himself Before Assyrian King, *Black Obelisk, British Museum*
The Prophet Amos, *Gustave Doré*
The Elders of the Northern Tribes Rebel Against King Rehoboam, *Julius Schnorr von Carolsfeld*
Ancient Jerusalem, *Hartmann Schedel*
The Death of Athaliah, *Gustave Doré*
Ancient Jerusalem
King Josiah Having the Book of the Law Read Out to the People, *Matthaeus Merian the Elder*
The People of Judah Driven Into Exile by the Babylonians, *Julius Schnorr von Carolsfeld*
Cyrus Liberating the Jews From Their Babylonian Exile, *Gustave Doré*
Rebuilding the Temple, *Gustave Doré*
Antiochus Pillaging Jerusalem, *Bible Picture Gallery*
Herod the Great, *Barbara Gelb*
Jewish Prisoners and Temple Treasures Paraded in Rome, *Arch of Titus, Rome*

BIBLIOGRAPHY

The Bible (Tanakh)
First and Second Book of Maccabees

Ackroyd, Peter, *Exile and Return*
Aharoni, Y., *Land of the Bible*
Albright, William, *From Abraham to Ezra*
Armstrong, Karen, *Jerusalem*
Anderson, Bernhard, *The Living World of the Old Testament*
Ben-Sasson, H. H. (editor), *A History of the Jewish People*
Brandon, S. G. F, *The Fall of Jerusalem*
Bright, John, *A History of Israel*
Brodsky, Alyn, *The Kings Depart*
Cassius Dio, *Roman History*
Epstein, Isadore, *Judaism*
Farmer, W. R., *Maccabees, Zealots and Josephus*
Finkelstein, Louis, *The Jews: Their History*
Furneaux, Rupert, *The Roman Siege of Jerusalem*
Goodman, Martin, *The Ruling Classes of Judaea*
Gottwald, Norman, *The Tribes of Yahweh*
Grayzel, Solomon, *History of the Jews from the Babylonian Exile*
Heaton, E. W., *The Hebrew Kingdoms*
Hengel, Martin, *The Zealots*
Herodotus, *The Histories*
Herzog, Chaim and Gichon, Mordechai, *Battles of the Bible*
Horsley, Richard A., *Bandits, Prophets and Messiahs*
Isserlin, B. S. J., *The Israelites*
Josephus, *Jewish Antiquities*
Josephus, *The Jewish War*
Kaufmann, Yehezkel, *The Babylonian Captivity*
Kirsh, Jonathan, *King David*
Law, David, *From Samara to Samarkand*
Letwin, Thomas, *The Siege of Jerusalem by Titus*

Lowery, R.H, *The Reforming Kings*

Magolis, Max and Marx, Alexander, *History of the Jewish People*

Miller, J. Maxwell and Hayes, John H., *A History of Ancient Israel and Judah*

Neusner, Jacob, *First Century Judaism in Crisis*

Newsome, James, *By the Waters of Babylon*

Payne, David, *Kingdoms of the Lord*

Pearlman, Moshe, *The Maccabees*

Pfeiffer, Charles, *Exile and Return*

Pritchard, James, *The Ancient Near East*

Rhoads, David M., *Israel in Revolution*

Robinson, T.H., *Decline and Fall of the Hebrew Kingdoms*

Russell, D. S., *The Jews From Alexander to Herod*

Sicker, Martin, *The Rise and Fall of the Ancient Israelite States*

Sievers, Joseph, *The Hasmoneans and Their Supporters*

Stern, Menahem, *Greek and Latin Authors on Jews and Judaism*

Tacitus, *The Histories*

The *Tanakh* is the primary source for the earliest history of the Jews. It is a gathering of sacred scriptures which tell the story of their origins and their early evolution as a people, a nation, and a religious community. Its contents were initially transmitted orally from generation to generation, to be written down and edited by scholars and scribes. It is an interpretation of events, pronouncements, procedures, laws and beliefs central to the religious and secular experiences of the Jews in ancient times.

INDEX